D0929861

JOURNAL FOR THE STUDY OF THE PSEUDEPIGRAPHA
SUPPLEMENT SERIES

3

Editor
James H. Charlesworth

JSOT Press
Sheffield

The HISTORY of the QUMRAN COMMUNITY

An Investigation

Phillip R. Callaway

Journal for the Study of the Pseudepigrapha
Supplement Series 3

Published by JSOT Press
JSOT Press is an imprint of
Sheffield Academic Press Ltd
The University of Sheffield
343 Fulwood Road
Sheffield S10 3BP
England

Typeset by Sheffield Academic Press
and
printed in Great Britain
by Billing & Sons Ltd
Worcester

British Library Cataloguing in Publication Data

Callaway, Philip R.
The history of the Qumran community : an investigation. - (Journal for the study of the pseudepigrapha supplement series ; 3)
1. Jordan. Khirbet Qumran. Cultural processes, B.C. 780 - A.D. 135
I. Title II. Series
306′.0933

ISBN 1-85075-107-2

CONTENTS

PREFACE

In this study, 'The History of the Qumran Community' is viewed as an unresolved historical issue. From this basic perspective it became necessary to reexamine all of the available documentary and nondocumentary data that is usually adduced as evidence for Qumran history. The reconstruction of this history, as is largely true for creative and imaginative historical reconstruction in general, depends heavily on the documentary evidence. In the case of the history of the Qumran community, which is apparently never mentioned in other historical documentation, the historian must turn to CD, 1QpHab, 4QpPs37, 4QpNah, 4QTest, and 1QH. In these ancient documents statements are made that seem to refer to or allude to persons, events, and controversies. These statements have enticed many biblical specialists to speculate on the identity and history of the people who authored, collected, and preserved the Dead Sea Scrolls. Since the Scrolls preserve few statements that would help to date the persons and events thought to be mentioned in the Scrolls, historians became very appreciative of the general chronological periodization that could be inferred from archaeological work done at Qumran, from palaeographical analysis of the scripts in which the Scrolls were written, and from the ancient reports about the Essenes. These three bodies of evidence seem therefore to complement the information in the Scrolls themselves.

This study was also conceived as a dialogue with representatives of the current consensus on Qumran history, that is, the Maccabean thesis, which understands the references and allusions in the Dead Sea Scrolls against a Maccabean context. This approach was not adopted in order to slight or ignore hypothetical reconstructions outside of the current majority view. Rather, it was felt that the evidence should be allowed to speak for itself and to judge the gamut of theories on the history of the Qumran community.

The conclusions reached in this investigation urge much less speculation than has hitherto been the case, for the available evidence just cannot sustain the detailed reconstruction of historical events involving the Dead Sea or Qumran community that has characterized Qumran studies from their beginnings. Of course, any new and relevant documentation would be welcomed that might potentially verify, modify, or even falsify the conclusions of this study. If such documentation exists, it should be made available for widespread scholarly evaluation. Elisha Qimron and John Strugnell have suggested that 4QMMT, soon to be published in full, is a letter from the Teacher of Righteousness to the Wicked Priest (Jonathan or Simon Maccabeus). According to their preliminary indications, however, there is not a shred of evidence in this document for the specific identities of the writer and the addressee of 4QMMT. It is claims such as theirs, which seem to persist largely unquestioned, that constitute the *raison d'être* for this investigation.

The completion of this study was made possible by a large body of supporting actors. I would like to express my gratitude to my mother, Mrs Loraine F. Floyd, who has supported my academic interests in general and the writing of this study in particular. My faculty also contributed by reading and critiquing the original dissertation (1986), which remains essentially unmodified—Professors Carol A. Newsom, John H. Hayes, J. Maxwell Miller, Martin J. Buss, members of the Old Testament faculty at Emory University, and Vernon Robbins of the New Testament faculty. As adviser, Professor Newsom deserves a special word of appreciation for her numerous suggestions about the structure and argumentation of the dissertation. Professor Hayes introduced me to the Dead Sea Scrolls and was the actual inspiration for the comprehensive evaluation of evidence bearing on a history of the Qumran community. Having supervised my MTS thesis, in which I demonstrated that I was a staunch supporter of the Maccabean thesis, Professor Hayes could not have foreseen the radically conservative conclusions of this investigation. I am also indebted to Professor Dr Dr Hartmut Stegemann of the Georg-August Universität in Göttingen, West Germany for allowing me to work as one of his assistants in the framework of the Qumranforschungsstelle in Marburg and Göttingen. My dialogue with his study of the history of the Qumran community is obvious throughout. I also want to thank my friend Hartmut Pabst, a longtime Mitarbeiter at the Qumranforschungsstelle, for our many discussions about the Qumran community and related matters during the period October 1980—March 1985.

My appreciation goes also to Dr Philip R. Davies for his interest in this investigation and our conversations about CD (see Chapter 5).

Most importantly, I must register my deepest gratitude to my wife Birgit Brössel-Callaway for her enduring support, while I researched and wrote this study. Not only did she make life easier for me during this time, but she also contributed directly from her art-historical perspective to my discussion of 1QH (Chapter 8). This investigation is dedicated to her.

Chapter 1

INTRODUCTION

A. *The Basic Concern*

This work has the goal of reassessing the evidence for reconstructing the history of the Qumran community. There exists to date no comprehensive appraisal of the evidential foundations upon which scholars have based their reconstructions of the community's history. Clearly, a start was made by Solomon Zeitlin, but his critique was made to some extent in support of his own view that the Dead Sea Scrolls were more recent documents that had derived from the medieval Karaites.[1] The most extensive, and perhaps the best, critique of almost every aspect of historical reconstructions of Qumran history—including attention to palaeography, archaeology, the Essene reports, and internal analysis of the Dead Sea Scrolls—remains that of G.R. Driver.[2] He, too, interpreted the data in favor of his own hypothesis, identifying the Dead Sea Covenanters with the Zealots. Therefore, his critique belongs with others emerging from within the camp of those who actually attempt to reconstruct Qumran history. Unlike Zeitlin, Driver, and practically all others who have been concerned with reconstructing the history of the Qumran community, Hartmut Stegemann has presented a comprehensive analysis of the Qumran documents that are potentially relevant for such a reconstruction. His analysis is significant above all, because he lays out his assumptions and his methodology with a clarity that remains unrivaled. Since his study belongs to the current consensus on Qumran history, it will be discussed below in section C, and throughout this investigation.

Despite their differences of opinion about the correct historical context to which the evidence witnesses, all the Qumran historians share the working premise that a history of the Qumran community can be reconstructed by means of literary study of the relevant Dead

Sea texts and the application of a historical hermeneutic to them. Some of these scholars prefer, however, to use the archaeological and palaeographical evidence in a methodological first step to determine the proper historical background against which to reconstruct the history alluded to in the texts.

Since the primary concern in this context is to understand the ancient data itself, we are not beginning with a prior commitment to any of the published historical reconstructions. Only after the data has been investigated in regard to its historical import will we address this issue. Our analysis of the data cannot, however, presume to proceed without consideration of the immense amount of groundwork that precedes us. Therefore, before the several bodies of evidence for the history of the Qumran community are subjected to separate analyses, it would be helpful to review briefly the various perspectives on the history of the community as well as the prevailing consensus on that history.

B. *Reconstructions of the History of the Qumran Community*

Since the discovery of the Dead Sea Scrolls, a plethora of scholarly theories and reconstructions of Qumran history has been published, which, taken together, span a period of about one thousand years from the early second century BCE to the Middle Ages. While sharing the working premise that sufficient and necessary evidence is available to identify the key actors and to reconstruct important episodes in that history, these theories and reconstructions vary principally according to when one dates the 'origin' and earliest history of the Qumran community. The 'origin' of the community is sometimes used to refer to the initial occupation of the site Qumran in the mid-second century BCE or later. In contrast to this strictly archaeological understanding of the community's 'origin', two chronological notes in CD I,5-11 are thought to refer to a community that had come into existence self-consciously even before settling at Qumran. This group is sometimes called the pre-Qumran community. The first chronological note seems, on the face of it, to date the emergence of this community 390 years after the exile, i.e. to the early years of second century BCE (I,5-7). According to the second note, God gave this community a teacher twenty years after its historical emergence (I,9-10). This event is sometimes thought to coincide chronologically with the settlement of Qumran. Of course, the documentary and archaeological evidence has been variously interpreted. Several overviews of most of these theories of the community's history are accessible in the secondary literature.[3] For the sake of brevity, only a sketch of these theories is presented here.

The pre-Maccabean theory dates the origin of the community c. 200 BCE, associating allusions in some of the Dead Sea texts with persons involved in the so-called Hellenistic crisis in Judaea and identifying the Qumran community with the Essenes or forerunners of the Hasidim.[4] Closely related to this view is the Maccabean theory, which dates the origin of the community c. 175 BCE and identifies characters alluded to in the scrolls with the Maccabee family and its contemporaries, including the Hasidim.[5] Two versions of this theory are represented in the secondary literature: one identifies the Wicked Priest with Jonathan Maccabeus and the Teacher of Righteousness with a contemporary Zadokite high priest; the other identifies the Wicked Priest with Simon Maccabeus, no identification postulated for the Teacher. The Hasmonean theory dates the community's emergence between 130 and 90 BCE: one version identifies the Wicked Priest with Alexander Jannaeus; the other identifies him with Aristobulus II.[6]

According to the Roman theory, dating the existence of the community c. 47 BCE to 70 CE, the community came into being about the time of direct Roman involvement in the affairs of Jerusalem and Judaea—approximately at the time of Herod the Great. One strand of the Roman theory associates the Qumran antagonists and protagonists with figures of early Christian history.[7] The other strand identifies the Qumran community with the Zealots.[8] Although one may not characterize it strictly speaking as a historical reconstruction of the Qumran community, some scholars date certain Qumran compositions from the end of the first century to the sixth century CE.[9] For the sake of convenience it will be called the Late Roman theory. Similarly, a few scholars consider the Qumran compositions to be Karaitic in origin, but they never actually begin to reconstruct the community's history based on this perspective.[10]

Most of the scholars presenting these reconstructions agree that the antagonist of the Teacher and his community, the Wicked Priest, is an identifiable, historical personality. Several candidates have been suggested for this individual. The usual process of identification is as follows: once one has postulated the identity of the Wicked Priest, one may then postulate the identity of his contemporary, the Teacher. According to the prevailing consensus, the Maccabean theory, these figures were active about 150 BCE, but the Teacher's community continued to exist until c. 70 CE. Most scholars agree that the community's life at Qumran ended with the Roman destruction of Qumran c. 70 CE. The Christian and Zealot datings have been criticized (as have the Late Roman and Karaite theories) for attempting to fit the history of the Qumran community into too short a period of time and for not taking into account the chronological controls derived from archaeological and palaeographical analyses.

There are also significant differences of opinion about how one proceeds with the reconstruction of the community's history. The division among scholars has often been recognizable in the debate over the correct methodological starting-point. Does one begin with the 'external' chronological controls provided by archaeology and palaeography, which are thought to be independent and more objective than exegetical conclusions? Or does one rely chiefly upon a study of the allusions to historical characters and events in the literary data? Those who argue for the primacy of the so-called 'external' controls over against internal analysis of the relevant texts argue that the archaeology of the site Qumran and the palaeography of the Dead Sea scripts provide crucial evidence for establishing the correct periodization against which to understand the statements within the texts themselves.[11] Others have been critical of the claims to chronological precision in Qumran archaeology and palaeography. According to representatives of this latter view, the so-called 'external' controls are not objective. For that reason, the historian is that much more dependent upon the evidence provided by the literary documentation.[12]

Since all of the reconstructions of the history of the Qumran community cannot be analyzed individually in the present context, we will restrict our investigation to several scholarly proposals that belong to and continue to contribute to the prevailing consensus, which associates the origin and early history of the Qumran community with the Maccabean period. This decision is not intended in any way to discredit theories *a priori* that stand in some respect outside the pale of the consensus. Rather, as will become apparent in the course of the investigation, the strengths and the weaknesses of the prevailing consensus can also be found in other non-accepted, yet competing reconstructions of the community's history. It is hoped, therefore, that the conclusions of this study reflect not solely on the current consensus concerning that history, but also on the enterprise of reconstructing such a history itself.

C. *The Prevailing Consensus*

In the 1950s Geza Vermes associated the events alluded to in some of the Dead Sea Scrolls with the history of the Maccabees Jonathan and Simon.[13] Despite intermittent dissenting voices, this thesis has been generally accepted. Vermes has recently asserted that the superiority of his thesis, in contrast to the many others, is that it takes account of all the evidence—the archaeological, the palaeographical, and the literary data.[14] While the general historical background associated with this thesis—the Maccabean context—has often been taken for granted, differences in the use of the sources and concerning details of the community's history are emphasized in several investigations. Four names are often associated with the further elaboration and stabilization of the Maccabean thesis—Gert Jeremias, Hartmut Stegemann, Jerome Murphy-O'Connor, and Frank M. Cross, Jr. The general thrust of each scholar's contribution to the question of Qumran history is sketched below.

Gert Jeremias

Gert Jeremias's book, *Der Lehrer der Gerechtigkeit*, arose from his work in the Qumranforschungsstelle in Heidelberg, West Germany.[15] Its abiding value lies less in his identification of characters involved in the history of the Qumran community than in his own systematic analysis of the relevant sources. This work consists of two parts. In Part I, 'Die Person des Lehrers der Gerechtigkeit',[16] he investigates the Kittim (=Romans), the Wicked Priest (=Jonathan Maccabeus), the Man of the Lie, and the enemies in 4QpNah in order to home in on the period of the Teacher's activity (Chapters 1-4).[17] In Chapter 5, he investigates statements about the Teacher in 1QpHab, 4QpMicah, 4QpPs 37, and CD.[18] In Part II, 'Der Lehrer der Gerechtigkeit als geistliche Persönlichkeit', he argues that the Teacher wrote 1QH II,1-19, 31-39; IV,5-VII,25, and VIII,4-40. These *hodayot* are classified under the heading 'Das Selbstzeugnis des Lehrers'.[19] Understanding these *hodayot* as historical sources for the life and experiences of the Teacher has come to play an important, although not entirely uncontroversial, role in the reconstruction of the history of the Teacher and his community.[20] In the present context, Jeremias's comparison of the Teacher of Righteousness and Jesus need not be examined (see his Part II, Chapter 9).[21]

Hartmut Stegemann

Like Jeremias, Hartmut Stegemann was also an assistant to K.G. Kuhn in the Qumranforschungsstelle in the early 1960s. One of his doctoral dissertations, *Die Entstehung der Qumrangemeinde*, has become an oft-cited study of the history of the Qumran community.[22] After an introduction (Chapter 1), in which he expresses his acceptance of the results of palaeographical and archaeological studies as well as his advocacy of the widely accepted identification of the community with the ancient Essenes, Stegemann indicates how his work differs from that of his colleague Jeremias.[23] He does not start with an investigation of the Kittim, because they are nowhere in the Qumran texts associated with *the beginnings* of the community.[24] Likewise, difficulties in the identification of the Teacher of Righteousness, or rather the sheer plurality of possible identifications, induce him to reject a discussion of this character as a starting-point for investigating the origin of the community.[25] He chooses rather to focus his investigation on the inner-Jewish opponents of the Qumran community.[26] Unlike his colleague Jeremias, who investigates the enemies in order to learn more about the teacher, Stegemann is primarily interested in clarifying the relationship of the individual enemies to one another.[27] Secondarily, he wants to answer the question whether the Teacher was the founder of the community as Jeremias and others have claimed.[28] Accepting the chronological indicators arising from the palaeographical and archaeological studies, he maintains that the community came into existence between 200 and 37 BCE and that the latest non-biblical texts from Qumran could theoretically have been authored as late as 68 CE.[29]

In Chapter 2, he deals with the problem of which texts provide clues to the early history of the community. Because they preserve statements about the Teacher in conflict with his enemies, his crown witnesses are the pesharim. In particular, 1QpHab, 4QpNah, and 4QpPs 37 fall into this category.[30] Other pesharim are eliminated from the historical discussion either because of their future eschatological stance or because of their fragmentary condition.[31]

4QFlor, 4QPB, 4QTest, 1QSa, and 1QM are also excluded from the historical discussion because of their eschatological or ideal character. With some reservations in mind, Stegemann includes CD as a valuable historical witness to the early history of the community.[32] Because 1QS presents the opponents of the community in a rather stereotypical and undifferentiated fashion, that is, as a homogeneous body, it too is excluded from use in the historical reconstruction.[33] Finally, Stegemann appropriates Jeremias's claim that the Teacher wrote many of the thanksgiving hymns in 1QH II–VIII, thereby attributing to them a crucial historical value.[34] His Chapter 3 is devoted to the investigation of previously unpublished fragments of 4QpPs 37.[35]

With Chapter 4, Stegemann begins his discussion of the opponents of the Qumran community. In his primary source, the pesharim, he discovers nine terms referring to enemies: the Man of the Lie (the Liar),[36] the Violent Ones of the Covenant,[37] Ephraim,[38] the Misinterpreters of the Torah (=Seekers after Smooth Things),[39] the Deceivers in Jerusalem,[40] Manasseh,[41] the Wicked Priest,[42] the Priests of Jerusalem,[43] and the Lion of Wrath.[44] Building upon Jeremias's analysis of CD, Stegemann discusses its references to the community's enemies as viewed through the categories of enemies found in the pesharim.[45] Finally, the enemies of the so-called *Lehrerlieder* in 1QH are discussed.[46]

In Chapter 5, 'Historische Auswertung des Befundes: Die Entstehung der Qumrangemeinde und der "Lehrer der Gerechtigkeit"', Stegemann proceeds from analysis of the primary historical sources to a synthesis of their data with information preserved in Josephus and the books of the Maccabees.[47] Like Jeremias, he identifies the Wicked Priest with Jonathan Maccabeus and the Teacher with an unknown Zadokite high priest in Jerusalem whose office had been usurped by the Wicked Priest.[48] With that chronological datum firmly established, he retreats twenty years from the time of the Teacher's first association with the community (CD I,11), where he discovers the precipitating cause and date of the community's origin—the murder of Onias III c. 172-171 BCE.[49] The community emerged, therefore, as a traditionalist (pro-Zadokite) response to the Jerusalem Hellenists.[50]

Chapters 6–10, on the origin of the Pharisees, the Zadokites in relation to the later Sadducees, Qumran's view of history, its way of writing history and use of scripture remain unfinished.[51]

Jerome Murphy-O'Connor

While viewing himself as belonging to the same literary-critical tradition of Qumran scholarship as represented by Jeremias and Stegemann, and sharing many of their conclusions, Murphy-O'Connor is also critical of certain historical theories of the community's history, e.g. the Roman-Christian-Zealot theories, that do not accept the chronological framework inferred from palaeographical and archaeological study, which would preclude any such late reconstructions.[52]

Murphy-O'Connor has made a distinctive contribution to the discussion of the history of the Qumran community. He is primarily recognized in Qumran studies for his literary-critical studies of 1QS and CD.[53] In our study, we shall focus on his work on the latter. Whereas Jeremias emphasized 1QH II–VIII as an invaluable historical source concerning the Teacher, and Stegemann made the pesharim his strategical fulcral point for understanding all the other sources for Qumran history, Murphy-O'Connor draws attention to CD as his major witness for the early history of the community, prior to its being joined by the Teacher.[54]

In contrast to Stegemann, who also finds literary seams and ideological unevenness in CD, but who characterizes it as a Qumran document,[55] Murphy-O'Connor finds a pre-Qumranic Essene Missionary Document in CD II,14–VI,1[56] as well as a Memorandum in VII,4–VIII,3[57] that were not authored in the Qumran community. These sections of CD are attributed to a Babylonian Essene community that had returned to Palestine during the wars of the Maccabees against the Seleucids and their supporters in Israel.[58] I,1–II,13 (the historical and theological introductions),[59] VI,2–VIII,3 (the Well-Midrash),[60] and VIII,3-19 (the Critique of the Princes of Judah)[61] are attributed to later Qumran-Essene authorship.

Murphy-O'Connor should be credited with first attracting attention to the composite nature of CD and presenting an alternative way of explaining its literary components historically. His major assumption, which he undergirds with a source-critical analysis of CD, is that its earliest literary layer should be interpreted radically differently than it had been. According to him, the earliest community, which composed the Missionary Document and the Memorandum, was not formed simply as a traditionalist reaction against Palestinian Hellenism, but rather as the expression of a nationalistic Babylonian group inspired by the victories of Judas Maccabeus (c. 165 BCE) to return from their exile to the homeland.[62] Against Stegemann, who, he says, dissolves all of CD's geographical references into symbols because they derive from scripture, Murphy-O'Connor interprets the name Damascus as a reference to Babylon.[63] He takes the first chronological note in CD I,5-6 somewhat loosely, locating the Babylonian Essene group in the environs of Jerusalem c. 165 BCE.[64] He interprets the reference to twenty years of groping like blind ones (I,10) as a round number meaning a half-generation or ten years.[65] In these ten years, after the arrival of the Essenes in Judaea, the Teacher grew to be a man.[66] Around 152 BCE the Teacher, who had meanwhile become the de facto high priest in Jerusalem during the so-called Intersacerdotium (159-152 BCE), joined the newly repatriated Babylonian Essenes, who already had a decisively anti-Temple disposition that stamped their ideology until their annihilation during the First Jewish War against the Romans.[67]

On both literary and historical levels, Philip R. Davies's recent study of CD is a refinement of all previous work, especially that of Murphy-O'Connor.[68] Since he does not present a comprehensive analysis of the history of the Qumran community, discussion of this work is reserved for the chapter on CD.

Frank M. Cross, Jr

Frank M. Cross, Jr, differs from Jeremias, Stegemann, and Murphy-O'Connor both in his selection and interpretation of the sources. Unlike Stegemann, who explicitly rejects 4QTest as a historical witness because of its eschatological character,[69] Cross views it as a central piece of evidence for his identification of the Wicked Priest with Simon Maccabeus.[70] He argues that the 'accursed man, one of Belial' (l. 23) refers to none other than Simon Maccabeus and the 'instruments of violence' (l. 25) allude to his sons Judas and Mattathias.[71] He finds supportive documentation for this general historical scenario in 1 Macc. 14.41-49, which refers both to the selection of Simon as leader and high priest of the Jews until a trustworthy prophet should arise and to Simon's prohibition of unallowed assemblies in the countryside. Cross believes this prohibition was directed potentially against the rebellious Qumran community.

The scholars discussed above have made enduring contributions to the investigation of the Dead Sea Scrolls and the history of the community that wrote and preserved them. Jeremias, Stegemann, and Murphy-O'Connor are in agreement on the identification of the Teacher and the Wicked Priest, but diverge concerning the details of the history. Associating these figures with a slightly later historical context, Cross's analysis of the data remains on the fringe of the current consensus. These four analyses were chosen for the present discussion because of their contributions to the consensus and because each emphasizes a different body of literary evidence: Jeremias, 1QH; Stegemann, some of the pesharim—1QpHab, 4QpNah, 4QpPs 37; Murphy-O'Connor, CD; and Cross, 4QTest. Furthermore, all four scholars agree that one should first establish the periodization for the history of the Qumran community on the basis of archaeological and palaeographical studies before addressing the problem of decoding the allusions in the literary data from Qumran. Finally, they also share the view that the Qumran community should be identified with the ancient Essenes.

D. *The Evidence*

In order to reconstruct the history of any human association, the historian must examine all the potentially relevant data. In the case of the Qumran community, the evidence is represented by the remains of the Qumran complex itself and the documents coming from the nearby caves. Until the caves and the Qumran complex had been brought into connection with these documents, on the basis of the proximity of the caves to the complex and a shared material culture, there was practically no concern with reconstructing the history of a Jewish community that occupied Qumran from the middle of the second century BCE to the last quarter of the first century CE. The Damascus Document, the only 'specifically Qumranic document' known before the discovery of the scrolls, had been studied, but there was no consensus on the identity of its author nor on the identity of the community whose history it presumably relates. Only after the discovery of the scrolls, which included older fragments of the Damascus Document, did a consensus begin to emerge identifying the inhabitants of Qumran with the people alluded to in the Damascus Document and the other scrolls. These people have gradually come to be identified with the ancient Essenes known from Philo, Josephus, and Pliny.

The archaeological work carried out at Qumran, which has produced an important corpus of artifacts, also requires reassessment in order to determine its relevance and possible contribution as evidence to the historical reconstruction of the history presumably alluded to in the Dead Sea Scrolls. Likewise, the young discipline of Hebrew-Aramaic palaeography needs to be examined for its contribution to the historical issue under consideration. One important palaeographer, Frank M. Cross, Jr, has maintained that palaeographical and archaeological analyses provide more objective chronological information necessary for establishing the proper historical background against which to reconstruct the community's history than does internal analysis of the statements within the community's historical writings themselves.

Although the archaeological data and the ancient reports about the Essenes continue to function as valuable circumstantial evidence for the existence and identity of the group settled at Qumran, the burden of reconstructing the details of its history lies on the relevant information culled from the Qumran documentation itself. Since the Dead Sea Scrolls comprise the most important body of literary data pertaining to this particular history, it is to this documentation that the historian must turn.

Among the writings found in the Qumran caves, sometimes thought to have been a storehouse for the library of the Qumran community, there are both biblical and non-biblical texts. The former category may be excluded from classification as specifically Qumranic writings, since they are not peculiar to Qumran authorship and use. The non-biblical category may be subdivided into non-Qumranic, e.g. *Jubilees*, *Enoch*, and Qumranic writings, e.g. 1QS, CD, 1QH, the pesharim. Although the debate continues on the distinction between these two sub-categories of non-biblical texts, several texts are now widely accepted as being Qumranic.[72]

Since a community was occupying Qumran in the second half of the second century BCE, according to archaeological study at Qumran, and the earliest script (1QS) of specifically Qumranic documents dates to the end of the second or early first century BCE, it is thought that documents composed between c. 150 BCE, the *terminus a quo*, and 68-70 CE, the *terminus ad quem*, could have been composed by members of the Qumran community. Documents which may have been composed before and after these termini and which do not mention figures like the Teacher of Righteousness, the Wicked Priest, and the Liar, are automatically disqualified from consideration as specifically Qumranic documents. Within this widely accepted chronological framework, the pivotal criterion for Qumran authorship or redaction would therefore have to be the presence of certain interests emerging out of the community's ideology, institutions, and history.

Stegemann has mentioned a few internal criteria for the designation of 'specifically Qumranic' literature that seem to be generally accepted among Qumran scholars.[73] (1) Texts that credit the Teacher of Righteousness with an authoritative function may be designated as specifically Qumranic. (2) Those that know the specific way of life of the community may also be considered specifically Qumranic. (3) Texts that reflect the Qumran community's special position in the framework of Judaism of the Second Temple period (specifically from the second century BCE to the first century CE) belong to this category. (4) Those that are related to the above three criteria by virtue of shared literary forms, e.g. the pesharim, and/or shared terminology, e.g. the Teacher of Righteousness (מורה צדק), the Wicked Priest (הכוהן הרשע), and the Liar (איש הכזב) may also be categorized as specifically Qumranic. Based on these criteria, Stegemann ascribes all of the pesharim, CD I-VIII, XIX-XX, CD IX-XVI, 1QS, 1QSa, 1QSb, 1QH, 4QFlor, and 11QMelch to Qumranic authorship.[74] Other analysts have drawn up slightly different lists or made statements about what characterizes specifically Qumranic literature.[75]

Criteria (1) and (4) are useful in the historical inquiry, because they focus on one of the specific historical issues under scrutiny—the relationship of the Teacher of Righteousness to the Wicked Priest and the Liar. Criterion (2) refers above all to CD IX-XVI and 1QS, which preserve information about the community's structure and halakhot. This criterion is independent of criteria (1) and (4), for these documents never mention specific historical figures entitled the Teacher of Righteousness and the Wicked Priest. In fact, the conflict alluded to in these legal texts is presented as one of infraction of accepted norms of behavior rather than as a personal conflict or communal strife between two or more influential figures. Criterion (2) answers the question which community wrote and preserved these prescriptions. Criterion (3) seems to refer to texts like CD, 1QpHab, and 4QpPs 37, that preserve statements about hostilities and polemics between the Teacher's community and that of the Wicked Priest and the Liar. Thus this criterion is not clearly independent of (1) and (4).

Within Stegemann's list of specifically Qumranic documents, there are only a few texts that are widely accepted as having direct relevance for the reconstruction of episodes in the history of the Qumran community. These are CD I–VIII, XIX–XX, 1QpHab, 4QpPs 37, 4QpNah, 1QH, and, according to Cross, 4QTest (see section C, above).

While Stegemann's list of possible sources for the history of the Qumran community agrees with that drawn up by most other analysts (an exception being Cross's inclusion of 4QTest), he illustrates perhaps better than most others that the historian is involved in weighing pieces of potential evidence, sometimes giving preference to one source over another and sometimes interpreting the remaining sources in light of a central source. He concludes that all the relevant Qumran sources are not of equal historical value.[76] Therefore, he designates one body of literary evidence as primary and central for understanding the other literary evidence. These are the pesharim.[77]

He chooses the pesharim, because he believes that they can inform the historian best about the earliest conflicts between the Teacher of Righteousness along with his (Qumran) community and the Wicked Priest, the Liar, and their adherents.[78] For him, the pesharim provide a stylistically homogeneous body of evidence, which often demonstrates an overlap in terminology related to the history of the Qumran community.[79] This history appears, however, under the guise of sobriquets and veiled allusions to historical personalities and events. The most important pesharic texts are 1QpHab, 4QpNah, and 4QpPs 37.[80] Other pesharim that are preserved only fragmentarily, e.g. 1QpMicah, 1QpZeph, 1QpPs 68, 3QpIsa, 4QpIsa^{a-d}, and 4QpHos, are thought to be practically unyielding for the historical analysis.[81]

The overlapping terminology referring presumably to the history of the Qumran community is the chief feature of the pesharim that makes them attractive to Stegemann and others as historical sources.[82] Although this terminology is not entirely identical from one document to another, Stegemann suggests that this may be due to slight differences in the main subjects of the individual pesharim, or to the biblical texts being cited and their peculiar formulations, or to differences in the interests of their authors (i.e. different dates of composition).[83]

Both 1QpHab and 4QpPs 37 speak of the Teacher of Righteousness, the Wicked Priest, the Liar, and the Violent Ones of the Covenant.[84] None of these expressions is found in 4QpNah.[85] On the other hand, the Seekers after Smooth Things (=Misinterpreters of the Law), known from 4QpNah, are never mentioned in 1QpHab and 4QpPs 37.[86] In spite of this incongruity, both 1QpHab and 4QpNah are interested in the Kittim, not found in 4QpPs 37.[87] The latter document and 4QpNah share the expressions Ephraim and Manasseh, lacking in 1QpHab.[88]

Although Stegemann rightly warns against the uncritical mixture of statements from the different pesharim, he maintains that the great amount of overlap in terminology does allow analysts to associate one pesher with another.[89] He admits that 4QpNah differs greatly in content from 1QpHab and 4QpPs 37, but suggests that this may be due to its bad state of preservation.[90]

For Stegemann and others CD and the *Lehrerlieder* of 1QH are also valuable sources for the history of the Qumran community.[91] Unlike most other Qumran scholars, however, he states quite lucidly that these two literary sources cannot function as primary evidence due to their *Tendenzen*, their styles, and their lack of a historical framework.[92] CD, for example, lumps the opponents of the Qumran community and its Teacher together, thus producing an undifferentiated and skewed presentation of several opponents that probably existed over a longer period of time.[93] The *Lehrerlieder* are written in a highly personal style, focused around the 'I' that is speaking. This 'I' is difficult to interpret historically, because it makes use of standard biblical expressions found in the Old Testament psalms and prophets.[94] Thus Stegemann suggests that CD and the *Lehrerlieder* can be understood properly only after the historical framework and particular details within the framework deriving from the pesharim have been made intelligible.[95]

E. *Methodological Considerations*

None of the sectarian documents from the Qumran caves takes the form of a work of history in the sense that 1 Samuel–2 Kings, 1 & 2 Chronicles (Ezra and Nehemiah), Josephus' *Antiquities* and his *Jewish War* do. None of them presents a continuous narrative about events and persons that can unequivocally be identified as having lived and acted in public history of a particular historical period. This is due to the nature of the documentation, whose historiographic intent has usually been assumed rather than demonstrated. Certainly, the pesharim, CD, and the *Lehrerlieder* are not histories in the usual sense, but they are often implicitly treated as such.

The history of the Qumran community is not explicitly alluded to in the historical works of the period in which the community presumably lived, i.e. 1 & 2 Maccabees, Daniel, and Josephus. If such a history can be told at all, the information for the narrative must come from the sectarian Dead Sea Scrolls themselves. Therefore, one should carefully scrutinize each of the pertinent documents in regard to its character, literary structure, and language before making any claims about their historical usefulness.

Martin Noth has aptly pointed out that the historian has not completed his task merely by collecting (*zusammentragen*) and arranging (*ordnen*) the pertinent historical reports.[96] In fact, prior to arranging the reports, they require accurate interpretation in regard to their usefulness (*Verwertbarkeit*) and significance (*Tragweite*) as historical sources.[97] Noth emphasizes the working principle that sources should be questioned about their intention and character before the weight of their contents can be evaluated for the presentation of a history.[98] Realizing that source study is the very heart of historical research and reconstruction, he says it is necessary to discover the conditions under which particular sources were composed (this would include a knowledge of the history of the growth of a document) and what the sources/their authors actually wanted to convey. Then one may ask why a source related just that which it does and why it tells it in just the way that it does.[99] By asking these questions, the historian can determine what kind of information can be retrieved from a literary source and what weight this information should carry in the historical reconstruction.[100] Noth counsels that one should address these kinds of questions to each and every possible piece of literary evidence. Otherwise, one runs the risk of failing to appreciate the historian's special situation, thereby giving answers that are not justifiable and which cannot hold up under more careful scrutiny.[101]

CD, the pesharim, 4QTest, and 1QH are not historical narratives that refer directly to known historical characters such as Jonathan or Simon Maccabeus and their contemporaries as the Deuteronomic History, the Chronicler, and the Gospels seem to refer literally to Israelite-Judaean and early Christian personalities. If historical reconstruction of Israelite-Judaean history and of Jesus and his early followers is difficult, even where an abundance of history-like narrative documentation is available, how much more difficult will it be to retrieve historical information from literature not bearing the narrative form and whose language is not self-explanatory.

1. Epithets like the Wicked Priest, the Liar, and the Teacher, must be studied within their individual literary contexts. One needs to ask two related questions when one encounters such sobriquets: whether the author intended, *vis-à-vis* the literary context, to refer to discrete historical figures, and, if so, whether one can identify them by name or function with figures from the historiographical works of the time.

2. The texts should be interrogated about the geographical locality of these historical figures and their respective communities. In the historically relevant Qumran texts, reference is sometimes made to geographical and ethnic entities such as Israel, Judah, Ephraim, Manasseh, Damascus, and Lebanon. Do these names correspond to known peoples or locations of the past or are they used in some other way in their present contexts, e.g. as ideal literary or theological constructs or perhaps in some non-literal, transferred sense?

3. Above all the historian requires more than just a general periodization in order to begin to speak about individual and group history at a particular location. He must have at least one solidly dated event that is mentioned in the texts under consideration or from some external source (for example, in the ancient reports about the Essenes). These three issues in combination, the identification of historical characters, the determination of the geographical setting, and the chronological background, if they can be determined positively, allow one to entertain the possibility of sound historical reconstruction.

A final working principle is that *possible* and *actual* identity of an entity is not equivalent to its historical development through time. In order to reconstruct a history, an already identified entity, perhaps even an identifiable one, in this case a person or a community of persons, must be associated with an accurate date and their development should be traceable either forward or backward, ideally both, from that given date. The accurate description of an episode in such a history would serve as a minimal requirement for initiating historical reconstruction. As an example of this particular problem, one may take the ancient reports about the Essenes. Although Josephus' reports on the Essenes (as well as the other reports) do not comply with this important requirement of some historical development in time, they *may* help to identify his Essenes with a first-century branch of the Dead Sea community (but only after that group is already known from reliable historical sources). While valuable for the question of the character and make-up of the Essenes, Josephus' digressions on the Essenes reveal nothing at all about the all-important historical episodes, presumably related in some of the sectarian scrolls, which in combination could be used to reconstruct a historical narrative.

The central goal of this work is to reassess all the evidence that could potentially bear on the historical background, the historical locality, and the reconstruction of episodes in the history of the Qumran community, which is widely thought to be identical with an Essene group localized at Qumran from the second century BCE to the last quarter of the first century CE and which wrote and preserved the manuscripts discovered in the eleven main Qumran caves.

This reassessment is based on an analysis of the non-literary and literary evidence for such a history. The non-literary/external evidence includes the results of archaeological work carried out in the late 1940s and 1950s at the site Qumran (Chapter 2) and the results of palaeographical study of the Dead Sea Scrolls themselves and other relevant palaeographical data (Chapter 3).

Another important body of external evidence that deserves attention, in this case literary evidence, is the ancient reports written by Philo, Josephus, and Pliny concerning the Essenes (Chapter 4). 1 & 2 Maccabees will also be reviewed for possible contributions to the historical reconstruction. The internal/literary evidence for the historical reconstruction of Qumran history consists of CD (Chapter 5), the pesharim, 1QpHab, 4QpPs 37, and 4QpNah (Chapter 6), 4QTest (Chapter 7), and the *Lehrerlieder* of 1QH (Chapter 8).

Each piece of evidence will be investigated and assessed independently in terms of its possible contribution to the reconstruction of the history of the Qumran community. Where it is appropriate, the discussion of the primary evidence will require a more extensive dialogue with the literary and historical theories represented by the prevailing consensus on Qumran history. From time to time other reconstructions and hypotheses standing outside of this consensus may be mentioned. Once all the potential evidence has been reviewed, we will be in a position to determine which, if any, reconstruction of the history of the Qumran community the evidence favors.

Chapter 2

ARCHAEOLOGY AND THE HISTORY OF THE QUMRAN COMMUNITY

A. *Introduction*

A central issue distinguishing some hypotheses and reconstructions of the history of the Qumran community from others is the attitude of historians to the relevance and significance of the Qumran archaeological data for this particular problem. Despite the continuing presence of skepticism among some scholars about the role that archaeology at Qumran can validly play in discussions about Qumran history,[1] representatives of the prevailing consensus (see Chapter 1 §C) agree that the results of archaeological work carried out at Qumran—in conjunction with the contribution of the palaeographical study of the Dead Sea Scrolls—can be used to establish the correct periodization against which to reconstruct the historical events alluded to in the literary evidence. The chronological information inferred from the archaeological evidence is sometimes thought to be more objective than the more elusive and ambiguous data found in the Scrolls themselves.[2] This claim is based upon the widely accepted view that Qumran provides a known empirical location for the ancient Essenes, if not their central headquarters, over an extended period of time.

In order to reassess this claim, the nature of archaeological evidence in general as well as the character of the specific evidence from Qumran must be discussed.

B. *The Nature of Archaeological Remains*

As is the case with the literary data, tangible archaeological remains of the past also require interpretation.[3] The historian is aware that the archaeological data are essentially different in kind from the literary data. While the former rarely elicit unambiguous information about specific historical events, the latter may preserve information about such historical happenings.[4] By nature archaeological data are restricted in what they can prove and cannot prove.[5] According to Martin Noth, archaeological data can offer insights into the presuppositions and the conditions of life as well as into their transformations in the course of time, thus painting the historical background against which particular historical characters may have acted in particular situations.[6] The historical background is a valuable ingredient of historical reconstructions, but it does not usually provide the detail concerning human actions and identities within a specifically known chronological context without which the historian cannot formulate continuous narrative accounts about human groups in the past. This crucial detail derives predominantly from the literary evidence.[7]

Known both for his work in biblical studies and for his archaeological work at Qumran, Roland de Vaux also shares this view, but perceives the relationship between the literary and the archaeological data to be potentially complementary.[8] The archaeological data can sometimes verify the literary evidence,[9] but can also function as a control in historical reconstructions, even providing a corrective to the traditions found in the literary documentation.[10] Because these two bodies of data offer basically different kinds of information, the historian has to be careful not to produce an invalid harmonization of the archaeological facts and the literary statements.[11] In order to avoid such harmonizations, the value of each body of evidence for the historical reconstruction must be determined on its own merits.

In regard to Qumran, de Vaux admits that the relevant literary data, primarily the sectarian Dead Sea Scrolls, provide necessary and sufficient information about the particular history of the people who lived at Qumran and wrote the Scrolls. Having a different character, however, the archaeological data may aid in the interpretation of the texts by indicating a historical framework, a human milieu, or a provenance against which to understand the textual information.[12]

C. *The Archaeological Remains from Qumran*

Already in the mid-nineteenth and early twentieth centuries Qumran and its environs had been visited and explored by biblical scholars, archaeologists, and naturalists.[13] Not until the discovery of the Dead Sea Scrolls in the nearby caves, however, did the name Qumran become well-known and the site become identified with the headquarters of the group known from several ancient reports as the Essenes. De Vaux's account of the archaeological work done at Qumran in the late 1940s and the 1950s has come to be definitive for later discussions of Qumran's archaeological remains.[14]

Based on several years of excavation at Qumran, de Vaux postulates three broad periods of human occupation there—the 'Israelite', the Hellenistic-Roman, and the Byzantine and later occupations. The following review of Qumran archaeology derives entirely from de Vaux's own reports which are summarized in *The Archaeology of Qumran*. The 'Israelite' occupation is represented by Iron II sherds, one of which is a jar-handle bearing the *lmlk* stamp, and by ruins dating to the eighth and the seventh centuries BCE.[15] In connection with the scrolls, de Vaux's archaeological report emphasizes chiefly the next period of occupation, the Hellenistic-Roman occupation which encompassed a time-span of c. 220 years (c. 150 BCE–70 CE).[16] Later occupation or traces of human life at Qumran are mentioned only in passing.

Following the 'Israelite' or Iron II settlement, Qumran lay in ruins for several centuries before a new Jewish group resettled there in the second century BCE. This new Jewish occupation is thought by de Vaux to have been continuous, with the exception of a thirty-year abandonment toward the end of the first century BCE, from its genesis in the second century BCE to its abrupt end in the second half of the first century CE. The evidence for this continuity of material culture derives from the stratigraphy at Qumran. Stratum I is associated with a late Hellenistic occupation. At the bottom of this stratum the archaeologists found indications of considerable destruction, which was presumably so severe that Qumran's inhabitants were forced to abandon the site. According to de Vaux, the same historical group resettled Qumran about thirty years later. Stratum II witnesses this period of reoccupation which lies immediately above the signs of the destruction in stratum Ib. In historical terms, this would be Period II. The homogeneous occupational history of Qumran, represented by strata I and II, comes to a violent close at the end of Period II and is replaced by a non-Jewish occupation in Period III (=stratum III).

The Qumran Complex

Stratum Ia of the late Hellenistic occupation was built upon the remains of the 'Israelite' period (see de Vaux Pl. IV).[17] A channel was constructed to increase the water supply to a round cistern left from the 'Israelite' period. Beside this cistern, two rectangular cisterns and a decantation basin (loc. 117-118) were dug out. Another channel running from the south to one of the two new cisterns was also constructed. To the south of the building complex a corner was enclosed and two covered buildings were annexed (loc. 101-102). North of the wall which was surrounding the round Israelite cistern, a few rooms were added (loc. 115-116, 125-127). Even farther to the north some smaller rooms were constructed (loc. 129, 133, 140-141). The plan of stratum Ia is not completely discernable in the east. A few small rooms seem to have been built, but the southeastern rooms were replaced by two pottery kilns (Pl. Vb).

The exact date for the beginning of the Ia settlement cannot be determined, for the sherds and pottery of this stratum are indistinguishable from the following phase of occupation, Ib. Since there is no numismatic data that might add some precision to the dating of this period, the remains of stratum Ib serve to date the preceding stratum relatively.

According to de Vaux, stratum Ib (=Period Ib) represents the 'definitive form' of the Qumran complex.[18] Next to the main entrance on the northern side of the site, a two-story tower was installed (loc. 9-11). A smaller gateway was located on the southwestern side (loc. 139). A third entrance was built on the eastern side near a kiln (loc. 84). After entering by the main entrance in the north, a main building was located to the east and a smaller one was on the west. These constructions were separated by a space containing three cisterns and rooms from Period Ia. De Vaux thinks these rooms came to function as workshops in Ib. Access to this entire complex was gained through a gateway between the buildings (loc. 128).

The two-story tower is slightly separated from the rest of the architectural complex by open spaces in loc. 12 and 18. The eastern gateway led into a small courtyard (loc. 13), which gave access to several rooms, one of which was perhaps an assembly room (loc. 4). This room had benches along the walls. Next to it was a larger room (loc. 30), perhaps also used as an assembly area.

On the eastern side of the complex a courtyard was located, adjoining a paved rectangular room with fireplaces (loc. 38 and 41).

De Vaux surmises that this room may have been a kitchen. To the north of this lay a narrow courtyard; to the east, two rooms (loc. 39-40). In the south of the large courtyard there are some buildings and basins whose function is unclear (loc. 34). Farther to the east of this courtyard there was an uncovered area where two cisterns were found (loc. 49-50). The larger of the two was provided with steps (loc. 48) that had been built upon the kilns of Period Ia. Next to this construction was a washing-area accompanied by a stone basin and a sump (loc. 52). Loc. 53, where several iron tools were discovered, seems to have functioned as a storeroom. The space left between the 'Israelite' and the Ib walls was used to create storage areas or workshops (loc. 44-45, 59-61).

A large stepped cistern was dug out in Ib to the south of the main building (loc. 56, 58). Adjacent to this and outside of the older, 'Israelite' wall was a long room (loc. 77), measuring twenty-two by four and one-half meters. A courtyard in the west was added (loc. 111) along with two storerooms (loc. 129, 121). Another cistern was located in the south (loc. 91) and a courtyard sat upon the southwestern ridge (loc. 96). A 'lean to' was erected against this wall (loc. 97).

Besides the many storage areas attributed to Period Ib, it is characterized by its many cisterns.[19] Thus water supply was a chief concern at Qumran during this period. Water reached the complex itself by way of an aqueduct running to the northwestern corner of the site (loc. 137). At the point where the aqueduct meets the complex, the masonry dispersed the water into a broad decantation basin (loc. 132 and 137). Close by was a bath (loc. 138. Pl. VIIIa). After leaving the decantation basin the purified water filled up the cisterns at loc. 110, 117, and 118. Overflow was drained off to the north. The water channel turned toward to south, opening into a smaller decantation basin at loc. 83, and continued toward the large rectangular cistern at loc. 85 and 91. From here the channel ran on toward an elongated cistern to the south of the main building (loc. 56 and 58). After winding around the northern corner of this building and crossing a square basin at loc. 67, the channel headed southward. A peripheral channel ran on toward two cisterns in the east (loc. 49-50), continuing to a small bath (loc. 68, Pl. VIIIb), then to a decantation basin (loc. 69), and finally it arrived at a large cistern to the southeast of the Qumran complex (loc. 71).

Of special interest to the archaeologist are several rooms where important material remains were uncovered.[20] Adjoining the large room at loc. 77 is another (loc. 86, 89, Pl. IXb). Its ceiling had collapsed and debris covered more than 1000 vessels. At the western end of the room twenty-one small jars, thirty-eight dishes, and eleven jugs were uncovered. Against a pilaster 210 plates were stacked up (Pl. Xb). To the east 708 bowls were stacked up in rows forming a rectangle (Pl. Xa). Seventy-five beakers were found in front of these bowls. Pieces of pottery were scattered over the entire floor. Large jars, lids, pots, juglets, and lamps were absent from this important discovery. De Vaux thinks this area was used as the community's crockery in Period Ib.[21]

In open spaces between and around the buildings, deposits of animal bones were discovered.[22] These lay between large sherds of pitchers or pots (Pl. XIb), sometimes being found in closed jars. De Vaux associates these deposits with stratum Ib and dates them circumstantially on the basis of the coins of Alexander Jannaeus that were found nearby (loc. 130). Alexander Jannaeus reigned from 103 to 76 BCE. Similar deposits located above the sediment of loc. 130 and the old decantation basin at loc. 132 are recorded for the following period. This sediment is found above the destruction layer at the end of Ib. Associated with coins of Agrippa I and the Procurators, the sherds found covering these later deposits are attributed to stratum II (=Period II). Agrippa I reigned from 37 to 44 CE. The Procurators of Palestine reigned from 44 to 66 CE.

While the pottery of stratum Ib is similar to that of II, it is not identical.[23] One exception in all the ceramic material found at Qumran is an ovoid jar with a neck that has been reinforced from the outside (Pl. XVb right). The only identical counterpart to it belongs to a third-century BCE stratum in the Citadel of Jerusalem.[24] Certain characteristic features in the ceramic wares are helpful in distinguishing the two phases of Jewish occupation at Qumran.[25] The plates of Ib lack the molded edge typical of plates from stratum II. The large flared and thin-walled beakers of Ib are manifestly distinct from the smaller, thicker, and generally ribbed exemplars from stratum II. The distinction between the Hellenistic and Herodian lamps is even more apparent.

De Vaux maintains that the observable differences between the wares of strata Ib and II correspond approximately to a known historical line of demarcation: the wares of Ib belong to the late Hellenistic age in Palestine, ending around the middle of the first century BCE; those of II not only preserve forms that are similar to the earlier ones, but also newer forms that are documented for the period of the first Roman presence in Palestine.[26]

This broad periodization that is inferrable from the ceramics at Qumran can be made more precise, according to de Vaux, when brought into conjunction with the numismatic evidence.[27] The coins associated with Ib include eleven silver Seleucid coins, six dating from the years 132-129 BCE, another from somewhere within this range of years, and another dating possibly to the reign of Demetrius II (c. 145-139 and 129-125). Five other Seleucid bronzes come from the reigns of Antiochus III, IV, and VII (c. 223-187, 175-163, and 139-129 BCE). As for the coins from the Jewish mints, one from the reign of John Hyrcanus I (c. 134-104) and one from the reign of Judas Aristobulus (d. 135) are represented. In contrast to this paucity, one hundred forty-three coins from the reign of Alexander Jannaeus (c. 103-76) are extant. There is one from the reign of Salome Alexandra (c. 76-67), one from the time of Hyrcanus II (c. 63-40), and four from the time of Antigonus Mattathias (c. 40-37). None of these Jewish coins are dated precisely by inscriptions on the coins themselves. Nevertheless, the inscriptional references to various Jewish leaders do enable one to date them within particular known years of office. The coins attributed to Ib, which may include several deriving from Ia, range from the first quarter of the second century BCE into the early second half of the first century BCE. The Herodian coins, which de Vaux introduces while discussing Ib, are attributed to stratum II and will be discussed in that context.

If the numismatic evidence for Ib may be taken as a reliable indicator of the general range of human occupation at Qumran, the coins of Antigonus Mattathias serve to date the end of Ib, the *terminus ad quem*, to c. 37 BCE or slightly later. It is much more difficult to determine the *terminus a quo* of Ib with confidence.

Although no evidence exists that would allow one to date the beginning of Ia, its end, or the beginning of Ib precisely, de Vaux employs an important piece of circumstantial evidence to mark the chronological watershed between Ib and II: evidence of severe earthquake damage at Qumran. This damage is found on the eastern side of the Qumran complex running in less than a straight line from north to south across loc. 46, 40, 39, 51, 50, 49, 48, 43, 66, 73, 72 and 76.[28] It is most clearly witnessed in the steps and the floor of a large cistern (loc. 48-49, Pl. XVI), which are split and have sunk about fifty centimeters below the western side. The earthquake shook the tower only twenty-five meters to the west. Its eastern wall cracked and the ceiling and lintel of the tower's ground floor collapsed (loc. 10-11, 18-19). The northwestern corner of a building to the west was also affected by this seismic activity (loc. 129-130). The only signs of damage in the south are found in loc. 86 and 89, where the large store of pottery covered by ceiling and other debris was found.

De Vaux attributes this damage to the famous earthquake of 31 BCE.[29] According to Josephus, who preserves two succinct reports of this catastrophe, this major earthquake caused extensive destruction throughout Judaea both to animals and humans, especially to those dwelling in houses and other buildings.[30] He reports that 30,000 people died. This occurred, according to his statement in the *War*, in the spring of the year that Caesar fought Antony at Actium—31 BCE. Should this be the event that is responsible for the severe damage and evidence of a fire at the end of Qumran stratum Ib, it would serve as an absolute historical benchmark for the end of Period Ib and as a relative date for the beginning of Period II. The dating of the *terminus a quo* for the remains of stratum II depends upon whether one discerns continuity in occupation at Qumran immediately after the earthquake or whether one postulates abandonment of the site for a short period of time, as de Vaux has done.

De Vaux postulates a period of abandonment, since a layer of sediment covers the destruction layer associated with the earthquake of 31 BCE.[31] The remains from the following period, II, resettled presumably by the same group, lie above this sediment. The sediment, a result of the overflow of water once the earthquake had damaged Qumran's water system, had accumulated in the large decantation basin at loc. 132 (see also loc. 130). Its accumulation measures approx. seventy-five centimeters near the northwestern corner of the secondary building (loc. 129-130). Toward the east this layer of sediment thins out. The settlement of Period II used it here as a foundation for a supporting wall. The shaken outer wall of loc. 89 was also reinforced in this way. Therefore, its foundation was provided not only by the remains of Ib but also by the accumulated sediment.

At the beginning of Period II, apparently no consistent attempt was made to remove all of the debris from the previous occupation and the destruction that brought it to an end nor to rebuild the Qumran complex just as it had been in Ib.[32] The decantation basin (loc. 132) was not cleared of debris. A smaller basin at loc. 137 was used instead. The elongated cistern to the south of the main building was divided into two (loc. 56, 58). Split by the earthquake, two other cisterns in the east (loc. 49-50) were abandoned. The channel feeding them was blocked up. The small basins at loc. 34 were filled in, but the washing-area in loc. 51 continued to be used. Several rooms were covered; others were divided.

An especially interesting find was the covered workshop at loc. 125.[33] This consisted of a furnace and a drainage conduit (Pl. XIXb). De Vaux is not sure of its function. To the south of the round cistern, loc. 101 (Pl. XIXa) was newly paved. A furnace made of brick and a smaller oven were found there as well as a wooden cylinder coated with plaster.[34] A flight of steps led either to a terrace or to an upper story through which the furnace's chimney projected.

At loc. 100 (Pl. XXa) evidence was found of milling activities.[35] On a pavement of large stones a round platform with a carved-out trough was found. This construction's function is apparent. Mill-stones were placed on the platform for grinding, and the flour fell into the trough. Two fully intact basalt mill-stones were found in a pit at loc. 104. Other vestiges of mill-stones were also found there.

The long assembly room of Ib (loc. 30) was filled with debris from the upper story.[36] Fragments of plaster-covered mudbricks were found there. The reconstruction of these fragments has produced a writing-table measuring about five meters (length) by forty centimeters (breadth) by fifty centimeters (height).[37] De Vaux thinks that the additional discovery of two inkwells, one of bronze and another of earthenware known from the Roman period in Egypt and Italy, indicates that the upper story was a writing-area.[38]

Although the numismatic material recovered from this stratum seems to belong to a later period than that of Ib, two exceptions to this generalization may exist—ten coins of Herod the Great and one of Herod Archelaus. Despite the fact they come from mixed levels, de Vaux attributes the ten coins of Herod to stratum II.[39] They are associated with the later coin: in one case one of Herod's coins appears in a context with four of Alexander Jannaeus and one of Antigonus Mattathias that is associated with eight of Alexander Jannaeus. These were located close to one coin of the Procurators. Although de Vaux never clarified what he meant by his expression 'mixed levels', he was apparently referring to the possibility that the Herodian coins could empirically belong either to the end of Ib or the inception of II. He chooses the latter possibility, associating them, some or all of which may have come into circulation after 31 BCE, with the reoccupation in Period II. He recognizes, however, that this particular numismatic material cannot function as hard evidence supporting his dating of the *terminus ad quem* of Ib to 31 BCE.[40]

On a slope to the north of the ruins, archaeologists excavated Trench A, which preserved pottery and coins identical with those from Period Ib at the site, with the exception of one coin.[41] This find includes one silver tetradrachm of Antiochus VII Euergetes dated to 131/130 BCE, a tetradrachm of the autonomous Tyrian currency (pre-CE), an undated bronze of Antiochus III, and an undated bronze of Antiochus IV, nineteen coins of Alexander Jannaeus, one of Hyrcanus II, and one of Herod Archelaus. The last coin, dating between 4 BCE and 6 CE, is susceptible to two conflicting interpretations. De Vaux maintains that it was probably lost during the clearance work carried out at the beginning of Period II.[42] Accordingly, this coin would serve as circumstantial evidence for the resettlement of Qumran Period II. Along with the ten problematic Herodian coins, it could also be used to argue that Period Ib continued beyond 31 BCE. While both a theory of continued settlement and one of reoccupation are possible, the ambiguous evidence of this one coin can hardly tilt the balances in favor of one or the other.

Another group of coins belongs to Period II.[43] These include sixteen of Herod Archelaus (4 BCE–6 CE), ninety-one of the Procurators (6–66 CE), of these thirty-three were struck during the reign of Nero (between the years 54 and 58 CE), seventy-eight of Agrippa I (37–44 CE), and Jewish coins of the First Jewish Revolt against the Romans (66–70 CE). Associated with the destruction marking the end of stratum II, these Jewish coins of the First Revolt provide a valuable body of circumstantial chronological evidence for the *terminus ad quem* of Period II: represented are ninety-four bronze coins, eighty-three of which come from the second year (67 CE), five from the third year (68 CE), and six that cannot be identified due to extensive oxidation. Outside of the western containing wall, loc. 103, a clump of thirty-nine oxidized coins was also found. In the decantation basin at loc. 83, one coin of the Procurators, one of Agrippa I, a silver one struck under Nero in 62/63 at Antioch, and thirty-three of the First Revolt were found in debris and sherds from stratum II that the inhabitants of Period III had thrown into the basin. De Vaux argues, on the basis of the presence of Jewish coins from the year 68 and the absence of any from the fourth year, 69 CE, that Jewish occupation at Qumran came to an abrupt end at the hands of the Romans in the third year of the rebellion, 68/69 CE.[44] Taken together, these coins provide a broad periodization against which to understand the occupational history of Period II. They range from 4 BCE to 68 CE.

In loc. 120 a hoard of 561 silver pieces in three pots was found, one containing 223 pieces, one 185, and another 153.[45] Two of these pots are small, large-mouthed pots without handles that were closed up with a stopper of palm fiber: the forms are never otherwise found at Qumran. The third pot whose form is common to Qumran wares had a hole in its side through which coins could be deposited. This hoard was located above stratum Ib and below stratum II. It consists almost entirely of Seleucid silver tetradrachmae. Some of the coins come from the last rulers of the Seleucid dynasty, but most of them represent the autonomous currency of Tyre. The latest coin preserved in this hoard is dated to the year 118 of Tyre (=9/8 BCE); other pieces are countermarked to this year. Not until the year 126 (=1 BCE/1 CE) do new issues of Tyrian currency begin to appear anywhere. This collection of coins was made in or after 9/8 BCE and, as de Vaux surmises based on the absence of newer Tyrian issues, was buried before 1 BCE/1 CE.[46] De Vaux postulates two possible occasions when this burial may have occurred—between the time of the abandonment of Qumran Ib and the new settlement of Period II or at the beginning of Period II.[47] Two pieces of numismatic evidence induce de Vaux to date the *terminus a quo* of II toward the turn of the era.[48] First of all, the latest coin of the hoard comes from the year 9/8 BCE. It provides, therefore, a *terminus post quem*. Secondly, de Vaux thinks that a coin of Herod Archelaus (4 BCE–6 CE) found in Trench A belongs to the clearance of Qumran at the beginning of II.

Not the oldest coin of this hoard but rather the many Jewish coins of the First Jewish Revolt against the Romans date the end of Period II.[49] Along with (Roman) arrowheads, these coins were found in a layer of a black powdery substance. Therefore, the youngest of these Jewish coins is contemporary with or earlier than the time of the destruction of Qumran Period II. As was mentioned above, the absence of coins from the fourth year of the rebellion (69/70) leads de Vaux to date this destruction to 68/69 CE.[50] He refers to the context of the coins from the following period to support his claim.

Nine coins of Caesarea during the reign of Nero date to 67/68 CE and four of Dora from the same year were discovered.[51] De Vaux views these non-Jewish coins as circumstantial evidence for a Roman occupation of the site in Period III. Since they were not found in the layer of destruction associated with the end of Period II, but rather above it, they must derive from the following Period III.

Other coins associated with stratum III include one undated coin from Antioch during the reign of Nero (pre-68 CE), one bearing the names of Nero's daughter and wife, Claudia and Poppaea (65 CE at the earliest), one silver coin from Antioch in the reign of Vespasian and Titus in 69/70 CE, two from Ashkelon dating 72/73 CE, four of *Judaea Capta* (no earlier than 72 CE, perhaps even later), and one of Agrippa II from 87 CE. Because this last coin was discovered outside of the building, de Vaux doubts its attribution to stratum III and disqualifies it as evidence for this period.[52] Therefore, the presence of non-Jewish coins dating after 67/68 CE that are associated with the stratum III as well as the absence of Jewish coins of the First Revolt from this level indicate indirectly a non-Jewish, probably Roman, presence at Qumran about the year 68 or 69 CE.

As for the ceramic data, forms from Period II are present, but those peculiar to Qumran itself are lacking.[53] Along with the numismatic data, one could construe such an absence as an indicator of the new, albeit short-lived, occupation associated with stratum III.

The architectural evidence seems to point in the same direction (Pl. XXIII).[54] In the main building to the north, the two-story tower was reused, the walls running toward the east were reinforced, and the rooms to the northeast were modified slightly. South of the tower, the layer of destruction had been leveled out and the orderly arrangement of the rooms gave way to a haphazard juxtaposition of a group of several small rooms. The southeastern part of the main building was left unoccupied, but was reinforced. The central court of the older building was closed off by a large wall. Along the western wall, a ditch was dug, but the western section of the site was left in ruins.

The water system was greatly simplified.[55] The Romans reused only the large cistern in the southeast. The large reservoir in the south-west (loc. 91) was filled in, and a new channel was built over it connecting to the older channel in loc. 100 (Pl. XXIVb). This channel extended to the cistern at loc. 91 and crossed the annex (loc. 89) to the assembly room (loc. 86). It continued along the outside wall of this room and rejoined the older channel at loc. 72.

This stratum III represents a 'radical transformation'[56] of the earlier building design, characterized by simplification of the older building structures and the water system, attention given to reinforcement at places, perhaps for defensive purposes. There seems to be no recognizable concern for collective assembly, work-areas, or kilns. Outside of the ruins at the foot of the tower, however, one oven for bread baking was found (Pl. XXIII).

The Roman occupation was not extensive and appears to have been followed by transitory occupation during the time of the Second Jewish Revolt against the Romans in 132-135 CE.[57] Except for the construction of a wall dividing the cistern at loc. 58 in two, which was erected upon the rubble of stratum III and a (later) natural deposit, these inhabitants were not involved in large-scale reconstruction at the site. In the upper layer of the main building, a Jewish coin of this time has been found. Several others derive from the ground-floor of the tower to the north, where they were conserved under the bottom of a bowl.[58] This find includes five bronzes, one silver denarius of the Second Revolt, one denarius of Vespasian (69–79 CE), and three denarii of Trajan (98–117 CE). Some of the Jewish coins are undated, while others date to the second year of the Second Revolt, 133 CE. De Vaux thinks that the undated coins may be the latest of the lot.[59]

The final period of human presence at Qumran is represented by a small group of coins dating from the third century CE to the period of Turkish occupation of Palestine.[60] The remains of this period are not associated with the human occupation of Qumran in the Hellenistic-Roman age and, therefore, require no further discussion.

Other Material Remains

Four other bodies of material remains do deserve some attention, however, since they are materially related to the finds at the Qumran complex—the artifacts from the Qumran caves, Qumran cemeteries, 'Ain Feshkha, and 'Ain el-Ghuweir.

Outside of the Qumran site the most important body of material remains is that from the caves where the Dead Sea Scrolls were discovered. Besides the textual discoveries, the Qumran caves yielded many other ceramic remains that are thought to confirm the connection of the habitation of Qumran with the occupation of the caves.[61] According to de Vaux's report, Caves 1–4, 6–10, 17, and those in the marl terrace preserved broken pottery that is identical to the wares at Qumran in Periods Ib and II—late Hellenistic and Roman wares of Judaea. These include sherds of cylinder jars, lids, bowls, jugs, juglets, goblets, pots, and lamps. Alongside the ceramic remains, archaeologists recovered remains of foodstuffs, e.g. olive and date-stones and dessicated dates (Caves 1 and 7–10), scraps of cloth dated by a carbon-14 test to 33 BCE +/- 200 years (Cave 1), palm fibers (Cave 1), hides and papyrus (Cave 3), the ends of mats and ropes, scraps of leather (Caves 7–10), leather phylactery cases (Caves 1, 7–9), an inscribed ostracon (Cave 10), and wooden tentposts (Cave 17). With the singular exception of the cylinder jars known elsewhere only from a tomb at Quailba near Abila in the upper Transjordan,[62] the ceramic wares from the caves are identical to those found at Qumran strata Ib and II. No coins were discovered in the caves.

Although de Vaux was originally skeptical of the relationship between the Qumran complex and the nearby caves,[63] the presence of these shared ceramic wares convinced him that the same group inhabited both Qumran and the caves, the former being a communal center and the latter dwelling- and storage-areas.[64] Appealing also to the argument of proximity, de Vaux points out that Qumran is located centrally in relation to the caves. None of the caves in the marl terrace lies more than 100 meters from the Qumran complex.

A large cemetery to the east of the ruins consists of about 1100 tombs. Most of those that have been excavated preserved male skeletons, but a few female skeletons were also discovered.[65] Mudbricks used in the construction of these tombs consisted in part of sherds from strata Ib and II. One tomb preserved fragments of a jar from Ib, and another preserved a lamp from II. Except for a modicum of rare ornaments, beads, and earrings found near two of the female skeletons, the tombs yielded no other objects.

To the north of Khirbet Qumran and to the south of Wadi Qumran at the base of the marl terrace, two other secondary cemeteries were also discovered.[66] De Vaux does not report any other artifacts found in these tombs, such as ceramics or coins, that would further support the association of these two smaller cemeteries with the material remains at Qumran and the main cemetery.

De Vaux thinks that the Feshkha complex south of Qumran was occupied by the group settled at Qumran in Periods Ib and II.[67] Located to the north of 'Ain Feshkha, the building complex consists of a building measuring twenty-four by eighteen meters, an enclosure to the south of it, and a courtyard with basins. This complex yielded remains of ceramic wares that are identical to those associated with Qumran strata Ib and II. Although Feshkha I shows no signs of violent upheaval, as was the case at the end of Qumran Ib, Period II apparently ended by some sort of violent destruction. A single coin of the second year of the First Revolt is associated with this destruction layer. Therefore, the archaeological data from Feshkha are consistent with those from Qumran Ib and II.

P. Bar-Adon has postulated that ʻAin el-Ghuweir, located c. fifteen miles south of Qumran, was also inhabited by the people of Qumran and Feshkha.[68] The Ghuweir building complex consists of a walled-in courtyard, four rooms, a hall, a large kitchen, and two rooms in the east. Two periods of occupation, separated by a layer of burned material, are discernable. In this layer five undated coins of Herod the Great, one of Herod Archelaus, and one of Agrippa I struck in his sixth year, 42/43 CE, were unearthed.[69] Although de Vaux emphasizes that this site preserves mostly ceramic wares known from Qumran and Feshkha stratum II,[70] Bar-Adon finds a general correspondence with the wares of Qumran Ib and Feshkha I as well.[71] If overlap does exist, the numismatic data indicate this would have been from the time of Herod the Great or Herod Archelaus to at least 42/43 CE. The absence of coins of the First Jewish Revolt induces de Vaux to minimize the possible historical connection between Qumran, Feshkha, and ʻAin el-Ghuweir.[72]

D. *The Significance of the Archaeological Remains for Historical Reconstruction*

The most significant contribution of de Vaux's report of the archaeological data recovered at Qumran and in its vicinity for the historian of the Qumran community lies in its confirmation that the general area—Qumran, its cemeteries, Feshkha, and the caves where the Dead Sea Scrolls were found—witnesses to a homogeneous material culture that dates from some time in the second century BCE into the last half of the first century CE. Although the material culture shared by Qumran and the caves does not conclusively prove that the group living at Qumran during this time also composed the Scrolls and hid them away in the nearby caves, it is an important element—along with the argument of proximity—in the view that one and the same group inhabited this area.

The continuity in material culture extends from Period Ia or Ib to the end of Period II. Signs of destruction date the end of the Jewish settlement c. 68–69 CE. The non-Jewish numismatic data found in stratum III above the layer of destruction and associated with the end of Ib no longer evidence Jewish coins of the First Jewish Revolt. This absence is taken to indicate the beginning of a new non-Jewish occupational phase in or after 68–69 CE.

The inception of Jewish settlement in the late Hellenistic period at Qumran in Ia is not absolutely dateable due to the fact that one can neither demonstrate that any numismatic data comes unequivocally from this stratum nor can one clearly distinguish the ceramic wares of Ia from those of Ib. Therefore, the historian must settle for an open-ended date for the beginning of the Ia installation at Qumran—at some time in the late second or early first century BCE.[73]

De Vaux claims that Ib witnesses the 'definitive form' of the Jewish settlement at Qumran. Although one cannot assign an absolute date to the erection of this expanded complex, the presence of ceramic wares and coins can give an indication of the approximate periodization. The ceramic wares fall into two categories that are more or less typologically and stratigraphically distinguishable: Ib forms are attributed to the late Hellenistic period (roughly to 50 BCE) and II forms to the Roman period (roughly after 50 BCE to 70 CE). The coins range from the reign of Antiochus III (c. 223–187 BCE). This large quantity of coins from the latter's reign is sometimes thought to argue circumstantially for the building expansion that occurred at the beginning of Ib. The large number of coins from his reign does not sufficiently support this claim. In conjunction with the general periodization of the ceramic wares, the numismatic evidence as a whole does, however, seem to restrict the Ib settlement to the pre-Christian period.

Various opinions also exist on the date for the end of Ib. The chief debate concerns explaining the cause of evidence of damage found below stratum II and assigning a secure date to it. De Vaux attributes this damage, which runs on the eastern side of the ruins from north to south as well as signs of burning to the earthquake of 31 BCE.[74] Since the most recent numismatic evidence from Ib, that is, coins found below the layer of destruction, seems to date at the latest to the year 37 BCE, de Vaux rightly looked for an explanation after this date but before 1 BCE/1 CE. Because seismic damage could explain evidence of a conflagration but not vice versa, de Vaux is convinced of the seismic explanation.

Besides the earthquake of 31 BCE, D.H. Kallner-Amiran records two other earthquakes for this general period, one in 64 and another in 24 BCE.[75] A. Schalit opts for the former, which is mentioned by Dio Cassius (*Roman History* XXXVII,11).[76] While the pottery from Ib might permit this explanation, its coins dating as late as 37 BCE would not. No one seems to have argued for the earthquake of 24 BCE, although it could account for the ceramic and numismatic evidence just as well as the earthquake of 31 BCE would. In fact, seismic activity in the area of Qumran in the year 24 BCE could account for the presence of coins of Herod the Great that may have been issued after 31 BCE but which would also belong to stratum Ib. Nevertheless, there is no hard evidence that would favor one earthquake over the other.

Another explanation questions the earthquake thesis entirely, interpreting the crack in the cistern at loc. 48-49 differently. This particular damage could have resulted from faulty construction of the cistern, which could not have sustained the weight of the water.[77] This view cannot be ruled out as a possibility but it would not seem to account for the more extensive damage found along the entire eastern side of the ruins.

According to Karcz and Kafri, any so-called earthquake-induced damage is difficult to evaluate.[78] They point out three sources of limitations in the use of such archaeological data as an independent instrument for the verification of historical records.

> First, the decision of an individual archaeologist to assign features of destruction to seismic causes may well be affected by his awareness (or lack thereof) of historic references to establish a chronological reference horizon for the site in question. Second, in some cases, an earthquake may provide a *deus ex machina* explanation of otherwise inexplicable desertion or decay of a prosperous township in peacetime, adding a touch of drama to the site history. Finally, in restricted excavations and isolated ruins, features of seismic damage are difficult to distinguish from those due to poor construction or adverse geotechnical effects.[79]

Karcz and Kafri point out that the earthquake thesis is at best inconclusive and that the situation at Qumran can be explained in another way. The Qumran compex was built upon unstable Lisan Marl, consisting of alternating calcareous and clayey layers. This geological formation is subject to swelling, seepage, and percolation that could directly contribute to the destabilization of architectural structures.[80]

Not only do Karcz and Kafri doubt the cause of the damage at Qumran Ib(?), but they also question our ability to date it accurately. They mention a regional geological study of the Judaean desert in 1931 carried out by Picard (bibliographical information not given), in which he speaks of 'a N-S "cleft" produced in the strong earthquake of 1927'.[81] While not specifically attributing the damage at Qumran to the massive earthquake of 1927, they do emphasize the ambiguity in dating earthquake-induced or geologically-tectonically induced damage such as that at Qumran. As loc. 48-49 are not directly associated with coins, that is, none were found in these loci, or pottery, nothing can be said conclusively about the relationship of damage at this location to the Qumran stratigraphy. Thus, while the absolute dating of the end of Ib to 31 BCE or even 24 BCE is possible, the evidence need not be restricted to this time-frame. Therefore, it cannot function as hard evidence for the sudden demise of Qumran Ib.

The ambiguity in dating the end of Ib is also due to the difficulty in determining the actual stratigraphic context of the coins of Herod the Great.[82] While de Vaux assigns them to stratum II, he does recognize that some or all of them might date after 31 BCE and could be used to argue circumstantially for continued settlement of Qumran Ib even after that date. Nevertheless, the most that the archaeologist and historian can say in face of the reported evidence is that the Herodian coins may not function as hard evidence for dating the end of Ib or the beginning of II precisely, because they come from mixed levels.

The situation is similar with regard to determining the context of a single coin of Herod Archelaus found in Trench A. Since all the pottery types from this trench are known from other Ib loci on the site itself and almost all the numismatic data predate the reign of Herod the Great, no coins of his reign having been discovered in this trench, de Vaux believes that the one coin of Herod Archelaus derives clearly from the next phase of settlement, Period II. There is no hard evidence for this claim, and the historian must be content to say that this coin, like the ten coins of Herod the Great, also derives from a mixed context; it should not be allowed to function as hard evidence for dating the end of Ib or the inception of II.

The difficulty in interpreting the numismatic data in order to date the beginning of Ia, its end, the beginning of Ib, and the end of the Ib settlement at Qumran is paralleled by the problem of assigning an exact date to the pottery of the Ib/II transition. Both I and II forms are represented at the site, in the tombs, and in the caves. But only at the site is the distinction between the ceramic forms thought to be corroborated by distinctive stratigraphic contexts. While noting the similarity of the ceramic wares from Ib and II, de Vaux does also mention a few stratigraphic contexts that would support the distinction in the wares of the two periods. For instance, deposits of animal bones were discovered under Ib bowls, which were dated by association with coins of Alexander Jannaeus. Above a layer of sediment that de Vaux associates with a period of abandonment of Qumran between Ib and II (31-4 BCE), other animal bones were found under pottery attributed to stratum II. This is clearly an argument based on stratigraphy. In another case, the ceramic wares of Trench A turn out to be identical with some of those of Ib as known from other places at the site. This is a stratigraphic argument supported by the absence of ceramic wares known from stratum II.

In addition to his observations on the pottery in relationship to its stratigraphic context, de Vaux also lists several typological distinctions.[83] He points out, first of all, that the distinction between late Hellenistic and Herodian lamps is marked. Furthermore, the plates of stratum Ib lack the molded edge typical of stratum II. The large flared and thin-walled beakers of stratum Ib are unlike the small, thick, and ribbed wares of II.

Speaking of trends and developments in the ceramic wares, Paul Lapp supports de Vaux's analysis of the wares of Ib and II. He notes that the collared rim gradually lengthens, others lose the rim with a rounded section, and a ridged or grooved neck appears in the first century CE.[84] The neck of flasks gradually lengthens above the upper handle attachment.[85] The craters of the first century CE have everted rims with concave ends.[86] Lapp does admit, however, that such a form is also represented in the Ib horizon of loc. 89. Although squat forms of Ib cooking pots persist into II, a tendency is recognizable toward a shortened and less differentiated neck.[87]

While not explicitly dealing with the stratigraphy at Qumran, Lapp's typological observations on the ceramic wares at Qumran agree with de Vaux's typological delineations. He also agrees in general with de Vaux's dating of the types, but based on the general rule of thumb that pottery found in a layer comes from its end, he offers a more restricted relative dating of the ceramic wares of Ib and II.[88]

	Ib	*II*
De Vaux	100–31 BCE	4 BCE–68 CE
Lapp	50–31 BCE	50–68 CE

A difficulty with this chronological framework is the postulation of a gap in settlement based on an absence of ceramic production at Qumran in the years 31–4 BCE. This gap was first proposed by de Vaux in the historical form of an abandonment of the site after the earthquake of 31 BCE. Lapp later accepted this thesis and claimed that no ceramic wares were produced at Qumran during this time.[89] But de Vaux later pointed out that these wares were less autonomous than he had previously thought.[90] This is supported by the presence of wares, which are usually designated as 'Qumran' wares, at the Jewish Citadel C, Sam Rom Ia, Sam Vlt C2, Jer T. Val, and Bethany C. 61 during the period 31–4 BCE.[91] Thus the wares that are designated as 'Qumranic' were neither restricted locally to Qumran alone nor were they non-existent for the years 31–4 BCE, the period when Qumran was presumably abandoned.

In sum, the chronological framework pre-/post-31 BCE = Ib/II is problematic. Neither the seismic/geological damage nor the numismatic data supports such a precisely dated watershed. Furthermore, the abandonment thesis can be shown to be weak based on the nature of the remains of Ib-II. According to the evidence, the new settlers of Qumran II seem to have made no attempt to restore the water system to its previous state in stratum Ib=Period Ib. Nevertheless, they apparently continued to function in some way in spite of the presence of immense damage to the water system. Finally, while one can speak of Ib and II pottery, one can no longer date Ib forms before and II forms after 31 BCE, because the so-called 'Qumran' wares are represented at other sites for the supposed period of abandonment.

P. Bar-Adon offers a more open-ended approach to dating the ceramic data. He notes that the ceramic wares of 'Ain el-Ghuweir correspond to those at Qumran. Unlike de Vaux and Lapp, he does not date the ceramic material according to a pre-31/post-31 BCE scheme. Rather, he discerns a general continuity in many of the ceramic forms between the years 200 BCE and 70 CE, and sometimes even into the Bar-Kokhba period.[92] Some bowls are dated roughly 75 BCE–70 CE and some are dated 50 BCE–70 CE and into the second century CE.[93] Robert Smith dates Herodian lamps between 37 BCE and 135 CE. Type I would date between 37 BCE and 35 CE and Type II between 50 and 135 CE.[94]

Since any attempt to draw a rigid chronological line between Ib and II wares is plagued with difficulties, despite their distinctions, it would seem better to accept Bar-Adon's less precise dating of the ceramic forms at 'Ain el-Ghuweir and Qumran, admitting the possibility of forms overlapping from one period to another, and to avoid an overly precise attempt to date the latest Ib form to any particular year.[95] The ceramic evidence from Qumran cannot be dated so exactly.

Conclusion

Some scholars have doubted that study of the archaeological remains from Qumran can contribute directly to the reconstruction of the history of the people of the scrolls. Once one recognizes that the caves and the Qumran complex witness to the same material culture and that their proximity suggests habitation and use by one and the same Jewish group, one is naturally tempted to infer that the scrolls found in the caves were preserved, stored, and in part composed by this group—known widely as the Qumran community.

Many of the skeptics were rightly concerned about the nature of archaeological evidence, particularly that from Qumran, and its appropriate use in reconstructing the history of the Qumran community. Certainly, the archaeological remains from Qumran and the caves do not identify their inhabitants nor do they shed light on particular historical events that may have occurred there. They do, however, contribute to the determination of the historical period against which to understand potentially useful statements in the scrolls themselves.

De Vaux's archaeological research revealed that Qumran was inhabited in Iron II and the Hellenistic/Roman periods. The 'definitive form' of the Qumran complex and the material culture represented by the contents of the caves are directly associated with the latter period. The material culture of the caves and the Qumran complex dates approximately from the late second century BCE to c. 70 CE. Thus one infers that the people that placed the scrolls in the caves lived at Qumran during this time. It is widely believed, however, that the scrolls were hidden in the caves c. 70 CE by the most recent Jewish inhabitants of the Qumran complex, thereby preserving historical information about the early history of the Qumran (=the Teacher's) community.

Difficulties arise when one attempts to date particular phases of the community's settlement history more precisely. It is impossible to give a precise date to the installation of the late Hellenistic settlement at Qumran (Ia), because the ceramic data for this archaeological stratum is indistinguishable from those of the next stratum, Ib. Similarly, one cannot say with certainty when new construction at Qumran brought Ia to an end and constituted the inception of Ib, Qumran's 'definitive form'. While some Qumran scholars would date this installation as early as the middle of the second century BCE, the Ib ceramic wares, which are paralleled at other sites in Judaea in the late Hasmonean period, and the coins enable one to date the beginning of Ib roughly to the end of the second century BCE or the first century CE.

The two most controversial issues have been the determination of the cause of the damage and destruction at Qumran Ib and its dating. The evidence of burning was found beneath an accumulation of sediment. Above this, ceramic wares of Period II were found. Therefore, the destruction must have been coterminus with the end of Ib. De Vaux and others also associate the evidence of burning with geological damage discovered running from the north to the south on the eastern wing of the Qumran complex (loc. 46, 40, 39, 51, 50, 49, 48, 43, 66, 73, 72, 76). He associates both the conflagration and the geological destruction with the famous earthquake of 31 BCE.

Karcz and Kafri have argued that the evidence of damage, which de Vaux attributes to a specifically known earthquake, is not necessarily the result of seismic activity. They point out, in contrast to this, that Qumran was constructed on unstable Lisan Marl. The so-called 'earthquake' damage may just as easily have been caused by swelling, seepage, or percolation. Besides offering an alternative to the questionable earthquake thesis, Karcz and Kafri doubt that one can determine precisely when the site was damaged.

Once de Vaux's dating of the end of Ib to 31 BCE is questioned on geological grounds, it is no longer necessary to postulate a long period of abandonment of the site at this time. The accumulation of debris does suggest some period of absence from the site, but its extent cannot be determined. Even the settlers of Period II did not find it necessary to repair the damage of the water system (see loc. 48-49). Since it is not clear when the conflagration occurred or what actually caused it nor the time of the geological damage, one can hardly speak of dating the end of Ib with any confidence. Nor can one date the latest of the Ib and the earliest of the II ceramic wares to a particular year.

In contrast to the difficulties involved in dating the beginning of Ia, the beginning of Ib, and the end of Ib, scholars generally agree that a group of settlers, presumably ideologically and historically related to the group of Ib, came to Qumran during the reign of Herod Archelaus (4 BCE–6 CE). This was the beginning of Period II. Based on the absence of Jewish coins from the fourth year of the First Jewish Revolt against the Romans, 69 CE, de Vaux infers that Jewish occupation at Qumran ended in 68/69 CE. Despite the difficulties in determining precise dates for the transitional phases from one settlement period to another, the broader periodization is clear—approximately from the late second century BCE to c. 70 CE. Thus, while the archaeological remains do provide information on the periodization for Qumran history, the burden of producing details of that history rests on the relevant literary sources.

Chapter 3

PALAEOGRAPHY AND THE HISTORY OF THE QUMRAN COMMUNITY

A. *Introduction*

Hebrew-Aramaic palaeography, which has become an independent discipline during the last 100 years, has come to play a special role in discussions of the history of the Qumran community. The palaeography of the Qumran documents has gradually acquired an important, if not central, function in determining when the documents were copied, thereby establishing—presumably without the speculation involved in exegetical study—the general historical background against which the allusions to historical persons and events become meaningful.

Some analysts insist that the palaeographical datings of the Qumran texts are an evidential *sine qua non* for any valid reconstruction of the community's history.[1] Already a decade after the first discovery and publication of several of the Dead Sea Scrolls, Frank M. Cross, Jr made a statement on the function of palaeography as a chronological index for historical purposes that now seems to be widely accepted.

> the elusive character of the data suggests that we can achieve sound historical results only by utilizing outside controls to limit the framework within which our sources operate. Concretely this means that we must approach the problems relating to the historical interpretation of our texts by first determining the time period set by archaeological data, by palaeographical evidence, and by other more objective methods before applying the more subjective techniques of internal criticism.[2]

This statement about the 'elusive character of the data' refers to the difficulty in dating the historical events alluded to in the Qumran documents solely on the basis on their contents. Cross advocates using 'outside controls' in the form of archaeological and palaeographical studies as an objective solution to this dilemma. In combination, the results of these two independent disciplines enable one to establish a chronological framework against which to understand the textual statements themselves.

Cross makes three key assumptions in his position as palaeographer quite clear. (1) The documents themselves, including those customarily used in historical reconstructions of the community's history—CD, 1QpHab, 4QpPs 37, 4QpNah, 4QTest, and 1QH—and others reflecting its liturgies, laws, and rules, are neither internally dated nor do they preserve demonstrably reliable chronological information. The allusions in the scrolls to persons and events are themselves susceptible to various identifications and concomitantly to different chronological settings. (2) In contrast to unreliable guesses based on the interpretation of textual statements, palaeographical analysis allows one to arrange most of the scripts within a typological sequence, which can be assigned chronological values. Thus palaeographical datings attain a chronological precision that has no comparable counterpart in internal criticism of the textual statements themselves. (3) Relative palaeographical datings can sometimes be further refined by association with dated archaeological strata.

Cross is certainly correct in maintaining that the events and persons alluded to in the Qumran texts cannot be unequivocally dated on internal grounds alone. To a great extent, this fact accounts for the many diverse theories concerning the time of the community's origin, its continuing history, and the identification of its key characters. The crucial issue is the contribution that palaeographical analysis can make in determining the period when the documents were copied. Once the approximate date of copying is established, one is then able to view the information in the documents themselves against a known historical period. Cross's third claim, that dated archaeological data can be used to refine the dating of the scripts in the Qumran texts, may be ignored in the present context, since the slight inscriptional evidence, the ostraca, from Qumran does not contribute directly to the potential reconstruction of Qumran history.

The chronological limits against which to date the hands of the Dead Sea Scrolls are set by other non-Qumran documents.[3] The upper limit for dating the Qumran hands is marked by the

Elephantine papyri written in the standard Aramaic cursive of the fifth century BCE. The Edfu papyri, also written in a cursive hand, date to the beginning of the third century BCE. They provide a *terminus post quem* for discussing the palaeography of the Dead Sea Scrolls. At the lower end of the chronological scale, the Masada and Wadi Murabba'at documents provide the *terminus ante quem* for the scrolls. A Bar-Kokhba letter is dated internally to 134 CE. Excavations at Masada have unearthed an ostracon and a papyrus that were deposited there before its destruction in 73 CE. A contract from Muraba'at is dated to the second year of Nero—55/56 CE. Hence, the Edfu and the Masada/Murabba'at hands provide the absolute datings missing in the Qumran hands—from the early third century BCE to 73 CE.

B. *The Palaeography of the Dead Sea Scrolls*

Building upon earlier palaeographical studies, Cross presents a hypothesis on the development of the Jewish protocursive and semicursive hands as well as the formal hand in the Hellenistic-Roman period.[4] He designates the formal hand either as Archaic dating c. 250–150 BCE, or as Hasmonean c. 150–30 BCE, or as Herodian c. 30 BCE–70 CE. This typological periodization is based upon the most characteristic traits in each script. The book hand of the Archaic period is recognizable by virtue of the differing size of the letters (the lack of a uniform size) and the variety in the width of their strokes (shading). In the Hasmonean hand, the letters differ in size, but a tendency toward uniformity is recognizable. Shading is idiosyncratic, and the letters hang from an upper line. The Herodian script is characterized by the standardization of letter-size, the emergence of a base-line as well as an upper line, the proliferation of 'tittles', and the appearance of ligatures.

In lieu of absolutely dated scripts, especially for the Archaic and the early Hasmonean periods, Cross postulates the relative age of a script on the basis of its use of archaic and novel forms of the letters of the alphabet. If a script should predominate in archaic forms rather than the younger ones, its age would be closer to that of the established norm; if novel forms should outweigh the archaic forms, the script would then be younger than the norm. Avigad and Birnbaum follow this principle also.[5] The latter added, however, a questionable mathematical operation to his palaeographical analyses. After establishing a particular script as his chronological norm, he proceeded to analyze other scripts converting archaic and novel letter-forms into percentage points, each corresponding to a certain number of years.[6] Without its mathematical dimension, this approach is in principle correct. Still, it assumes that the development of scripts is straightlined and not more complex.

Cross dates both the biblical and the so-called sectarian documents from the Qumran caves to the Archaic, the Hasmonean, and the Herodian periods. The oldest documents, the biblical manuscripts, are dated before the emergence of the Qumran community as expressed in the Maccabean thesis to the Archaic period and may, for that reason, be excluded from the following discussion. These include 4QEx[f] (protocursive, c. 250 BCE).[7] 4QSam[b] (proto-Jewish formal, late third century BCE),[8] 4QJer[a] (proto-Jewish formal, c. 225–175 BCE).[9] 4QQoh[a] (semiformal, c. 175 BCE),[10] 4QTemple (c. 175 BCE),[11] 4QPriéres liturgiques A (semiformal, c. 175 BCE),[12] and 4QDeut[a] (c. 175–150 BCE).[13] Little is known concretely about the relationship of the copyists of these manuscripts to the Qumran community. None of these documents contain references to the Teacher of Righteousness, the Wicked Priest, or the Liar. Therefore, it is wise provisionally to exclude them from the discussion of Qumran influenced documents. It should be kept in mind, however, that Cross and his student Eugene Ulrich maintain that the copyist of 1QS, 1QSa, 1QSb, and 4QTest is also responsible for copying 4QSam[c].[14] This suggests that scribal activity on traditional, biblical and nonbiblical manuscripts by one and the same person was by no means an impossibility at Qumran. Strictly 'Qumran' sectarian writings are absent from the Archaic period. They appear in the late Hasmonean and Herodian periods.

It is widely accepted that several of the sectarian Dead Sea Scrolls were authored and copied by members of the Qumran-Essene community. Some of these documents are thought to preserve information about the community's ideology and history. These are 1QS, 4QS, 1QSa and b, 4QTest, CD (4QD, 6QD), 1QpHab, 4QpNah, 4QpPs 37, 1QM, 1QH (hands 1 and 2). It must be emphasized that the palaeographer is concerned above all with the age of the scripts, that is, the time of copying in most cases. These scripts are arranged according to their postulated palaeographical typology and age as follows:

1QS	Hasmonean semiformal(?)	*Cross*: 100–75 BCE[15] *Avigad*: later than 1QIsa[a] (second century to c. 50 BCE, the *terminus ante quem*)[16] *Thiering*: Herodian[17]
4QS	Hasmonean protocursive(?)	*Cross*: early Hasmonean, same horizon as 1QS[18] *Thiering*: difficult to date [19]
1QSa and b	Hasmonean semiformal(?)	*Cross*: same hand as that of 1QS[20] *Thiering*: Herodian semi-formal with specific Palmyrene influence[21]
4QTest	Hasmonean semiformal(?)	*Cross*: same hand as those of 1QS, Sa and b[22]
CD	Hasmonean/Herodian	*Cross*, *Milik*: 4QD, 75–50 BCE; 6QD, first century CE[23] *Thiering*: Herodian[24]
1QpHab	Herodian	*Cross*, *Birnbaum*:[25] *Avigad*: younger than 1QM, ranging from beginning of Herodian period to 70 CE[26]
4QpNah	Herodian	*Cross*, *Birnbaum* *Strugnell*:[27]
4QpPs 37	Herodian	*Strugnell*: 30 BCE–20 CE[28]
1QM	Herodian	*Cross*: 30–1 BCE[29]
1QH(hand 1)	Herodian	
1QH(hand 2)	Herodian	probably younger than 1QH (hand 1)[30]

Except for Thiering, who differs from Cross and Milik especially on the dating of 4QS, 1QS, 1QSa and b, 4QTest, and 4QD, the palaeographers of the Qumran documents seem to agree that their scripts range from the beginning of the first century BCE to some time in the first century CE.[31]

C. *Palaeographical Analysis and the Historical Reconstruction*

Palaeographical study of the sectarian Dead Sea Scrolls helps to determine the general period against which to understand statements in the documents themselves. 1QS, 1QSa, 1QSb, and 4QTest are, according to palaeographical analysis, the oldest copies of the sectarian Qumran literature, dating at the earliest 100–75 BCE. These documents were presumably copied by one person. Except for 4QTest, whose relevance to the reconstruction of the history of the Qumran community is questioned below (Chapter 7), these documents are not of central importance for the historical reconstruction since they never mention the Teacher of Righteousness, the Liar, the Wicked Priest, the House of Absalom, and the Seekers after Smooth Things. These figures are mentioned in CD, 1QpHab, 4QpPs 37, and 4QpNah. 1QH presents a peculiar case, because it is widely held that the one speaking in these thanksgiving hymns is the Teacher of Righteousness and the conflicts which he depicts are those between himself and his adversaries, who are never named nor entitled as the Liar and the Wicked Priest. It does speak of traitors and Seekers after Smooth Things.

According to the palaeographical analysis of Cross and Milik, the oldest script in which a sectarian document was copied is that of 1QS, dating c. 100–75 BCE. The year 75 BCE provides, therefore, the *terminus ad quem* for copying 1QS. CD is represented by 4QD that dates c. 75–50 CE. According to this dating, historical characters and events, thought to be alluded to in CD, would predate the year 50 BCE. The *terminus ante quem* 75 BCE, which Cross and Milik propose, suggests additionally that 4QD may have been copied as early as 75 BCE, but not earlier. If this dating should be correct, then CD's historical allusions must apply to the years preceding 75 BCE. However accurate the dating of 4QD to 75–50 BCE may be factually, it is consistent with the literary evidence in CD itself. Technically speaking, 75 BCE is the maximum upper limit for dating the copying of 4QD. The lower limit is also only a rough estimate, for, as Cross and other palaeographers point out, one must allow for a scribe whose handwriting did not change noticeably over the period of his lifetime. The chronological notes in CD I,5-6 and 10 indicate that the Teacher and the remnant lived four hundred and ten years after the Babylonian exile. The accuracy of this chronological information is discussed below (Chapter 5). The compiler of CD lived at some time after the death of the Teacher (CD XIX,23-24; XIX,35–XX,1). On the basis of the textual information alone, one cannot determine the time of CD's compiler. Palaeographical analysis would date the copying and implicitly the composition of 4QD before 75 BCE. But it cannot tilt the scales in favor of a particular theory that reconstructs the history of the Qumran community in those years. Should the *terminus ad quem* 50 BCE be correct, the figures of Qumran history could not have been active after that time, thus discounting the Early Roman, both the Zealot and Christian identifications of the Qumran community, the Late Roman (post-70 CE), and the Karaite theories (see Chapter 1 nn. 1, 2, 7-10).

According to palaeographical analysis, 1QpHab dates to the Herodian period—approximately 30 BCE to 70 CE. Cross and Birnbaum characterize the script of 1QpHab as early Herodian. While the *terminus ad quem* is not certain, potentially as late as 70 CE, the *terminus ante quem non* 30 BCE is probably accurate. That would suggest that 1QpHab was copied in the last third of the first century BCE at the earliest. Since other copies of 1QpHab are not extant, it has been suggested that the preserved copy of it is identical with the original composition.[32] That means that the conflict between the Wicked Priest and the Teacher of Righteousness (I,12-13; IX,8-12; XI,2-8), the indifference of the House of Absalom during this conflict, and the Liar's as well as his adherents' disobedience to the words of the Teacher occurred in the period before 30 BCE. While the broad Herodian dating would not exclude the Christian and Zealot identifications, it does allow one to dismiss the Late Roman and Karaite theories from serious consideration. If the early Herodian dating should be correct, one could also dismiss the Christian and Zealot theories. In any case, the Herodian dating is consistent with the view that its writer lived in the period of Roman occupation of Palestine, during the time of the Kittim (II,10–V,6). The juxtaposition of II,6-10 with II,10–V,6 implies that the Teacher's message about the future concerned the Kittim=the Romans in the age of the pesharist.

The same claims can be made for 4QpPs 37. It was copied, if not originally composed, in the Herodian period. Cross and Birnbaum think its script is also early Herodian. Thus statements about the Liar, Ephraim, Manasseh, the Priest, the Teacher of Righteousness, and the Wicked Priest in conflict with the Righteous One (IV,7-9; cf. 1QpHab IX,8-12; XI,2-8) would refer at the earliest to persons and events in the time before 30 BCE. This is consistent with the periodization established by palaeographical study for 1QpHab and 4QD (implicitly also CD).

4QpNah is also dated on palaeographical grounds to the Herodian period, indicating that the pesher was a literary form of the late first century BCE. Accordingly, the *terminus ante quem* for its copying was c. 30 BCE. Thus the pesharist could only have been writing about his contemporary period or the past. While the pesharist of 4QpNah is not explicitly concerned with the Teacher of Righteousness and the Wicked Priest, one of his chief interests is the group called the Seekers after Smooth Things. Below (Chapter 6) this group is identified as the Liar's community. Admittedly, the chronological relationship of this group to the Liar and the conflict between the Wicked Priest and the Teacher of Righteousness is unclear. In CD I, which presumably dates to 75–50 BCE (based on palaeographical study of 4QD), the Seekers after Smooth Things are mentioned in a context that juxtaposes the Teacher and the Liar. The chronological notes in CD I suggest that these figures existed around or after 177 BCE (see below Chapter 5, on CD). There is, however, no cross-reference to a known historical event at this time. 4QpNah I presents the Seekers after Smooth Things in collusion with a certain Demetrius, presumably Demetrius III Eukeros (95–88 BCE), referring therefore to historical events c. 90 BCE. These historical findings are clearly consistent with the Herodian dating of 4QpNah. Thus, it would seem that 4QpNah, whether a copy or an original, is concerned with events that occurred approximately sixty years before the earliest date established for its copying on palaeographical grounds.

Conclusion

The palaeographical datings enable one to establish a general periodization against which to interpret the statements made in the sectarian Qumran literature. None of the documents discussed above could have been copied after 70 CE, thus eliminating the Late Roman and Karaite theories from further consideration. Palaeographical analysis suggests that these documents were probably copied before the beginning of the Common Era. Based on this observation, one can rather safely dismiss the Zealot and Christian identifications of the Qumran community as well.

At the earliest, CD (actually 4QD) was copied c. 75 BCE; at the latest, c. 50 BCE. 4QD is the oldest copy of a text containing historical allusions, i.e. the Teacher of Righteousness, the Liar, and the Seekers after Smooth Things. The three pesharim—1QpHab, 4QpPs 37, and 4QpNah—and 1QH were copied in Herodian scripts, the earliest of which could have been copied c. 30 BCE. Thus the five documents most relevant to the historical reconstruction date palaeographically to the late Hasmonean and Herodian periods—from c. 75 BCE to 30 BCE (or later).

These palaeographical datings are consistent with the textual evidence, primarily that of CD I and 4QpNah I, that seems to refer to persons and events in the period before 75 BCE. 4QpNah I alludes to historical events involving the Liar's community=the Seekers after Smooth Things of the year 90 BCE. CD I dates the Teacher, the remnant, the Liar, and the Seekers after Smooth Things after c. 177 BCE, if one takes its chronological information at face-value. The compiler of CD was active after the Teacher's death (see cols. I, XIX–XX)—but before 75 BCE.

Chapter 4

THE ESSENES AND THE IDENTITY OF THE QUMRAN COMMUNITY

A. *Introduction*

Much of the secondary literature on the Dead Sea Scrolls has been devoted to the identification of the community that presumably wrote and preserved the scrolls. The Dead Sea community has been identified with almost every known Jewish group in the Hellenistic-Roman period, e.g. the Pharisees, the Sadducees, the Essenes, the Therapeutae, the Zealots, the Ebionites, Jewish Gnostics, and Christians. While this variety of identification might suggest that the Dead Sea community resembled in one way or another all the reported Jewish groups of that time, and consequently had no distinctive identity of its own, a scholarly consensus has emerged identifying this community with the ancient Essenes.[1]

Despite the fact that the designation Essenes has sometimes come to be used synonymously with the expression Dead Sea or Qumran community, it refers first and foremost to the group(s) about which Philo, Josephus, Pliny, and others have written.[2] Philo preserves two essays on the Essenes—*Quod omnis probus liber sit* 72-91 and *Pro judaeis defensio* 1-18. Flavius Josephus also has two valuable digressions concerning them—*De bello judaico* 2.8.119-61 and *Antiquitates judaicae* 18.1.18-22. Unlike Philo and Pliny, Josephus mentions individual Essenes: Judas the Essene (*Bell* 1.78-80), Simon the Essene (*Bell* 2.111-13), and John the Essene (*Bell* 2.20.566-68). He reports also on an Essene gate in the Jerusalem wall (*Bell* 5.144). Significant for appreciating him as a historical source for the Essenes is his claim to have lived and studied with them for a while (*De vita sua* 10-12). This claim, which only he makes, leads one to suspect that he is the historian's only possible eyewitness to the inner workings of the Essene communities. Pliny the Elder provides a short but invaluable statement about the Essenes in his *Naturalis historia* 5.17.4.[3]

These three writers—representing three significant cultural centers in antiquity, Alexandria, Jerusalem, and Rome—comprise the first-century witnesses to the Essenes. Later reports are thought to be dependent upon them.[4] While it is often thought that Hippolytus' report about the Essenes in the *Refutatio omnium haeresium* 9.23.28 depends on Josephus, he does preserve information that may be his own. The status of the material peculiar to him as evidence for the Essenes remains controversial.[5]

It is obvious that the immense interest in the Essenes from the first to the eighteenth century was sparked predominantly by dogmatic concerns.[6] Various Christian writers sought to demonstrate the affinity between early Christianity and the Essenes. Essenism was often cited as the immediate historical ancestor of early Christianity. At the same time, medieval Jewish scholars searched the Talmudim for references to the Essenes. In the last half of the eighteenth and early nineteenth centuries, the investigation of the Essenes was driven by the question whether the religion of Jesus derived from the human religion of the Essenes or whether he had received his wisdom in a supernatural revelation.

Around the middle of the nineteenth century a more critical attitude toward the sources began to be taken on a broader scale than ever before. During the second half of that century, scholars debated the genuineness of the ancient reports about the Essenes (and the Therapeutae in Philo's *De vita contemplativa*). While the credence of Philo's *Quod* and *De vita* was called into question, Josephus was widely trusted, since he had claimed to have spent time studying with the Essenes. By the beginning of the twentieth century, the ancient sources were credited with a basic trustworthiness, with Josephus at the top of the list. In fact, the current, continuing discussion about the identification of the Essenes with the Dead Sea community seems to take the reports of Philo, Josephus, and Pliny more or less at face value.

In this chapter, the ancient reports about the Essenes will be examined. In particular, the information presented by Philo and Josephus will be compared and contrasted in order to demonstrate that these two ancient writers are sometimes in agreement on their general characterizations of the Essenes, but differ significantly in regard to specific information about the internal workings and the ideology of the Essenes. After examining Philo, Josephus, and Pliny on the geographical location, the antiquity and size, and the occupations of the Essenes, attention will be directed to the apologetic interest of Philo and Josephus, both of whom were concerned with depicting the Essenes as an ideal society to their respective audiences. In spite of this apologetic interest, both writers know the Essenes as a volunteer association devoted to a rigorous communal existence. Only Josephus presents information concerning the community's entrance procedures, its daily regimen, its concern with prophecy, and names of particular Essenes of the Roman period. Once the ancient sources have been evaluated in terms of trustworthy information about the Essenes, the debate between A. Dupont-Sommer and G.R. Driver concerning the identification of the Essenes with the Qumran or Dead Sea community will be reviewed. Then Pliny's report on the Essenes will be examined. Only at that point will it be possible to determine the relevance of the ancient reports about the Essenes for the reconstruction of the history of the Qumran community.

B. *The Sources: Philo, Josephus, and Pliny*

These sources require comparison with each other and cross-examination in order to determine the special tendencies which may either support their usefulness in historical reconstruction or obviate such a use. Such a critical analysis could highlight agreements as well as apparent inconsistencies that would indicate the relative reliability of the ancient reports about the Essenes. Thereafter, one can deal with the question of the relevance and usefulness of these sources for the specific problem of the identification of the Essenes with the Dead Sea or Qumran community.

Philo, Josephus, and Pliny agree that the Essenes originated in Palestine (*Quod* 75; *Apologia* 1; *Bell.* 2.8.119; *Ant.* 18.1.19; Pliny). Philo says they flee the corrupt cities of Palestinian Syria and live in villages (*Quod* 76); elsewhere (*Apologia* 1) he locates them specifically in the towns and villages of Judaea. Saying that they dwelled in towns forming colonies (*Bell.* 2.124), Josephus introduces them alongside the Pharisees and Sadducees as a major religious group into the political history of Jerusalem in the time of Jonathan Maccabeus c. 150 BCE (*Ant.* 18.171-73). From this it can be inferred that the Essenes were not strangers to the environs of Jerusalem. In fact, Josephus associates particular Essenes and the Essene gate explicitly with Jerusalem. Pliny locates them, however, north of Masada and Engedi near the western shore of the Dead Sea. It is peculiar that Josephus, who claims to have known Essenes, makes no mention of the Essene community residing near the Dead Sea (*Vita* 10-12).

Philo, Josephus, and Pliny speak of the Essenes as their contemporaries in the first century CE. Although not writing about the ultimate origins of the Essenes, Josephus knows them as a recognized philosophical or theological grouping in the middle of the second century BCE. He even says that they had existed from remote times (*Ant.* 18.1.20). He does mention individual Essenes at later periods, reporting that some of them behaved as heroes or martyrs during the First Jewish War against the Romans (66–74 CE). Pliny reports that the Essenes had existed for thousands of centuries. Accordingly, one may infer that the Essenes were not a newly-formed association among the Jews in the first century CE.

Both Philo and Josephus estimate the Essene population (membership?) at more than 4000 in Palestinian Syria/Judaea (*Quod* 75; *Ant.* 18.1.20). Although Pliny knows no such exact figure, he does say:

> Owing to the throng of newcomers, this people is daily re-born in equal numbers; indeed, those whom, wearied by the fluctuations of fortune, life leads to adopt their customs, stream in in great numbers.[7]

The round figure 'more than four thousand' found in Josephus and Philo does not seem to be based upon their own eyewitness accounts nor upon a census. Perhaps Philo and Josephus derived this number from an unknown common source. It could be a rather modest estimate—referring perhaps to average membership in a major religious center like Jerusalem.[8] On the other hand, we have no way of determining whether this number is accurate. Pliny's information is independent of Philo and Josephus, but he clearly does not offer specific demographic statistics.

Josephus alone designates the Essenes as Jews by race, but notes that 'they are more closely united among themselves by mutual affection than are the others' (*Bell.* 2.8.119). The 'others' to whom he refers are the Pharisees and Sadducees. Philo says that the Essenes formed a 'true brotherhood' not in name but in reality (*Quod* 79). While he does not speak of the ethnic origin of its members, perhaps presuming Jewishness, he does suggest that the fundamental principle of Essene organization and reception was not ethnic but was rather agreement on certain ideals and practices. Pliny is completely uninformed about the internal workings of the group to which he refers.

Philo and Josephus do agree that the main occupation of the Essenes was farming, but note that some members were shepherds, beekeepers, craftsmen, and officers of their various communities (*Quod* 76; *Apologia* 6, 8-10; *Bell*. 2.8.129; *Ant*. 18.1.18, 22).[9]

The uneven, sometimes conflicting, claims of the ancient reports about the Essenes leave one wondering whether they were in fact restricted to the western shore of the Dead Sea or to Judaea and Jerusalem, or whether they were scattered throughout Palestinian Syria. Did they live only within cities or outside of them, or both? When did they come into existence, c. 150 BCE or even as early as the time of Moses? What credence should we give to the statements of Josephus and Philo who claim that the Essenes numbered more than four thousand members? Were they strictly Jews by race as Josephus says or perhaps a voluntary association not subject to restrictions of birth alone?

These questions cannot be answered unequivocally and conclusively without giving more weight to one report and less to the other(s). Thus it is necessary to compare and contrast Philo and Josephus in a more detailed fashion with regard to Essene ideology and practices. Their reports deserve scrutiny in order to underscore a philosophical tendency shared by them and to salvage information that is, despite non-historiographic interests, historically valuable.

The Essenes: A Jewish Model of Virtue

Philo and Josephus apparently shared the goal of addressing non-Jewish audiences in Greek about a living Jewish model of virtue and holiness. While their Essene reports may be considered historically informative in a broad sense, they, nevertheless, represent a form of apology that not only lauds the best of Jewish piety, but one that also depicts it in terms of the best of non-Jewish virtue.

In their four essays on the Essenes, Philo and Josephus wanted to expound on the topics of virtue, holiness, and the saintly life. This life is characterized by a

> contempt for riches, glory and pleasure, and by their continence and endurance, and also frugality, simplicity, contentment, modesty, obedience to the rule, kindness, equality and a communal life (*Quod* 84).

Philo is clearly attempting in this passage to ingratiate himself with readers who have some appreciation of Greek philosophy and culture. Philo designates the Essenes as 'athletes of virtue' (ἀθλητὰς ἀρετῆς).

> Such are the athletes of virtue which this philosophy produces, a philosophy which undoubtedly lacks the refinements of Greek eloquence, but which propounds, like gymnastic exercises, the accomplishment of praiseworthy deeds as the means by which a man ensures absolute freedom for himself (*Quod* 88).

Philo apparently wanted his readers to believe this encomium, for he says, even the enemies of the Jews praised the life style of the Essenes as 'the clearest demonstration of a perfect and completely happy existence' (*Quod* 91; cf. *Apologia* 18).

Philo's apologetic intentions are similar to those of Josephus, but his philosophical concern predominates. He wrote his treatise *Quod omnis probus liber sit* in order to demonstrate the Stoic paradox that only the wise are really free. It was conceived as a companion tractate to his non-extant work 'every unwise man is a slave' (see *Quod* 1.1: listed in Eusebius' catalogue, *Ecc. Hist.* 2.18).[10] After an extensive introduction dealing with the meaning of the paradox 'the wise man alone is free', Philo begins to cite historical examples that demonstrate his point (12.73–13.97). For example, in Greece there were the Seven; in Persia, the Magi; in India, the Gymnosophists; and in Palestinian Syria, the Essenes.[11] Philo's concern to view the Essenes as a Jewish manifestation of a more widespread wisdom movement is often overlooked by scholars who are primarily interested in identifying the Essenes with the Qumran community. Once one recognizes Philo's philosophical direction, the temptation to use his reports about the Essenes uncritically as historically reliable information is diminished.

In contrast to Josephus, who viewed the Essenes as unique (*Ant.* 18.1.20), Philo is concerned to make a case for the universality of the virtuous life. His wide-ranging, almost ethnological, search for wisdom wherever it could be found is witnessed also in his *De vita contemplativa*, which was conceived as a counterpart either to *Quod* 75–91 or to *Hypothetica* 2.1-18 or to a third writing that has not survived.[12] In this work, he maintains that the Therapeutae could be found throughout the world, in Greece and in the barbarian world. He claimed that they were best represented by a group located in Egypt near the Mareotic Lake (21-23). It is obvious, in light of this, that Philo's interest in the Essenes and the Therapeutae is governed by his concern with the philosophical distinction between the lives of those who are truly free and those who are merely enslaved. In the case of the virtuous, he is concerned with shared features rather than with peculiarities that would distinguish them.

Although the philosophical interest in Philo is primary, and it is not absent from Josephus,[13] both writers preserve valuable information about the internal make-up and life style of the Essenes. Both agree that the Essenes lived in communities wherein all things were enjoyed by all members.[14] The common life tolerated no private property. Even the funds of the community were designated for common expenditure, the sick and the aged also being supported from the common purse.

According to Philo, the community consisted exclusively of 'men of ripe years already inclining to old age who are no longer carried away by the flux of the body nor drawn by the passions, but enjoy true and unparalleled liberty' (*Apologia* 3). He asserts, moreover, that there are 'no children of tender years among the Essenes, nor even adolescents or young men' (*Apologia* 3), because their character is at this age still unstable and not yet mature, and like women, they too might cause confusion in the ordered atmosphere of the communities. These statements stand in bold relief against Josephus' claim that the Essenes did adopt the children of others in order to teach them their customs (*Bell.* 2.8.120). This adoption could refer to the acceptance of disciples into the community, which Josephus claims to have experienced in his adolescence, even if only for a short time. On this question, Philo and Josephus stand in conflict. Pliny reports nothing about the ages of the Essenes; he only mentions the daily throng of newcomers.

A further inconsistency between Philo and Josephus may be found in their statements about the Essenes' attitude to women. While Philo depicts the Essenes unequivocally as monastic misogynists, who claim that women by nature work against the common good, Josephus offers a somewhat different understanding of their attitude toward women:

> It is not that they abolish marriage, or the propagation of the species resulting from it, but they are on their guard against the licentiousness of women and are convinced that none of them is faithful to one man (*Bell.* 2.8.121).

Despite this negative attitude toward women in general, Josephus writes about the Essenes who did marry for the purpose of propagating the species, for 'if everyone adopted the same opinion, humanity would very quickly disappear' (*Bell.* 2.8.160). Thus a conflict seems to exist between Josephus and Philo, who reports nothing about marrying Essenes. Philo suggests contrariwise that marrying was foreign to the virtuous life of the Essenes. He may simply have had no knowledge of marrying Essenes.

The uppermost concern of the Essenes, according to Josephus and Philo, was the welfare and preservation of the common good within the communities. To that end they established rules concerning the love of God, the love of virtue, and the love of men. The love of God entailed the rejection of oaths, the rejection of falsehood, the belief that God creates only the good and not the evil. The love of virtue consisted in contempt for riches, glory, and pleasure; a desire for continence and endurance, frugality, simplicity, contentment, modesty, obedience to the rule, and stability of character exemplified positively the life of virtue. The love of men required kindness, equality, and the communal life (*Quod* 83-89). Since Philo intended to portray the Essenes as the Jewish embodiment of virtue, his long list of praiseworthy qualities is not at all out of place.

Desiring to speak to a Hellenistic audience in terms understandable for that culture, Philo contrasts the Essenes with the Hellenistic athletes (cf. his similar statement in *Quod* 88, which is cited above).

> Performing their accustomed tasks from before sunrise, they do not leave them until the sun has almost set, devoting themselves to them with no less joy than those who train for gymnastic combat. Indeed, they believe their own training to be more useful to life, more agreeable to body and soul and more lasting than athletic games, since their exercises remain fitted to their age, even when the body no longer possesses its full strength (*Apologia* 6).

Whether Philo wanted merely to contrast Jews with Greeks or villagers with city-dwellers or both, it is certain that he desired principally to inform his audience about the most virtuous of men among his own people the Jews.

It should not be overlooked that Philo also mentions a few specifically Jewish traits of Essene ideology and practice (*Quod* 80-82). Although he speaks in terms of philosophical categories, he characterizes the Essenes as ethicists who are continually researching the ancestral laws. He says they do not indulge in logic and natural philosophy. Their ethical study of the law is central and is especially observable on the seventh day of the week, when they gather together in synagogues.[15] They sit according to rank and instruct themselves in the laws. Philo describes their form of instruction as follows: one of them first reads aloud from the ancestral laws; another then comes forward and explains any difficult passages,[16] often making use of symbolic interpretations. One need not doubt the accuracy of Philo's description of a representative Essene synagogue service, but it indicates chiefly an intimate acquaintance with Jewish practices and does not point to specific Essene practices that would sufficiently distinguish them from other Jewish associations.

At this juncture, one seems justified in claiming that Philo and Josephus are concerned with the same general phenomenon—the Essenes of Palestine. Some of the discrepancies between the reports of the two writers may derive from their actual geographical proximity to the Essenes, and hence from personal familiarity with them. While Philo never claims to have known any Essene community from personal experience, Josephus can boast that he had studied with them for a while. This may account for the fact that Philo knows no marrying Essenes. Another factor that may account for discrepancies in their reports is their different goals in writing. Since Philo presents very little specific information about the internal structure and ideology of the Essenes, but concerns himself chiefly with the aspects of their common life that are shared by other 'wise and free' societies in the world, one can safely say that he is involved primary in apologetics. He never associates the Essenes with the Jewish history of the Second Temple period. Most of his general information about the Essenes is consistent with that of Josephus, who was above all writing Jewish history. Nevertheless, Josephus presents much detail that only an eyewitness would have known. There is no reason to think that Josephus was fantasizing or lying about the Essenes. Of the two writers, Josephus is the only one who clearly associates the Essenes with the late history of the Second Temple period.

The Discipline and Ideology of the Essenes

Philo's insights into the organization and life of the Essenes are important, but it is Josephus who actually reports possible eyewitness information about their requirement for entrance into the community, their daily life, their rituals, and their laws. He alone elaborates on the process of initiation into the community's special life of purity (*Bell.* 7.137-43). After a prospective member had announced his desire to join the Essenes, he would receive his initiation equipment, consisting of a hatchet, a linen-cloth, and a white garment. For one year he would remain outside of the community proving his continence. During this time he continued to receive some sort of instruction from the community. If, after one year, he had proven himself worthy, he then attained purificatory baths at a higher level than before. He must continue to prove himself for two more years and, if he should be found acceptable, could then become a permanent member.

Before he could share the common food, which must have been one of the highest attainments in the Essene association, he had to make specific vows before his brothers, swearing to practice piety toward God, to observe justice toward men and to harm no man and to hate the wicked and fight together with the just. In addition, he swore, his loyalty to all those in power (for power comes from God), never to show insolence and arrogance, to love truth and pursue liars, and to avoid theft and unfair gain. He swore also to conceal nothing from the members of the group and also not to reveal anything about the secrets of the community to outsiders—even under the threat of death. Within the community he was required to transmit the community's doctrines accurately, to preserve their books, and the names of the angels. Flagrant disobedience was threatened with expulsion.

Once a new member had passed his third-year test and had made his vows, he would become privy to full association with the community. Full Essene association involved a particular daily ritual (*Bell.* 5.128-32). They would get up before sunrise and join together in one place in order to recite ancestral prayers eastwardly (as though entreating the sun to rise). When the prayer had come to an end, they would be dismissed by their superiors and proceeded to their work. At the fifth hour of the day (after sunrise), they would reassemble in the same place wearing their linen-cloths, take a purificatory bath in cold water, and reassemble in a special building designated for full members. Once seated, each man would receive a meager portion of bread along with some other dish. Then a priest would pray blessing God, the giver of life. At the end of the repast, the priest would say another prayer of blessing. Having removed their (ritual) garments, they would then return to work where they remained until sundown (cf. *Apologia* 6). The same procedure would take place at every meal (*Bell.* 2.8.128-32). The purificatory baths and the common meals were the two central, organizational events of the Essene communities.[17]

The Essenes are particularly noteworthy because of their attitude toward wealth and violence. Philo speaks of their antipathy to riches and private property (*Quod* 76-77; *Apologia* 4; cf. *Bell.* 2.8.122; Pliny).[18] They were not allowed to buy or sell to members of the Essene communities (*Bell.* 2.8.127). Philo says that they did not have 'the smallest idea, not even a dream, of wholesale, retail, or marine commerce, rejecting everything that might excite them to cupidity' (*Quod* 78). They held no slaves thinking it unjust and ungodly, since by nature all men are born equal. Not only did the Essenes take care to preserve order within their own communities by abolishing private property, they also avoided any behavior that might have contributed to war-making such as the manufacture of arrows, javelins, swords, helmets, armor, and shields (*Quod* 78). Josephus says, on the contrary, that they carried weapons for the sake of defense when traveling (*Bell.* 2.8.125). Elsewhere, he does not make it clear whether the Essenes who were tortured and died in the war against the Romans were pacificists or warriors, like the Zealots (*Bell.* 2.8.152). A certain John the Essene served as a Jewish commander in Thamma during the war against the Romans (*Bell.* 2.20.566-68). At no point in his discussions of the Essenes does Josephus depict them as pacifists. Hippolytus' report on the Essenes suggests that some of their extremists were inclined to violence and had for that reason received the names Zealots and Sicarii (*Refut.* 9.26). Even if the historical value of Hippolytus' report remains controversial, it is informative of how a later writer perceived the ancient Essenes.

Josephus presents information about the Essenes that Philo and Pliny never mention. For example, they regarded oil as a defilement (*Bell.* 2.8.123)[19] and were customarily dressed in white, wearing their garments until they were worn out. In public they would be inconspicuously recognizable, because they refused to swear by God (135), because of their strict sabbatarianism, even because of their refusal to relieve themselves on the Sabbath (9.147-49). Most of them lived to be 100 years old (10.150). They had their own juridical assemblies of at least one hundred participants, issuing very exact and impartial decisions (9.145). Furthermore, because they had their own laws of purification, the Essenes would send gifts to the temple in Jerusalem but sacrificed among themselves (*Ant*. 18.1.19). He also reports that there are four levels of distinction within the Essene discipline that are comparable to levels of purity: 'the juniors are so inferior to their elders that if the latter touch them they wash themselves as though they had been in contact with a stranger' (*Bell*. 2.10.150; cf. 10.150; Hippolytus, *Refut*. 9.26). He also makes the peculiar remark in *Ant*. 18.22 that they lived much like the Δακῶν who are called κτισταις. Rejecting a view that refers to a Thracian tribe, Dupont-Sommer explains this as a corruption of Σαδδουκαίων, but his argumentation is not entirely convincing.[20]

As an insider Josephus was able to report on their courteous conversation at meals, their prohibition of spitting in the midst of their assemblies (132, 147), and their respect for elders and majority rule at meetings of ten persons (146). Believing that one should always rely on God (*Ant*. 18.1.18), they studied works of the ancients—especially what was useful for the body and soul, e.g. the healing of diseases through roots and stones (*Bell*. 2.6.136). They are known as well for their study of the holy books and for their ability to foresee future events quite accurately (159; cf. 1.78-80 on Judah the Essene; 2.113 on Simon the Essene).

One of the most interesting aspects of Josephus' report in *Bell*. 2.153-158 is his association of Essene heroism with their belief in the immortality of the soul. Because of this belief, he says, the Essenes were able to triumph over their Roman torturers in the First Jewish War. This seems to be one of Josephus' favorite themes. Elsewhere in *Bell*. (7.323-36, 341-88) Josephus has Eleazar, the leader of the rebels at Masada, give an oration on the immortality of the soul. Josephus' emphasis on the Essenic belief in the immortality of the soul probably makes use of Hellenistic traditions, e.g. Sisyphus, Tantalus, Ixion and Tityus. In any case, Josephus clearly uses the notion of the immortality of the soul to appeal to the interests and entertainment expectations of his reading public in Rome.

Now that the Essene reports from Philo and Josephus have been compared and contrasted with each other, we are in a better position to reflect upon the historical value of each source for answering questions about the identity and history of the Essenes and the Qumran community. While we saw that Philo and Josephus both wanted to present a model of Jewish virtue to their readers, differences, if not contradictions, between their specific statements on identical features of Essene ideology and behavior induce one to avoid simply harmonizing their reports. Philo does provide information describing the common life of the Essenes and their religious services. Interest in the common life is well documented in Hellenistic-Roman antiquity, both as a literary topos and as a desired way of life.[21] Philo's description of the Essenes served above all to make his main point that 'the wise man alone is free'. Therefore, one may legitimately question his direct relevance and usefulness for identifying the Qumran community with the Essenes. Josephus presents more information than Philo about the inner workings, the daily life, and the beliefs of the Essenes.

Evaluation of Josephus as a witness for the Essenes proves to be difficult also, because he, like Philo, was an author aiming in large part to please and entertain his audience. At times he presents information that might suggest that he did in fact have some personal acquaintance with the Essenes; at other times, he is clearly offering his readers what he thought they might enjoy. Still, his testimony deserves careful attention, since he did claim to have studied for a short time with the Essenes and does present some particular information that one would expect an insider to know.

One should not forget that Josephus was speaking about the Essenes as a major religious association among the Jews in the Hellenistic-Roman period. In spite of his claim that they had existed from remote times, his report in *Ant.* is essentially a digression that has been interpolated into the political history of Jerusalem/Judaea at the time of Jonathan Maccabeus. The Pharisees and Sadducees are also given attention, but not nearly as much as the Essenes.[22] Josephus' inordinate attention to the Essenes is unexpected, for he did eventually join the Pharisees (*Vita* 12). It is also difficult to decide whether he is actually presenting reliable historical information when he speaks of individual Essenes as prophets and reports that one of them was a commander in the first war against the Romans.[23] Unlike Philo, Josephus deals with the Essenes in the course of narrating Jewish history.

Much of what Josephus considered praiseworthy in the Essenic life style and ideology were virtues that he saw in himself as well. Like the Essenes, he too devoted himself to the study of the holy books. He even claims that he was quite adept in the knowledge of Jewish law as an adolescent (*Vita* 8; cf. Gal. 1.14). He claims to have experimented with each of the religious factions of his time, the Pharisees, the Sadducees, the Essenes, and a certain Banus (*Vita* II).[24] Although he seems to have been quite enamoured of the Essenes, he chose finally to join the Pharisees at the age of nineteen (*Vita* 12).

Furthermore, the Essenes were known as prophets. Josephus mentions two in particular—Judah and Simon the Essenes. Josephus liked to regard himself also as a prophet. After he had surrendered to the Romans in 67 CE, he became the prisoner of Vespasian. Perhaps on the basis of Num. 24.1-17 or Gen. 49.10, oracles stating that a person or persons emerging from Judaea were at that time destined to rule the world, he predicted that Vespasian would become emperor (*Bell.* 3.354ff.; cf. Suetonius, *Vespasian* 5). This prophecy was fulfilled in 69 CE, when Vespasian did become the emperor of Rome, perhaps saving Josephus' head and convincing him of his prophetic abilities. His own belief that God or Psyche[25] is now on the side of the Romans in the Jewish War, and its political consequence that the Jewish people should leave this matter in God's hands, recalls his claim that the Essenes depend on God in all matters (*Ant.* 13.171), unlike the Sadducees who take matters into their own hands and the Pharisees who represent a sort of mixture of Essenic and Sadducean views.

Finally, it should be recalled that Josephus mentions a certain John the Essene who served as Jewish commander in Thamma during the war against the Romans, just as Josephus himself had done in Galilee. Josephus is clearly highlighting aspects of Essene behavior and ideology that he admired and that he might have considered to have special entertainment value for his Roman audience. Still, he preserves valuable details lacking in Philo and Pliny.

In sum, Josephus and Philo (where he is in agreement with Josephus) have presented information on several aspects of the Essene communal life. The historical reliability of this information has never seriously been questioned and is thought to urge the identification of the Dead Sea, Qumran community with a branch of the ancient Essenes. In order to reassess the validity of this claim, we should recall the important debate between its staunchest proponent, A. Dupont-Sommer, and his opponent, G.R. Driver.

C. *Dupont-Sommer and Driver on the Essene Identification*

The history of investigation of the Damascus Document shows that its attribution to Essene authorship was clearly accepted only by a few scholars before the discovery of the Dead Sea Scrolls.[26] There was in fact no widespread consensus on the identity of its author nor of the community to which it referred. After the discovery of the first of the Dead Sea Scrolls, Sukenik proposed the Essene authorship for several of these documents.[27] This claim was by no means immediately accepted, and other competing claims were proposed. It was not, however, Sukenik but rather A. Dupont-Sommer who was largely responsible for the elaboration of the theory of Essene authorship and identification.[28] It is often forgotten, in light of the recent popularity of this identification, that G.R. Driver presented a formidable challenge to it.[29] His precise objections to it have passed into oblivion more as a result of the growing tacit acceptance of the Essene identification than from sutained refutation of it.

The characteristic conclusions of Dupont-Sommer and Driver—two of the most significant advocates of the Essene and non-Essene identifications—are cited in order to provide the theoretical background for the details of the debate.

> Dupont-Sommer:
> it appears to me that *in all respects* where with regard to the *organization of community life, rites, doctrines*, or *customs*, there is *so much in common where essential characteristics and traits are concerned*, that it is almost impossible not to identify the Qumran sect with the Essenes, or in other words, conclude that the Qumran scrolls are of Essene origin.[30] (our emphasis)

> Driver:
> when every allowance is made, *the differences far outweigh the resemblances* between the Essenes and the Covenanters and while *the resemblances are incidental the differences are fundamental*; and other reasons for rejecting the identification of the two groups will appear hereafter.[31] (our emphasis)

These citations should demonstrate sufficiently that Dupont-Sommer's conviction is dictated by the weight he places upon similarities in the reports on the Essenes and in the information derived from certain Dead Sea Scrolls. Driver characterizes these similarities as incidental, because they are also applicable to other contemporary groups. He claims, in addition, that the distinctions between the Essenes and the

Dead Sea community are substantial and fundamental. What are the similarities and differences between these two groups according to Dupont-Sommer and Driver?

Dupont-Sommer finds a variety of agreements between statements in the Essene reports and several of the Dead Sea Scrolls.[32] (1) The name 'Essenes' derives from the Hebrew word עצה, which is often used in the Dead Sea texts. (2) The so-called novitiate period of the Essenes is sufficiently similar to that of the people of the Dead Sea Scrolls to allow one to postulate the identity of the two groups. (3) Josephus mentions a vow that a new member had to recite before his brethren before he was allowed to touch the common food (cf. 1QS V,7-11). Josephus' 'solemn vows' are, according to Dupont-Sommer, those of 1QS I,6–II,18. (4) Josephus' reference to the Essenes' concealment of secret doctrines (*Bell.* 2.141) is thought to be reflected in CD XV,10-11 and 1QS VII,10-12; IX,17-19. (5) In *Bell.* 2.132 and 146 Josephus speaks of the Essenes' respect for elders and superiors (cf. *Quod* 81); this is reflected in 1QS VI,3-4 and CD XIII,2-3. (6) Severe disobedience of the Essenic communal regulations is punished with excommunication (*Bell.* 2.143-44; 1QS VII,22-25; VIII,20–IX,2; cf. V,14; CD XII,2-8). (7) The Essenes and the Dead Sea community are known for their purification baths (*Bell.* 2.129, 138, 149-59; 1QS V,13-14; CD X,11-13). (8) Their morning prayers are reflected in 1QH IV, 23 (cf. *Bell.* 2.128). (9) The Essene concern with the hereafter (*Bell.* 2.154-58) is reflected in CD VII,5-6; 1QS IV,7-8, 12-13; 1QH III,29-36; 1QM XII,5. (10) The Essenic interest in angels is found in several documents (*Bell.* 2.142; 1QH; 1QM I,10-11; VII,6; IX,15-16; X,10-11; XVII,6). (11) The Qumran Essenes are strict sabbatarians (*Bell.* 2.147 and CD X,14–XI,18), who are absorbed in the study of the works of the ancients (*Bell.* 2.136,142; 1QS). (12) They hate pleasure and despise riches (*Bell.* 2.120, 122, 141; *Quod* 78; 1QS I,6-7; V,4-5; X,19; XI,21-22). (13) A similarity exists between their halakhah concerning the evacuation of bodily wastes (*Bell.* 2.148-49; 1QS VII,13-14; 1QM VII,6-7). (14) Essenic avoidance of oil is found also in CD XII,16. (15) Spitting in the midst of an assembly is prohibited by both groups (*Bell.* 2.147; CD VII,13).

This list of similarities should indicate Dupont-Sommer's position adequately and support his general claim that the pictures of the Essenes in the ancient reports and the group witnessed in the Dead Sea Scrolls—especially 1QS, CD, and 1QM—bear an obvious resemblance. But do these similarities unequivocally demonstrate the identification of the Essenes with the group depicted in some of the Dead Sea Scrolls or do they exist only at a superficial level?

Driver recognizes the similarities pointed out by Dupont-Sommer, but eliminates most of them as inconclusive when arguing for the Essene identification in particular. He points out that these same superficial similarities are found in other documents from and about other approximately contemporary religious groups.[33] For example, in every such religious conclave of the time there were both superiors and inferiors, the most learned and the novices (no. 5 above). In order that a modicum of community cohesion could exist and continuity be preserved, a certain degree of respect between pupils and teachers had to be present. As for the purification baths (no. 7), this ritual was more widespread than Dupont-Sommer admits. It is mentioned as well in the Mishnah *Demai* 2.3 and in the New Testament (Luke 7.34; 15.2; 1 Cor. 10.25-31). The prohibition against spitting in the midst of an assembly (no. 15) is known also among the rabbis: *Berakoth* 62b-63a. Special study of the ancients and observance of the Sabbath (no. 11) are typically Jewish and are not restricted to the Essenes. Christians also observed the Sabbath and studied the holy writings. Whether the stringent Sabbath regulations of the Essenes are to be identified with those of the Dead Sea community continues to be a matter of debate.[34] There is no similarity between the Essene and the Dead Sea regulations with regard to defecation (no. 13). Presumably, the Essenes did not evacuate on the Sabbath; the members of the Dead Sea group did. It is often pointed out that the Essenes venerated the names of the angels and kept them secret (no. 10). The Dead Sea texts do in fact demonstrate an interest in the angelic world, but this was hardly a concern of the Essenes alone.[35] Josephus, a Pharisee, argues under the guise of Agrippa that the Jews should not fight against the Romans for the sake of the city Jerusalem and the temple, calling both the temple and the holy angels as witnesses against the Jewish renegades (*Bell* 2.400-401). Neither is the avoidance of oil (no. 14) exclusively restricted to the halakhic interests of the Essenes (cf. *Yoma* 8.1; *Yoma* 76b; *Shabbat* 17b).

After emphasizing the superficiality of the similarities recognized by Dupont-Sommer, Driver addresses the concrete differences between the Essene and Dead Sea (Covenanter) communities. Noting that both Jewish and non-Jewish writers know the name

'Essenes', he says one would expect to find this name in the Dead Sea Scrolls as well. This is not the case. On the other hand, the title 'Sons of Zadok' is mentioned a few times in Dead Sea documents, but never in the Essene reports.[36]

Most relevant to the possible identification of the Essenes with the Dead Sea community is the issue of admittance to membership and the novitiate period (nos. 2-3).[37] In the Essene association the new applicant for membership received a hatchet, a girdle, and a white garment. This is nowhere mentioned in the Dead Sea Scrolls. Moreover, while Josephus speaks of a one-year probation period, when the prospective member would remain outside the Essene community but would continue to be instructed by it, the new member of the Dead Sea community seems to have been accepted immediately into the community (1QS V,8-12). According to the Essenes, once the new member had satisfactorily completed his probationary period satisfactorily, he was allowed to participate in the ritual baths. The Dead Sea Scrolls never refer to obligatory purification baths (cf. CD V,13-14). If the new Essene member should continue to make progress over the next two years, he would then be permitted to become a permanent member. 'Touching the purity of the Many' comes in the second stage among the Dead Sea community. But even a permanent member of the Essenes had to take an oath after this three-year period before being allowed to 'touch the common food'. Once the oath had been administered, the new member was permitted to enter into full association with the community. The Dead Sea community required the swearing of an oath at the very beginning of the novitiate (1QS V,8-12). 'Touching the drink of the Many' which is mentioned in CD VI,20, did not belong to the Essene novitiate. Furthermore, while Essene membership was apparently permanent, CD II,19 and V,23-25 refer to the annual renewal of covenant membership. The daily routine of the Essene community as reported by Josephus is never discussed in the Scrolls.

Driver thinks that the admittance procedures of the Dead Sea community, which he calls the Covenanters, and those of the Pharisees are more closely related than those of the Essenes and the Covenanters, but he never argues directly for this identification.[38]

It should not be overlooked that several specific interests of the Dead Sea Scrolls play absolutely no role in the Essene reports. (1) The chief characters of the pesharim, CD, and presumably also of

1QH, the Teacher of Righteousness, the Wicked Priest, and the Liar, are never mentioned by the ancient writers, one of whom, Josephus, claimed to have been a former member or at least an Essene disciple. (2) Important in the scrolls, the Zadokites play no role in the ancient reports. (3) The serious halakhic disputes that presumably existed between the Qumran community and the Jerusalem establishment are not even alluded to in the ancient reports. The calendar issue in particular, which some scholars place at the center of the polemics between the Qumran community and the Jerusalem priesthood, is entirely absent from the ancient reports.[39]

The above analysis of the ancient reports concerning the Essenes has revealed general agreement between the reports of Josephus and Philo on the nature of the Essene association. Both depict them as a group committed to a rigorous communal way of life. Information peculiar to Josephus was found to be more concrete and relevant to the question of the identification of the Essenes with the Qumran community. Still, much of his information proved to be of a generalizing nature, often applicable as well to other contemporary groups—as Driver has sufficiently illustrated. On the procedures for admittance to the communities, Josephus' Essenes and the Dead Sea community do bear impressive similarities. Nevertheless, Driver has demonstrated convincingly that distinctions between the two groups are also present in the documentation and that these differences would militate against their identification. Finally—and this point needs to be underscored—none of the ancient Essene reports presents information on the polemics that are usually associated with the origin and continuing history of the Qumran community. In fact, Josephus presents the Essenes as one of the three major religious association of this time, not as a rebellious sectarian conclave.

If the similarities between the Essenes and the Qumran community should serve as evidence for anything, it would be for the existence and resemblance of various religious associations in Hellenistic-Roman Judaea. While descriptive reports of such groups may enhance historical reports, the descriptive evidence for the existence of such religious associations should by no means be allowed to substitute for evidence for the historical development of such groups.

In a single paragraph the Roman historian, Pliny, presents valuable information on the Essenes (*Esseni*) located near the western shore of the Dead Sea.

> To the west (of the Dead Sea) the Essenes have put the necessary distance between themselves and the insalubrious shore. They are a people unique of its kind and admirable beyond all others in the whole world, without women and renouncing love entirely, without money, and having for company only the palm trees. Owing to the throng of new-comers, this people is daily reborn in equal numbers; indeed, those whom, wearied by the fluctuations of fortune, life leads to adopt their customs, stream in in great numbers. Thus, unbelievable though this may seem, for thousands of centuries a people has existed which is eternal yet into which no one is born: so fruitful for them is the repentance which others feel for their past lives! Below the Essenes was the town of Engag (Engedi), which yielded only to Jerusalem in fertility and palm-groves but is today become another ash-heap. From there one comes to the fortress of Masada, situated on a rock, and itself near the lake of Asphalt (*Nat. Hist.* 5.17.4).

Two pieces of information in this brief report are usually thought to clinch the identification of the Qumran/Dead Sea community with Pliny's Essenes. The first is the name Essenes, which the non-Jewish historian gave to this group. In combination with the name, the fact that these Essenes inhabited the general area of the Qumran complex would seem to weigh heavily in favor of identifying Pliny's Essenes with a local manifestation of the larger group about which Josephus and Philo wrote.

Clearly, Pliny preserves a significant piece of evidence on the geographical location of the Essenes, but he does not seem to know much about them concretely. Where he does present some information about them, it conflicts with Josephus, who claims to have known the Essenes by personal acquaintance. First of all, Pliny says the Essene community consists of persons who are wearied by the fluctuations of fortune. While this statement can be viewed as consistent with Philo's claim that the Essenes flee the corrupt cities (*Quod* 76), it does not agree with Josephus who reports that the Essenes formed colonies in towns (*Bell.* 2.124). Of these three sources, Josephus alone maintains that he had first-hand acquaintance with the Essenes. Furthermore, he presents the Essenes as a major Jewish faction in the late Hellenistic-Roman period (*Ant.* 13.171-73; 18.1.20), not as a group that had abandoned the rest of civilization. He located two Essenes in Jerusalem (*Bell.* 2.111-13, 566-68). One served as Jewish commander against the Romans in Galilee (*Bell.* 2.78-80).

Unlike Philo and Josephus, Pliny reports nothing about the life style, the inner workings, and the theology of the Essenes. Philo and Josephus describe the Essenes as a group that rejected individual wealth for philosophical reasons, favoring a communal life of sharing. Philo even says they have a contempt for riches (*Quod* 84). Pliny clearly suggests that the Essenes are made up of those to whom life has not been kind, not those who have willingly chosen a life of poverty.

On another aspect of Essene practice, Pliny's information conflicts with that of Josephus. After having written that women are absent from the Essenes (*sine ulla femina*), Pliny remarks that no children are ever born into the community. This statement is consistent with Philo (*Apologia* 3), but disagrees again with Josephus, who reports that marrying Essenes did exist (*Bell.* 2.8.160; cf. 121). The majority of graves seem to have contained the skeletons of males. Archaeologists have, however, discovered the tombs of women and children at Qumran, which might tend to cast doubt on the trustworthiness of Pliny and Philo.[40]

Therefore, Pliny, a non-Jewish source, also knows a group of Essenes. His most crucial piece of information is that they were located north of Engedi near the western littoral of the Dead Sea. This information suggests to most Qumran scholars that he is referring to the Dead Sea community. Unfortunately, he advances no information indicating that he had in fact visited the Essenes. Moreover, he never makes a claim to that effect. He does speak about them in the present tense, but since his use of sources is well-known, it is not certain whether his report reflects only his literary enthusiasm or whether it is historically accurate.

Leaney has pointed out that Pliny was writing around 77 CE about a group settled in the general vicinity of Qumran.[41] Thus, Pliny could hardly have been concerned with the Qumran-Essene community, whose headquarters was destroyed and reoccupied by the Romans in the year 68 CE. It seems, therefore, that the conflation of Pliny's information with that of Philo, and especially that of Josephus is illegitimate, even if his geographical information is enticing.

D. *Other Sources: 1 and 2 Maccabees*

Although Josephus introduced the Essenes alongside the Pharisees and Sadducees into the political history of Jerusalem during the high priesthood of Jonathan Maccabeus (c. 152 BCE), he in no way associated them with particular historical characters and events of the first half or, for that matter, of the second half of the second century BCE. In fact, named Essenes are reported only for the Roman period. Similarly, 1 and 2 Maccabees, the histories of Jerusalem and Judaea in the Hasmonean period, never speak explicitly about the Essenes. They do refer, however, to the Hasideans or 'pious ones', (συναγωγὴ Ασιδαίων, 1 Macc. 2.42; συναγωγὴ γραμματέων, οἱ Ασιδαῖοι, 1 Macc. 7.12-13), who are sometimes identified with the early Essenes or with their historical predecessors. Unfortunately, these sources tell us nothing about the organization, the inner workings, and the location of the Hasidim in second-century Judaism.

The Hasidim are often associated with the strict sabbatarians who preferred to die on the Sabbath rather than to violate it (1 Macc. 2.33). According to 1 Maccabees, this impression would be false, for some Hasidim clearly did join the Maccabeans against the Hellenizing Jews in order to fight on the Sabbath. The only other hint that we have about their interests is that they preferred Alcimus of the Aaronide line as high priest to his Hellenizing counterpart Menelaus (1 Macc. 7.14).

With one exception our sources report nothing about particular known Hasidim. This one exception is Judas Maccabeus, who is called the leader of the Hasideans in 2 Macc. 14.6.

> οἱ λεγόμενοι τῶν Ἰουδαίων Ἀσιδαῖοι,
> ὧν ἀφηγεῖται Ἰούδας ὁ Μακκαβαῖος

Based on the descriptions of Judas found in both 1 and 2 Maccabees, one might characterize him as one zealous for the law, for the ancient customs, and as a warrior whose aim was to restore the traditional way of life. In 2 Macc. 8.26 and 12.38, Judas is depicted as a strict sabbatarian, who ceased fighting on the Sabbath. This contrasts with the picture of his father in 1 Macc. 2.39-41 (cf. *Ant*. 12.274-76).

Josephus never speaks of Judas as a Hasid, but does know him as a politically and religiously influential person (cf. the situation involving Alcimus and the Hasidim in 1 Macc. 7.14). In fact, he maintains that the Jewish people gave the high priesthood to him when Alcimus died after serving only for four years, 162–159 BCE (*Ant*. 12.4.14, 419, 434). Yet that statement conflicts with 1 Macc. 9.56 that has Alcimus die after Judas and also with *Ant*. 22.237, where Josephus reports that there was no high priest in Jerusalem for seven years after the death of Alcimus. This period represents the so-called Intersacerdotium (159–152 BCE). This inconsistency in the sources may reflect either an actual high priesthood of Judas Maccabeus, since he did function with the required charisma and authority expected of such an important figure, or it may be an idealization of Judas that is consistent with his characterization in 2 Maccabees.

How much Judas shared with other Hasidim of this period or differed from them cannot be determined from the sparse information provided in 1 and 2 Maccabees. These historical sources for Jerusalem and Judaea in this period, therefore, do not speak directly to questions about the internal and external history of the Essenes and the Qumran community.[42]

Conclusion

The oldest reports on the Essenes exhibit agreements as well as inconsistencies in their descriptions of Essene life and thought. Both Philo and Josephus reflect a concern to present the Essenes as a Jewish embodiment of virtue and wisdom. Clearly, Philo wanted his audience to view the Essenes as a Palestinian manifestation of ideal human associations throughout the known world. Josephus presents them as the epitome of an ideal society. They agree that the Essenes form a communal organization devoted to a rigorous discipline.

Of these two writers, only Josephus preserves information that might substantiate his claim to have known the Essenes first-hand and to have studied with them. He elaborates on their communal entrance requirements and their daily regimen (*Bell.* 7.137-43). Dupont-Sommer has demonstrated that similarities do exist between the novitiate of the Essenes and the group behind CD and 1QS. On the basis of these similarities, he argues for the identification of the two groups. Granting the similarities, Driver points out discrepancies between the two groups that would argue against their identification. For example, none of the Dead Sea Scrolls ever states that an applicant for membership received a hatchet, a girdle, and a white garment. A more serious discrepancy is the fact that the new member of the Essenes had to submit to a one-year probation period before admittance to the community, whereas the Dead Sea community apparently accepted members immediately. Secondly, the Dead Sea Scrolls do not speak of obligatory purification baths, as Josephus does about the daily routine of the Essenes. Furthermore, the Essenes required a permanent member to swear an oath after a three-year period before he could 'touch the common food'. The Dead Sea community required an oath at the beginning of the novitiate. Finally, whereas CD refers to the annual renewal of covenant membership, the Essenes apparently considered membership to be permanent. Thus, the similarities do not outweigh the fundamental differences, which argue against confident identification of the ancient Essenes with the group that composed the sectarian Dead Sea Scrolls.

It was also discovered that Josephus would sometimes underscore aspects of Essene behavior that he admired. Like the Essenes, he had devoted himself to the study of his people's holy writings. Like Judah and Simon the Essenes, Josephus had prophetic powers, having predicted the fate of Vespasian. His belief that God (or Psyche) was on the side of the Romans in his days is consistent with the Essene view, as he reports it, that God controls history. Finally, Josephus was a Jewish commander in the war against the Romans, as was John the Essene. Consequently, it is difficult to decide where Josephus' self-praise ends and his historical reliability concerning the Essenes begins.

In the case of Pliny, it was determined that he had probably never visited the Essenes about whom he had written. The circumstance that he refers to *Esseni* located above Engedi near the Dead Sea does induce one to think that he was the only ancient source to speak of the Dead Sea community. One need not cast doubt on Pliny or his informant in respect to their information concerning this specific location of the Essenes. Two considerations weigh against his trustworthiness as an eyewitness. First of all, he seems to be writing about a group settled in the Qumran area after the year 68 CE, when the Romans attacked and reoccupied the Qumran complex. Presumably no Essenes lived at Qumran at that time. Secondly, he knows nothing about the characteristic features of the Essene community that would allow the historian to decide whether the group to which he is referring is indeed a local manifestation of the more widespread and influential group about which Philo and Josephus wrote.

In contrast to the Essene reports of Philo, Josephus, and Pliny, which are concerned with a group of the first century CE, 1 and 2 Maccabees are thought to offer some evidence for the early history of the Essenes or at least of a group which may have in part developed into the Essenes. Nowhere in these two books are Essenes referred to explicitly, but occasionally reference is made to the Hasideans. Since the Hasideans are associated with the strict sabbatarians, and since the sabbath laws of CD X-X1 would identify its author and his community also as strict sabbatarians, some scholars perceive an ideological lineage running from the Hasidim of the second century BCE through the Essenes of the first century CE. Clearly, 1 and 2 Maccabees report virtually nothing about the life style and specific theological views of the Hasidim. Only in 2 Maccabees is reference made to an individual Hasid: this is Judas Maccabeus. He is described simply as one who championed the traditional way of life and as a zealot for the law. One can hardly draw substantial and far-reaching conclusions about the early history of the Essenes from this scant piece of information.

In their Essene reports, Philo, Josephus, and Pliny are clearly concerned with a voluntary communal organization called Essenes. The first two writers elaborate on the common life—at least in part as a reflection of a Hellenistic ideal. They point out the Essenes' love of virtue and the saintly life. Josephus alone is able to report on the procedures for entrance in the Essene association and their daily routine. Furthermore, he can name Essenes, whom he clearly credits with prophetic or predictive powers. Not even Josephus, the self-acclaimed eyewitness, locates the Essenes near the Dead Sea. This information is provided, however, by the Roman naturalist Pliny. Thus the ancient reports about the Essenes confirm the vigorous communal life of the Essenes, and Pliny in particular knows an Essene group in the general area of Qumran. None of these sources speaks about the central conflict between the Teacher of Righteousness and the Wicked Priest as known from several sectarian Dead Sea Scrolls.

Chapter 5

CD AND THE HISTORY OF THE QUMRAN COMMUNITY

A. *Introduction*

Unlike the other so-called sectarian texts found in the Qumran caves, the Damascus Document was known already at the turn of the twentieth century. It came from the famous Cairo Geniza, which was visited by Saphir, Firkowitch, and Schechter in the second half of the nineteenth century.[1] Schechter is responsible for salvaging many medieval manuscripts from this geniza and is most noted among Qumran scholars for the discovery (1896) and the publication (1910) of the Damascus Document.[2]

Despite the medieval date of manuscripts A (cols. 1-16, tenth century CE) and B (cols. 19-20, eleventh to twelfth centuries CE), several theories were presented dating the original document variously from the second century BCE to the eleventh century CE.[3] The authors of this document were identified with almost every known Jewish group of the Hellenistic-Roman period: Zadokites, Sadducees, reformed Sadducees, Dositheans, Pharisees, a group akin to the Pharisees, Essenes, messianic groups in the time of Titus and Hadrian, and the Karaites. It is interesting to recall that the attribution of this document to Essene composition was scarcely entertained until the discovery of several fragments of it in Qumran Caves 4-6. One exception to that state of affairs was Riessler.[4] Whereas several specific non-Essene identifications proliferated in this period, many scholars attributed it to a pious Palestinian splinter group, offering no definite identification.[5]

After the discovery of the fragments of CD at Qumran, the majority of scholars became relatively sure that the original document was authored in the pre-Christian period. According to palaeographical assessments, the fragments from 4Q and 5Q date at least to the first half of the first century BCE and those from 6Q to the first century CE.[6] The palaeographical datings of the Qumran fragments confirm the composition and use of CD, therefore, even before the destruction of the Second Temple. But they do not date the original document(s) precisely.

Several of the fragments from Caves 4–6 correspond to passages in the medieval manuscripts: 6Q15 I,1-3=CD IV,19-21; 6Q15 II,1-2=CD V,13-14; 6Q15 III,1-5a=CD V,18–VI,2a; 6Q15 III,5=CD VI,2b; 6Q15 IV,1-4=CD VI,20-VII,1; 4QD[b] can be restored to XV,15-17, 4QD[e] X.iii?-20, 5Q12 I,2=CD IX,7-8a; 5Q12 I,3-5=CD IX,8b-10; 6Q15 V,1-5=CD XII,1-3.[7]

Other material not found in the medieval MSS of CD but presumably belonging to a more ancient, if not the original, document was discovered. Based on unpublished material from Cave 4, Milik suggests an outline for the oldest Damascus Document.[8] (1) Some material originally preceded col. I as we know it. (2) The next section consists of cols. I,1–VIII,26 + XIX,35–XX,34. (3) The following section is represented by prescriptions not documented in the medieval manuscripts dealing with the cultic piety of priests, sacrifices, diseases, the fluxes of men and women, the relationship between the sexes, marriage, agricultural life, the payment of tithes, the dealings with pagans, and a prohibition of magic. (4) These prescriptions are followed by cols. XV–XVI and IX–XIV in that order. (5) Finally, Milik places a liturgy for the Feast of the Covenant Renewal after the laws.[9]

If Milik's reconstructed outline should turn out to be correct, and the still unpublished 4Q material prevents one from checking it, the medieval manuscripts A and B would seem to represent not only a shorter version but also a qualitatively different document from that represented by the 4Q fragments. If CD originally concluded with a liturgy for the Feast of the Covenant Renewal, then one would need to reassess the document according to genre and historical relevance.

In the absence of Milik's so-called original document, Qumran historians must investigate the two medieval manuscripts for clues to the history of the Qumran community. The material that Milik would add to these medieval manuscripts in order to reconstruct the original document is chiefly legal and does not speak of the historical conflicts at the center of the reconstructions of the history of the Qumran community. The medieval manuscripts do preserve such information. MS A col. I,11 speaks of a teacher of righteousness, who is sometimes thought to be the founder of the Qumran community or at least its most influential personality. This figure is apparently referred to in VI,11; XIX,35–XX,1; XX,14,32. I,14 mentions the Liar, one of the Teacher's opponents. This figure is also mentioned in MS B col. XIX,25-26; XX,15. Several references are made to the location of a remnant community that formed a 'new covenant' in the land of Damascus (VI,5, 18-19; VII,14-15, 18; XIX,33-34; XX,11-12). These references would provide a possible historical location for the community, its Teacher, and the Liar. Debate continues, however, concerning the literal and symbolic understandings of the name Damascus. Both MS A and MS B preserve chronological information that has enabled Qumran historians to determine the approximate period when the Teacher of Righteousness, the Liar, and CD's author lived. In MS A col. I, 5-8, reference is made to the emergence of a remnant community 390 years after the Babylonian exile under Nebuchadnezzar. In II,9-11, the Teacher is said to have appeared twenty years later. Taken at face value, that would mean that these characters existed c. 197/186–177/166 BCE and later, if one allows for a period of activity. In MS B XIX,35-XX,1 and XX,13-14, the writer seems to presuppose the death of the Teacher. The latter passage suggests that CD's author lived during a forty-year period after the Teacher's death. The critical issue for the historian is whether all this information is concrete enough to enable him/her to determine the actual time when these various figures lived, to locate them accurately geographically, and to identify the chief actors unambiguously. After a survey of the literary analysis of CD, attention will be directed to the evaluation of the historically relevant information that it preserves.

B. *Literary-Critical Study of CD*

Any analyst who desires to understand CD should attend to the question of its genre. Work on this aspect has begun, but more may need to be done once the 4Q fragments are published. The one major difficulty in determining the genre and function of the document lies largely in our lack of sociological information, e.g. about why such a text was written in the first place and how it was used, whether privately or publicly. Nevertheless, one can safely assume that CD was written to communicate a message to some audience. Just what its central message was and who comprised its audience continues to be a matter of debate.

A certain amount of agreement exists that CD is a composite didactic work of post-exilic Judaism. Rabinowitz discerns three types of material in CD: a discourse of admonition, glosses and comments, and laws.[10] The last category, the laws (cols. IX–XVI), are usually left out of most discussions of the document as a whole. Iwry considers CD to be a hortatory missionary work.[11] This view is shared to a certain extent by Denis, who designates I,1ff., II,1ff., and II,14 as *monitions*.[12]

Stegemann characterizes CD as a *Geschichtsdarstellung* consisting of a *Grundschrift* (I,1-12, 18–II,1) along with interpolations (midrash, I,13-18; chronology, I,5, 10) dealing with God's *rîb* against all flesh and God's deeds,[13] II,2ff. dealing with the ways of the wicked,[14] and II,14–XX,34 dealing with a revelation of the ways of God.[15] For him, CD is essentially a historical presentation of the conflicts of the Qumran community with the Liar and his community.

Murphy-O'Connor also devotes considerable attention to the analysis of CD into its literary components, some of which he understands as pre-Qumranic in origin.[16] He calls II,14–VI,1 a pre-Qumranic Babylonian Essene Missionary Document addressed to possible converts.[17] The Memorandum, VI,14–VII,4, derives also from the pre-Qumranic period.[18] Based on the Holiness Code, this section is a legal document that defines the proper behavior for members of the community.[19] It concludes with material intended to motivate obedience—a promise in VII,4-6=XIX,1-2 and a warning in VII,9-VIII,3=XIX,5-15.[20] According to Murphy-O'Connor, the close relationship of the Missionary Document to the Memorandum is demonstrated by their shared hortatory tone.[21] Another document, the Well-Midrash in V,2-11a, was later created to link these two older documents. It seems to be related to the historical and theological introductions in I,1–II,1 and II,2-13 respectively.[22] The historical introduction functions to deter members from leaving the community. It does this by condemning those who have already abandoned it.[23] The theological introduction functions to inform the listeners/readers/members why some have remained faithful and others have apostasized.[24] What appears to be a matter of human choice in I,1–II,1 turns out to be an issue of divine predestination in II,2-13.[25] To this later literary period, historically understood as a critical era of apostasy, belongs VIII,3-19, which Murphy-O'Connor entitles a Critique of the Princes of Judah. This document, he says, is embued with a tone of 'bitter disappointment'.[26]

Despite his sensitive awareness of shifts in tone, which enable him to sort out documents and relate them internally to each other, Murphy-O'Connor's literary analyses seem to be guided by his own historical assumption that an earlier non-Qumranic Missionary Document and Memorandum were later received and supplemented by Qumran writers. Accordingly, an earlier hortatory missionary work has been transformed into a critical reflection on actual apostasy from the Teacher's community. Whether his overall analysis should turn out to be correct or not, Murphy-O'Connor does not offer a form-critical treatment of CD as a whole.

In his recent book on CD, Davies has tried to compensate for this deficiency. In order to gain clarity about the form-critical designation of CD, Davies maintains that it should be understood on its own terms and not in light of the pesharim.[27] This sets him apart from Jeremias, Stegemann, and Murphy-O'Connor among others, whose literary analyses use the pesharim to a greater or lesser extent to clarify the historical allusions in CD. Davies builds on and diverges from other scholars in his attempt to explain CD as a covenant formulary.

In his attempt to come to grips with the genre of CD, Davies is concerned almost exclusively with the *Admonition* in I,1–VIII,19 (MS A) and XIX,33b–XX,34 (MS B). He does not intend to treat the laws in IX–XVI extensively.[28] In Chapter 1, 'Structure and Plot of the *Admonition*', he maintains that the *Admonition* is not at all a haphazard composition, but rather 'the outcome of an extremely accomplished piece of redaction', whose coherence derives from a 'clear and simple plot' as well as links of vocabulary.[29] It bears the structure of a covenant formulary, comprising three main original sections and a supplement.[30] Davies views the *Admonition* as a pre-Qumranic document that was later redacted by a member (or members) of the Qumran community. The redaction is associated primarily with statements about a human Teacher of Righteousness and a Liar, which give the *Admonition* a more sectarian tone, and chronological notes in cols. I and XX. He describes its plot as a movement from a *rîb* addressed to outsiders to a warning against apostasy directed to insiders.[31]

Davies divides the *Admonition* into four sections: the History, the Laws, the Warnings, and the New Covenant. The History comprises three discourses, I,1–II,1; II,2-14a; II,14b–IV,12a, whose purpose was to reveal to a remnant what God had in fact already done, but which had not been understood until that time.[32] The *rîb* of I,1–II,1 concerns an existing dispute about the sins of pre-exilic Israel and the subsequent punishment in the form of didactic instruction. In other words, God's punishment is ongoing and not merely a future expectation brought about by the wickedness of contemporary Israel. Noting its theological and lexical similarities with 1QS II,14ff., Davies characterizes the second discourse, II,2-14a, as predestinarian in tone. It deals with the deeds of the wicked. It resembles the first discourse in that both say God himself will teach his remnant.[33] The third discourse, II,14–IV,12b, proceeds beyond a description of a *Heilsgeschichte* to a summons/challenge.[34] The thematic sequence of the material is destruction-remnant-covenant (renewal), the last of which comprises (1) the revelation, (2) the human response, (3) the divine forgiveness, and (4) the making of the 'sure house'.[35]

According to Davies, several expressions have been interpolated by Qumran hands into this historical section: 'and from His sanctuary' (I,3), '390 years from delivering them into the hand of Nebuchadnezzar king of Babylon' (I,5-6), 'and from Aaron' (I,7), 'for twenty years' (I,20),' and He raised for them a teacher of righteousness to lead them in the way of his heart' (I,11), 'the last generation' (I,12), I,13-18a, along with 'and those who despise it shall not live' (III,17).[36] The suggestion that the reference to the Teacher of Righteousness could also be secondary is provocative and will be addressed below in section C.

The legal section of this so-called covenant formulary is divided into four units: IV,12b–V,16; V,17–VI,11; VI,11b–VII,4a; VII,4b-6a, 9-10a.[37] Davies maintains that the theme of the law unites the material in IV,12b–VI,4a. V,16-17 serves as an introduction dealing with examples of halakhot outside the community. These laws are a product of the activity of Belial. V,17–VI,11 deals with the true halakhot as established by God. Davies discerns here a progression from criticism of outsiders' behavior (as a result of Belial's work) to a revelation of the insiders' behavior (as a result of God's work). This progression comes from the hand of 'a very able redactor'.[38] VI,11b–VII,9 deals with the community's own halakhot, which are the product of exegetical study of Leviticus 17–26.[39]

Several elements are again thought to be secondary: the references to Zaw (IV,19-20), the midrash concerning David (V,1-6), 'and without them they will not succeed' (VI,10), the references to the 'closers of the door' (VI,12-14), 'this is to rob the poor of His people, that widows become the spoil, and that they might murder the orphans' (VI,16-17), 'and the festival days and the Fast Days according to the finding of the members of the new covenant in the land of Damascus' (VI,18-19), 'and not to sin each one against his kinsman' (VII,1), and 'for each man not to defile his holy spirit' (VII,3-4).[40]

The 'Warnings' in VII,9–VIII,19 treat the topic of apostasy.[41] The original warning, VII,9-10a, is addressed to would-be converts in an increasingly severe tone. VII,11–VIII,2a and VIII,2b-18 deal with the fulfilment of the divine *rîb* against outsiders and are, according to Davies, probably not original.[42] VIII,2b-18 is a criticism of the authorities that was later added to the original *Admonition*; this critique of the 'princes' functions to typify the unacceptable behavior mentioned elsewhere in the *Admonition*.[43] Five critical issues are presented in this passages: lust, wealth, incest, separation from the people, and not loving one's brother. Davies thinks that this section is explicitly polemical, perhaps as a response to some sort of actual, historical persecution inflicted upon the Qumran community.[44] The following passages are thought to be secondary: VII,10–VIII,9; VIII,12-13,20; XIX,24b-26a.[45]

Cols. XIX,33–XX,34, 'The New Covenant', are characterized by two themes, adherence to a teacher and condemnation of apostates.[46] This section comprises six units: XIX,33b–XX,1a; XX,8b-13; XX,14-22a; XX,22b-27; XX,27b-34; XX,1b-8a. Davies believes that the B text of CD (and perhaps also the A test) represents a Qumranic recension of the document.[47] XIX,33–XX,34 addresses *actual* historical apostates, that is, either those disobedient to the Teacher or those living after the Teacher's death who did not accept him as the expected eschatological figure.[48] Davies believes that two topics, apostasy and the Teacher's death, provide thematic unity in this section.

In addition to the new emphasis on the Teacher, new vocabulary appears—יחד, שוב, צדק, and הברית החדשה בארץ דמשק. According to Davies, these new elements come from the pens of Qumran writers.[49] XX,1b-8a is an interpolation concerned with discipline within the community (related to 1QS);[50] XX,8b-13a is a warning to potential traitors;[51] XX,13b-22a deals with discipline in the community after the death of the Teacher;[52] and XX,22b-34 concerns the 'house of Peleg'.[53] Hereafter, Davies discusses the Teacher's possibly negative attitude to the Jerusalem temple and suggests that he was neither a high priest within nor outside of the community.[54] Later revised by a Qumran scribe, XX,27b-34 probably served as a conclusion to the *Admonition* and functioned as an introduction to the pre-Qumran laws in cols. IX–XVI.[55] For the Qumran community, these laws were the so-called 'former rules'. Presumably the instruction of the Teacher would have resembled 1QS.[56]

In 'Redaction of the Admonition' (Chapter 6), Davies speaks of three successive layers of material in the *Admonition*: (1) a work originally ending with VII,9, traces of which appear at the end of XX and the laws of IX–XVI; (2) warnings; and (3) a layer representing the ideology of the 'new' covenant, i.e. the Qumran community as well as glosses and minor expansions from the hand(s) of a Qumran (writers).[57] This secondary material falls into four categories: (1) allusions to an individual opponent of the Qumran community; (2) a Qumran community *Heilsgeschichte*; (3) warnings originally uttered in respect of outsiders now redirected toward members of the Qumran community; (4) hostile references to the temple.[58] Davies regards the last category as least certain. Concern with individual figures is thought to be a later Qumran concern as exemplified in the pesharim. Preoccupation with the Teacher and his enemies gives the *Admonition* a more sectarian flavor.[59] The interpolation of the '390 years' defines the 'period of wrath' no longer as beginning with the exile, but rather with a period shortly before the Teacher's joining the community.[60]

Davies concludes that the original Damascus Document—the *Admonition*—is a coherent composition containing the ideology and historical traditions of a well-developed community that believed it originated during the exile. Although this community had its own halakhot concerning the temple, it differed otherwise only slightly from the Judaism of its time.[61]

While Davies's work builds upon all previous studies of CD, it is clearly a literary and historical revision of them in light of Murphy-O'Connor's thesis concerning the Babylonian origin of the Qumran community. Its chief merit lies in attempting to see CD as a literary whole and to determine its genre. Nevertheless, a caveat may be issued even against his determination of the genre, which is both his exegetical starting-point and his heuristic measure for the division of CD into units of a progressing rhetorical argument. In spite of his awareness of discrepancies between the formal structure of Baltzer's post-exilic *Bundesformular* and that of CD, Davies proceeds to suggest a means for removing that major difficulty. Baltzer's *Bundesformular* consists of an antecedent history, a statement of substance, stipulations of the covenant, and blessings and curses.[62] CD does not demonstrate this structure perfectly. Therefore, Davies chooses to eliminate the laws in cols. IX–XVI from the discussion of CD's structure and regards VI,11–VII,9 as corresponding to the covenant stipulation of the *Bundesformular*. As a heuristic designation, covenant formulary is perhaps instructive, but it is not an accurate description of CD as we now have it, neither in the medieval manuscripts nor the published Qumran fragments. Once the 4Q Liturgy for the Feast of the Covenant Renewal is published, Davies's designation of CD's genre may require reconsideration.

Still, what does one do with the laws in cols. IX–XVI, if, as Davies maintains, they belong to the original, pre-Qumranic *Admonition*? He does not treat these laws as an integral part of the *Admonition*. In view of what he says about the 'Damascus covenant', they would be superfluous.

> . . . that unlike the Mosaic covenant, it demands not obedience to a 'revealed' law, but insight into a 'hidden' law. The covenant of this community is undoubtedly an esoteric one, in which the doctrine of election assumes a prominent role.[63]

Davies's observation may be accurate for the *Admonition* less the laws, but not for XV,9, 12 and XVI,1-2, 5, which speak of 'returning to the law of Moses'.

Although Davies did not intend to deal with the laws in IX–XVI extensively, his claim that the laws belonged to the original pre-Qumranic *Admonition* would seem to oblige him to establish the literary relationship between the two bodies of material. He has discerned quite accurately several thematic correlations between VI,11ff. and IX–XVI as well as between IV,13-19a, IV,19bff., and VIII,3ff.[64] Nevertheless, thematic correlations such as these are precisely what one would expect of the creator(s) of a complex composition like CD; the lack of such correlations would be surprising.

Two features of the laws might suggest their potential literary independence of the original *Admonition*—the superscriptions and terminology not or almost never found in the laws. The various superscriptions do not appear to be directly related to the *Admonition* as a whole. It is not clear whether they derive from one and the same hand.[65] Several expressions suggest strongly that new hands, or at least different hands are at work in the laws. For example, some expressions appear in the laws but never in the *Admonition*: ספר החגו, מושב, and משכיל; others appear *almost* exclusively in the laws: סרך (exception VII,6, 8), עת/ועת (exception I,13), גורל האור (exception XX,4, 6), and מחנה (exceptions VII,6; XIX,2; XX,26). The presence of these expressions leads one to suspect a closer relationship to certain sections of documents like 1QS, Sa and Sb, and 1QM than to the original *Admonition* as a whole. This evidence would seem to support the view that the legal material is associated with the material that Davies thinks belongs to the Qumranic redaction of CD. Admittedly, Davies has demonstrated that specific Qumran interests in the *Admonition* do not emerge in the laws.[66] Links between the laws and the present form of the *Admonition* do undisputably exist, but the compositional or redactional history of CD is not as clear as Davies has suggested.

Any form-critical account of CD needs to deal with this legal material, which makes up more than fifty percent of the entire document (cols. IX–XVI; IV,12b–VIII,10a). Cols. I–VIII and XIX–XX preserve lessons about those who return to the law and those who abandon it. There are several ways to pose a central literary and perhaps also theological question that deserves more attention in the future: what is the function of so much law in a narrative or instructional text? What is the function of the historical lessons in a basically legal text? Or, less value-laden, what is the rhetorical relationship of the narrative and legal materials to each other?[67] Clearly, both are in a general sense instructional. Davies characterizes the *Admonition*, itself containing some legal material, as catechesis.[68] Catechesis provides lessons whose values suggest forms of desired and despised behavior. The laws state clearly what kind of behavior is expected and what is not tolerated. In that respect narrative and law can be viewed as two modes of catechetical persuasion that were used in the composition of CD.[69]

However one may eventually classify CD as literature, and the resolution of this issue is important for the issue of CD's relevance to the issue of the history of the Qumran community, the scholars whose works are examined above agree that it is composite and recognize some of its component units as older than others. All agree that CD in its present form reflects use in the Qumran community. In contrast to Stegemann, Murphy-O'Connor and Davies view the original non-Qumran document(s) as hortatory or instructional in character. Stegemann considers it to be a presentation of history. Diverging somewhat from all earlier studies, Davies believes that the original *Admonition* has not been altered essentially by the Qumran redactors. This claim induces him to speak of a covenant formulary whose basic structure and plot has remained intact from the time of its composition and use outside the Qumran community to the time of its redaction and use within the community.

Such a view seems to advance beyond the evidence which Davies himself has amassed. The secondary elements that Davies has discerned are extensive and, according to him, the final redaction of CD is in fact related to the interests found in the pesharim. It is clearly these so-called specifically Qumranic elements in the redactional material that have lured most scholars to use CD as a document preserving historical memories of the history of the Qumran community.

C. *The Use of CD in Historical Analyses*

A consensus now exists in Qumran scholarship on the relevance of CD for reconstructing the history of the Qumran community. Most of this potentially valuable historical information belongs to the material which Davies associated with the redaction of the *Admonition* in the Qumran community. (1) Special attention has been devoted in the secondary literature to understanding the expression מורה צדק, Teacher of Righteousness, and variations of it. The identification of this figure has been of central importance, for he is generally considered to be the shaper of the community's ideology, if not its founder. Related to this figure and sometimes identified with him is the דורש התורה. A third figure, the Liar (איש הכזב), and his followers have also played a pivotal role in the reconstruction of the community's history. (2) The peculiar expression בברית החדשה בארץ דמשק has also been of considerable importance for answering the question about the provenance of the group that wrote the original *Admonition*. (3) Of all the Qumran texts, CD alone preserves potentially relevant and valuable chronological information associated with the emergence of the community and its conjunction with the Teacher. I,5-6 refers to God's allowing a remnant to survive the Babylonian exile: God caused a root of planting to sprout up 390 years after the exile. I,9-10 refers to a twenty-year period of searching, after which God raised up for this remnant a teacher of righteousness. XX,13-14 speaks of a forty-year period from the 'death' of the Teacher of the *Yahîd* until the end of all the men of war. Despite divergence in the interpretation of these three types of information, they remain central to any discussion of CD as a historical source. They correspond to the three necessary elements for any historical discussion—historical actors, geography, and chronology.

1. *The Historical Actors*

a. *The Teacher of Righteousness*

Although the prevailing consensus identifies the Teacher of Righteousness with a contemporary of Jonathan Maccabeus, the Wicked Priest, several other identifications of this figure have also been made.[70] Some scholars even claim that מורה צדק was an office filled at various times by different individuals.[71] In any case, the acceptance of any of these hypothetical identifications must be based on a solid understanding of the term מורה צדק within the literary context of CD.

Davies has recently drawn attention to CD's several references to a/the Teacher of Righteousness. Most notably, he cites מורה צדק (I,1), יורה לצדק (VI,11), מורה יחיד (XX,1), יורה היחיד (XX,14), מורה (XX,28), and מורה צדק (XX,32). He recognizes that a teacher also plays an important role in several of the pesharim, but cautions against confusing references to a teacher in the context of the latter with those in CD.[72]

In order to understand the references to a teacher in CD, it is necessary first of all to investigate their meaning in the immediate context. The following passages will be analyzed: I,1-12; II,11-13; II,14–III,8; III,12-15; III,19-21; III,21–IV,11; IV,12; V,17-19; V,21–VI,2; VI,2-11. With the exception of the last passage, they demonstrate a relative structural and thematic congruence, which clearly helps to grasp the fundamental message of the *Admonition* as well as the individual references to a teacher. This message is two-pronged. Throughout history there have been those who were faithful and obedient to God's word and those who have apostasized. The consequence of belonging to the unfaithful is always judgment and destruction, while the consequence of faithfulness and repentance is salvation. This basic message is reiterated in various forms in the *Admonition*. Sometimes God is clearly identified as the teacher.

Elsewhere, a human figure of the past seems to be meant. According to the formulation of one passage, VI,11, the teacher seems to be a future figure, who is still expected. This reference is embedded in a section which also speaks of a *dōreš hattōrâ*, who precedes this teacher. The analysis of these passages should effectively demonstrate both the consistency of the essential message and the variability of the meaning and referent of the 'teacher' in CD.

The first reference to מורה צדק appears in I,11. This unit (I,1-12) is usually interpreted as a historical report about the origin of the Qumran community and, for that reason, the two chronological references—the 390 and twenty years—and the mention of the מורה צדק are emphasized. The rhetorical point of this passage, even if it should also be of historical significance, is how God reacts to human repentance.

> (10) And he (God) discerned their deeds for they sought him with a perfect heart (11) and he raised for them a teacher of righteousness to guide them in the way of his heart (12) and he made known to later generations what he had (already) done with the most recent generation, with a congregation of traitors (I,10-12).[73]

The structure of the argument reflected in this passage consists of the statements (1) that God discerned (יבן) repentance and searching; (2) that God, for that reason, raised (הקים) a teacher (מורה צדק); (3) that it was the teacher's function to guide the repentant community (להדריכם) and to instruct it concerning something (יודע).

Several problems in this passage deserve the attention of the exegete and historian: the subject of the passage, the problem of the מורה צדק, and the temporal orientation of the passage. At first glance one recognizes that God is the subject of the verbs in ll. 10-11. Determining the subject of ויודע is problematic.[74] For Stegemann, the subject is clearly God.[75] Davies too considers God to be the subject, because he is the one acting in almost all of the verbs in I,1-12.[76] For that reason, Davies considers the phrase ויקם להם מורה צדק להדריכם בדרך לבו as secondary.[77] The difficulty arises in understanding the function of a מורה צדק in a passage dealing with God's response to disobedience and to repentance. Even the substance of the superscription induces one to anticipate a presentation on the works of God: ועתה שמעו כל יודעי צדק ובינו במעשי אל כי ריב לו עם כל בשר ומשפט יעשה בכל מנאציו. While it cannot be adequately demonstrated that the phrase referring to the teacher is secondary, the passage makes good sense with or without it. In order to establish whether it is secondary, more attention needs to be given to the language of CD.

Nevertheless, the problem of the temporal orientation seems to be soluble. The chief difficulty lies in translating the verb עשה (I,12). While Jeremias and Stegemann seem to understand עשה as a perfect form, both translate it as a future tense (like a subjunctive mood).[78] According to Jaubert and Davies, it refers to God's reporting what he had done in the past.[79] Davies offers three considerations in support of this view.[80] First of all, without a noun or pronoun the verb reads more naturally as a perfect than as an participle. Accordingly, l. 12 concerns God's future dealings with בדור אחרון בעדת בוגדים. Jeremias and Stegemann have apparently been influenced by the language of 1QpHab. In 1QpHab II,1-10, both *habbōg*^e*dîm* and *haddōr ha'aharōn* are mentioned. The context suggests that at least some of the *bōg*^e*dîm* are a plural entity of the past—from the writer's perspective (see the verbs in ll. 3-4, some of which are partly restored). In ll. 5-10 the writer has made a special effort to use the expression הבוגדים in conjunction with the imperfect יאמינו, the plural participle הבאות and לאחרית הימים. However one may understand these three groups of *bōg*^e*dîm* temporally, all of them share a disbelief in the Teacher's message about the last generation. The first group of *bōg*^e*dîm* is associated with the activities of the Liar, clearly a figure of the past in this context. The *dōr 'aharōn* may include the Liar and adherents as well as later *bōg*^e*dîm*. In CD I,13-18, a midrashic section, the last generation and the congregation of *bōg*^e*dîm* are identified with the סרי דרך. In order to clarify this expression, the writer appeals to Hos. 4.16. In the biblical context, Hosea is presumably speaking to his contemporaries. Had CD I simply ended with this citation (l. 14a), one might give credence to the future understanding of עשה and דור אחרון proposed by Jeremias and Stegemann. However, the writer goes on to identify Israel's stubbornness with the past activities of the Liar and the group that he misled (see the verbs in ll. 14-21). This past perspective is consistent with a translation of the verb עשה and the noun דור אחרון as referring to the past. This perspective may also be consistent with 1QpHab II,1-3, which also knows the Liar and his rebellious group as entities of the speaker's past. Secondly, I,21 refers to a former punishment by God, whose victims are called a 'congregation' (עדה). The superscription as well as the narrative context of I,1-12 speak of God's activity in the past. Several other passages in CD are structurally and contextually similar to I,11-12.

Perhaps the clue to understanding the temporal determination of the דור אחרון lies in 1QpHab VII,1-12. In VII,1-2, Hab. 2.1-2 is interpreted. It says that God told Habakkuk to write down what will come over the last generation (cf. II,7, 10; CD I,12), but had not revealed to him the completion of the age. Then VII,3 takes up Hab. 2.2c again and interprets it as referring to the Teacher of the Righteousness, to whom God revealed the secrets of the prophets' words. The secret, information about גמר הקץ, is partly revealed in the interpretation of Hab. 2.3. The last age (הקץ האחרון, l. 7) is said to be even longer than the prophets had said. Then the remainder of 2.3 is interpreted as referring to 'the men of truth/the doers of the law whose hands will not become tired in the service of truth, even when the last age is extended'. Thus the term בוגדים could refer to entities of the past, present, and the future. The statement in 1QpHab II,10-12 shows, however, that the fulfillment of the prophets' words is a matter of the future.

> 5 And likewise, this saying is to be interpreted [as concerning those who] will be unfaithful at the end 6 of days. They, the men of violence and the breakers of the covenant, will not believe 7 when they hear all that [is to happen to] the final generation from the 8 Priest [in whose heart] God set [understanding] that he might interpret all 9 the words of his servants the prophets, through whom he foretold 10 all that would happen to his people and [his land.]

The pesher functions to encourage the Doers of the Law in the writer's generation to continue believing in the words of the Teacher, presumably his words about the completion of the last generation.

Therefore, 1QpHab II,1-3 and CD I,13-18 seem to agree that the Liar and his group are figures of the past. One need not treat עשה and דור אחרון in CD as referring to the future. 1QpHab II,5-10 does clearly speak of the progressive present or future. It is concerned implicitly with God's eventual judgment on the *bōgᵉdîm*. Neither the narration of CD I,3-12 nor the midrash in I,13-18 makes an explicit reference to the future. The future perspective is implicit in the words of CD's superscription (I,1-2):

> (1) Hear now, all you who know righteousness, and consider the works (2) of God; for he has a dispute with all flesh and will condemn all those who despise him.

Those who know righteousness are asked to listen and to understand

God's quarrel with all flesh and his judgment on his despisers. It seems, therefore, that both CD I and 1QpHab II and VIII are concerned to give those hope who are living in the דור אחרון, which had begun even earlier.

In II,11-13 God is again the subject: הקים לו קריאי שם and ויודיעם ביד משיחי רוח קדשו וחוזי אמת. The verbs הקים and יודיעם reproduce almost identically those in I,11.[81] Although no teacher of righteousness is ever mentioned, the statement is made that God communicates to his chosen ones through his messiahs and seers. While it may at this point go beyond the evidence to identify מורה צדק of I,11 as a messianic or prophetic figure, the thematic similarity of the two passages could suggest this possibility. Furthermore, in II,15-16 the phrase להתהלך תמים בכל דרכיו seems to echo להדריכם בדרך לבו in I,11. The verbs whose subject is God refer exclusively to the past: הקים (II,11), ויודיעם (II,12), שנא and התעה (II,13).

A new discourse beginning at II,14 and running through at least III,19 deals with the perversion of many (רבים) from God's way. The עירי השמים, their offspring, all flesh, and the children of Noah and their families are lumped together representing those who 'did not observe the commandments of their creator'.[82] After a sketchy review of the history of the faithful—including Abraham, Isaac, and Jacob—the writer returns to his designation and characterization of the sons of Jacob and their sons as unfaithful ones who, like the עירי השמים, 'did not obey the voice of their creator, the commandments of their teacher' (III,8). This is an unequivocal reference to God as their teacher (יוריהם) in the past. Accordingly, God had become angry with the unfaithful congregation, destroying kings and warriors because of their disobedience. Does this reference to God the Creator (II,21) as teacher clarify the term מורה צדק in I,11? It does not clarify it, but it does suggest that the former reference to a teacher may be understood as referring to a figure distinct from God the Creator but dependent upon his action.

A parallel formulation to I,10-12 and II,10-13 is found in III,12-15.

> (12) But with those who held fast to God's commandments,(13) (those) who were left over from them, he (God) raised up his covenant with Israel forever in order to reveal (14) to them hidden things in which all Israel had gone astray . . . his truthful ways.

As in II,8 and also I,11, God is again the subject, and the issue under consideration here is how God deals with the remnant. Moreover, as in II,12, where God is the one imparting information, here too in III,12 he makes something known to or instructs 'those having a name' through the messiahs of his holy spirit and the seers of his truth.

Davies too has recognized the recurrent use of certain terms and phrases in the recitation of episodes from Israel's past history in II,14–III,12-13.[83] Emphasizing that CD is a rhetorical text, he maintains that these terms and phrases are reiterated in order to drive a message home.[84] He finds five motifs in this message: (1) keeping the commandments of God, (2) not walking in the stubbornness of heart, (3) not following one's own desires, (4) the anger of God being aroused, and (5) the succession of rebellion through the children, the motif which ends every episode.[85] In reverse order, from (5) to (1), these motifs represent the key elements in the message of CD to this point.

Davies is correct in observing that the thematic sequence in the first three discourses of CD (I,1–IV,12b) runs from destruction to remnant to covenant.[86] Against Stegemann, who views 'those who held fast to the commandments of God' (III,12) as a reference to the faithful in the second century BCE,[87] Davies relates this passage rightly to a remnant of the exile.[88] In deference to the latter's claim that this passage is merely of historical rather than of typological value,[89] it must be emphasized that both aspects are present and should not be separated from each other. CD employs historical examples that are already saturated with a theological veneer in order to express a theological message about the fates of the faithful and the unfaithful in the past and potentially those in the present and the future. For that reason, the passages that reiterate a structurally and thematically similar message provide clues for understanding the basic concerns of CD.

The structure of the statements in I,10-12, II,10-13, and III,12-14 is quite similar. This observation is central for understanding several other passages in CD.

III,19-21 presents a partial parallel to I,10-12, II,10-13, and III,12-14. The use of the verb הקים provides a direct verbal correspondence. Although בין is not used, the similar-sounding form ויבן (from בנה) may echo it. להם refers to the recipients of God's mercy (cf. I,11; לו, II,11; ישראל, III,13).

Another partial parallel begins with III,21: הקים אל להם ביד יחזקאל

הנביא. It is difficult to compare this passage with the others discussed above, because it appears simply to introduce a citation from Ezek. 44.15. As in other structurally similar passages, however, the verb הקים is used to refer to God's establishing (cf. Deut. 18.18 in 4QTest 5, 2 Sam. 7.12 in Flor I,10-11, Amos 9.11 in Flor I,12). In this case, it is clear that the perfect form of the verb is used to illustrate how (כאשר) God will deal with those in the present and in the future who hold fast to the covenant (המחזיקים בו). In other words, there is a typological correspondence between the citation, the reference to the past, and the following statement about the future. The reference to the sons of Zadok as בחירי ישראל and קריאי השם who (will) stand at the end of the days, while thematically associated with the 'sure house' (III,19), certainly recalls קריאי שם in II,11.

A new section begins at IV,12.[90] It is thematically connected to the preceding section by two temporal references: הקץ למספר השנים (IV,10-11) and בכל השנים האלה (IV,12).[91] The latter phrase refers certainly to a period of dominance by Belial. The following material deals with the three nets of Belial and the deeds of David.[92] This section concludes with the statement that God became angry because this people lacked understanding (IV,15-16).

Immediately after this section dealing with Belial, a dualistic section (V,17-19) appears that is also structurally similar to I,10-12, II,10-13, III,12-14 and III,19-21.

> (17) For in earlier times (18) Moses and Aaron arose with the help of the Prince of Lights and Belial raised up Jannes and (19) his brother in his cunning.

According to the context, the verb עמד is used synonymously with the verb ויקם, whose subject is Belial. Therefore, it seems valid to maintain that עמדו (ll. 20-21) refers to the typologically similar activity of the מסיגי הגבול. Whereas the other passages dealt with so far concern the activity of God as teacher, misleader, and destroyer, in this passage two groups are opposed to each other dualistically—that of the Prince of Lights and that of Belial.[93]

As is usual in CD, the reference to the destruction of the land in V,21 is followed by a reference to God's mercy (VI,2ff.). God remembered (the) covenant of (the) earlier ones, raised up men of understanding from Aaron and men of wisdom from Israel, and instructed them. The correspondences with col. I are instructive.[94]

I,4	he delivered them to the sword	V,21 the land become desolate
I,4	he remembered (the) covenant of (the) earlier ones	VI,2 *identical*
I,11	he raised up	VI,2 *identical*
I,3	from Israel and from his temple	VI,2 from Aaron and from Israel

As in I,11, God is clearly the subject in VI,2.

Although the Well-Midrash that follows in VI,2-11 may not seem to be strictly related to the structural analysis of passages that either explicitly or implicitly deal with God or any other figure as teacher, it requires consideration in this context because of its reference to the דורש התורה (l. 7). This expression is sometimes thought to be an allusion to *the* historical Teacher of Righteousness.[95]

Murphy-O'Connor, who restricts the Midrash to VI,2-11a, believes it is later than the Missionary Document and the Memorandum (II,14–VI,1; VI,15–VII,4).[96] He suggests that it may have been written in order to link those two documents.[97] On the literary level, he associates the Midrash with the introductions in I,1–II,13,[98] but seems to have overlooked the obvious verbal connection with the earlier material in III,16: ויחפרו באר למים רבים (cf. VI,3). It may go beyond the evidence to claim that III,16 is a partial citation from Num. 21.18, but it is widely accepted that VI,3-4 does preserve this citation.[99]

Davies makes a good case that the literary unit including the Well-Midrash should probably begin even earlier than VI,1. Several phrases anticipate the section beginning with V,17.[100] In the conclusion to IV,12b–V,16 the word מילפנים appears (V,15b). It is repeated in V,17 (using a defective spelling). The phrase ויחר אפו בעלילותיהם, whose individual words are found elsewhere in CD, is taken up again in the motif of the desolation of the land in V,10. Even more impressive is the catchphrase לא עם בינות in V,16, which is actually a citation of Isa. 27.14. It is repeated in a slightly different form in V,17—אין בהם בינה. This is a citation of Deut. 32.28. In connection with this last example, it may be that the Well-Midrash is presented, perhaps redactionally, in order to highlight the wise men (חכמים,נבונים, VI,2-3) who search for understanding by digging a well (=the torah). In that respect, the Midrash is thematically associated with the earlier material (I,1–IV,2a).

Accordingly, this unit, V,17–VI,11, begins with a citation of Deut. 32.28. This is followed by the dualistic lesson from history in V,17-

19. In V,20–VI,3 a less concrete example is taken from the more recent past (ובקץ חרבן הארץ עמדו). Although it is difficult to determine whether ויחפורו (VI,3) originally continued the line of thought established by the verbs ויזכר, ויקם, and וישמיעם, in the present literary context, the exegete must construe the plural subject of ויחפורו as those whom God had instructed. Therefore, God functions again as teacher.

The transition from the statement that God instructed the wise men at some time in the past to the Well-Midrash itself is accomplished by the use of the phrase 'and they (the wise men) dug the well'. This is followed by the quotation of Num. 21.18. Various elements of this citation are taken up one by one and identified: the 'well' is identified with 'the law' (תורה=באר); 'the diggers', with 'the returnees of Israel' (שבי ישראל=חופריה; 'the staff', with 'the one searching out the law' (דורש=מחוקק התורה); 'the noble ones of the people', with 'those who came to dig the well' (הבאים לכרות את הבאר=נדיבי העם).

It is significant that the citation from Numbers is preceded by the statement that God instructed *them*—the wise men from Aaron and Israel. This statement provides a transition as well as an introduction to a new subject. The transitional phrase, 'and they dug the well' shifts the attention from God's action to that of the wise men. These wise men are associated with the שבי ישראל, who are in turn called Princes because they sought God. The use of a 'this is that' equation illustrates that 'digging a well' is equivalent to 'digging the law' and 'searching for God'. In VI,7 the emphasis shifts once again abruptly from a plural subject to a singular one. The staff מחוקק is identified with the דורש התורה. Although there is a shift in number, the association with the foregoing is sufficiently lucid; דרשוהו echoes דורש התורה. Suddenly, the interpretation reverts to the 'nobles of the people', a plural entity, that came to dig the well with laws that the Staff had established. The Staff apparently refers to an authoritative interpreter either in the past or the present from the perspective of 'the nobles'. In order to understand the temporal perspective, one should recall that the Well-Midrash is framed by narrative report and is itself partially formulated about the past, e.g. ויחפורו (l. 3), ויגורו (l. 5), קרא and דרשוהו (l. 6), and חקק (l. 9). The word מחוקק in the citation seems at this point to refer to a historical figure.

Despite attempts to find the Teacher of Righteousness in the expression דורש התורה, one might argue against this view. Regardless how one interprets דורש התורה, this figure would appear to be chronologically anterior to the יורה הצדק in VI,11. The latter figure would seem to be identifiable with the Teacher of Righteousness. The midrashist understands the *dōreš* to be a figure about whom Isaiah had written (54.16). This figure is responsible for the legislation that is to be followed in the period of wickedness. This period of time, which cannot be calculated based on information in the present context, seems to be concluded by the appearance of the Teacher of Righteousness. Thus the *dōreš* is apparently a figure of the past; the Teacher is yet to come. If one were to interpret this passage in light of I,3-12, one could speak of the Teacher who emerged during the period of wrath that began with the exile and of the authoritative expositor as someone like Ezra. Of course, the identification of this figure is hypothetical, but according to VI,7-8 he would have preceded the Teacher of Righteousness.

Is it possible that other references to דורש התורה can resolve this dilemma? In CD VII,18 this expression explains the word taken from Num. 24.17. While the midrashic sections of VI,7 and VII,18 are in fact similar, the difficulty in using the former to illuminate the latter lies in the problem of determining its temporal orientation. The midrash of VII,18ff., which by itself has often been interpreted as referring to the present or the future, is clearly framed by a narrative past perspective. This suggests that figures mentioned in the midrash should also be viewed from that perspective.

> (12) When the two houses of Israel separated, (13) Ephraim fell away from Judah. And all the rebellious ones were delivered to the sword, but the faithful ones (14) saved themselves in the land of the north (VII,12-14).

This narrative report is subsequently illustrated by the citation of Amos 5.26f. and 9.11 (ll. 15-16), whose elements could be construed as referring to the present or the future. This temporal perspective is modified by the statement in VII,21 to the effect that 'these escaped at the time of the first visitation, but the rebellious ones were delivered up to the sword'. VIII,1-2 would seem to support the view that the material from VII,12 to VIII,21 presents historical examples of the kind of punishment that the unfaithful should expect.

> (1) And thus is the judgment for all those who have come into his covenant, but who (2) do not hold fast to these (commandments) (VIII,1-2).

As specific examples of the faithful and the unfaithful respectively, a group that escaped to the land of the north is contrasted with the rebellious traitors (VII,13-14). Insufficient information is given to enable identification of either of these groups. In VIII,3-16 the writer seems to refer to the Liar and the saved ones of Israel as living in the age of the Kings of Yavan. The identities of these figures may have been known to the writer, but cannot be identified on the basis of the information which he presents.

Four other references to דורש התורה should be mentioned in order to illustrate the difficulty in its interpretation. In 4QFlor I,11, this expression seems to refer to a figure of the future. In 4QPB 2, המחקק is equated with 'the covenant of the kingdom'. In 1QS VI,6-7, it refers to one who studies the law night and day within his quorum of ten. Without being able to achieve a satisfactory understanding of the expression דורש התורה and of the temporal orientation of the passages in which this expression is found in CD, which is prerequisite to taking the next step of identifying it with a historical figure, it seems warranted to conclude that all historical identifications based on vague references in the Well-Midrash are hypothetical.

Before addressing the final references to a teacher in CD, let us summarize the results of our analysis of passages dealing with the expression מורה or יורה. (1) The superscription in I,1 leads the reader to anticipate a lecture on the works of God. In I,1-12, God is the subject of almost all the verbs. Although מורה צדק is mentioned in I,11, God is apparently also the subject of the verb עשה in I,12. Nonetheless, it is not clear what the relationship is between God and the references to a teacher in I,11-12. (2) No 'teacher' is mentioned again explicitly until III,8, where it refers directly to God. (3) The application of a structural-thematic analysis to CD has demonstrated the probability that God is intended as a teacher in several other passages: ויודיעם (II,12), לגלות להם (III,13-14), and וישמעם (VI,3). הבדיל (VII,4) belongs also to this category. (4) VI,7-11 speaks of two apparently distinct figures, an authoritative interpreter and a teacher. The interpreter seems to have been a figure of the past from the perspective of the writer. The teacher was apparently a figure that was still expected to come. If we choose to identify the authoritative interpreter with the Teacher of Righteousness of I,11, then the *yōreh haṣṣedeq* in the last days would be an eschatological figure. Since there is no other evidence in CD for the teacher as an eschatological figure, one may interpret the *dōreš* as a figure preceding the Teacher, possibly Ezra, and the Teacher would be identical with the teacher of I,11. The remaining references to a teacher in CD deserve scrutiny before drawing any conclusions on this issue. In any case, the structural-thematic analysis has demonstrated that the references to a teacher in CD are by no means identical.

In the legal material, cols. IX–XVI, there is no reference to a 'teacher'. Rather, in XV,3, 9, 12 and XVI,2, 5, the Law of Moses is cited as the central legal authority for the community (living in the age of wickedness?). There is no hint elsewhere in these laws that a particular Teacher of Righteousness or his legislation should be followed.[102]

The thematic and structural similarities noted in the previous discussion are also present to a certain extent in cols. XIX–XX (MS B). In XX,3-4 the statement is made that any member of the community who is not entirely faithful will be sent away from the congregation like one whose lot did not fall among the disciples of God (למודי אל, l. 4). In this poetic formulation, it is clear that the community of perfectly holy ones is viewed as an entity standing under God's guidance. After repentance, the recalcitrant member may return to the community and again enjoy the divine tutelage (cf. col. I,1-12).

A 'teacher' is mentioned four times in cols. XIX–XX. In two cases, parallel and almost identical formulations are present: both are thought to refer to the death of the Teacher of Righteousness and the coming of the messiah (XIX,35–XX,1; XX,13-14).

XIX,35–XX,1 מיום האסף מורה היחיד עד עמוד משיח

If one takes this phrase literally and historically, it refers to two historical occurrences, the one at some undetermined time in the past and the other at an uncertain time in the future.[103]

In the parallel formulation in XX,13-14, this chronological indeterminacy is resolved.

XX,13-14 מיום האסף יורה היחיד עד תם כל אנשי
המלחמה . . . כשנים ארבעים

Although XIX,35–XX,1 and XX,13-14 are parallel, they are not identical. The former speaks of a messiah, the latter of men of war. The latter seems to function, however, as a clarification of the former. The reference to the forty years answers the question how long the period is from the 'death of the teacher to the end of all the men of war'. This is a calculation of how long one should expect to wait for the messianic age. The forty years is a theological construct representing a typological period of wickedness like the Old Testament wilderness period.[104] Whether this chronological reference should be interpreted as historically accurate and trustworthy—in addition to its typological use—is a question that cannot be answered with certainty.[105]

Following the reference to forty years, Hos. 3.4 is cited as documentary confirmation for the previous statement in XX,13-14: 'no king, and no prince, and no judge, and no one to instruct with righteousness'. Davies maintains that this (the citation and the reference to the forty years) refers to a period when there was no teacher.[106] The phrase אין מוכיח בצדק may be interpreted in this fashion. Nonetheless, the themes of 'forty years' and 'lack of guidance' refer essentially to the absence of divine rather than human guidance. In that sense, the themes of 'forty years' and 'absence of leadership' are related to several other passages in CD (I,3; II,8, 26; III,4, 6, 11; V,15-16; VII,13; VIII,1, 13, 18; XIX,13, 31). Although it is not always stated fully in these passages, the basic message is as follows: disobedience leads to destruction, divine anger, and the hiding of God's face from the remnant. Upon repentance a new situation of divine blessing and acceptance is ushered in.

In the post-exilic period and later, there was significant speculation on the presence and absence of the deity from the remnant and the holy land as well as calculations of the length of periods of wickedness, whose end would be followed by God's mercy. In Isa. 30.18-21 a documentary tradition is preserved that apparently influenced the ideology of CD in this respect.[107]

> (18) Therefore, the Lord waits to be gracious to you; therefore, he exalts himself to show mercy to you. For the Lord is a God of justice; blessed are those who wait for him. (19) Yea, O people in Zion who dwell in Jerusalem; you shall weep no more. He will surely be gracious to you at the sound of your cry; when he hears it, he will answer you. (20) And though the Lord give you the bread of adversity and the water of affliction, yet your Teacher will not hide himself any more, but your eyes shall see your Teacher. (21) And your ears shall hear a word behind you, saying, 'This is the way, walk in it', when you turn to the right or when you turn to the left. (RSV)

In this passage several key elements of the theology of CD are present. First of all, the divine mercy introduces the rationale for what follows. Secondly, this God of mercy (and justice) is characterized as a chastizer. Thirdly, the deity is designated as 'your Teacher' who will no longer remain hidden (cf. Isa. 8.17). Finally, the Isaianic passage speaks of 'the way', a central motif in CD.

Although the notion of God as teacher permeates much of CD, the reference to a teacher in I,11 and the apparent reference to the 'death' of a teacher in XIX,35 and XX,13 suggest that another figure is viewed as the teacher. How do these passages correlate with others referring to a teacher in CD? At only one other place does a similar formulation appear—VI,11. In this passage, the teacher is treated as a future figure in relation to the מחוקק=דורש, who is apparently a figure of the past. Above it was suggested that the *dōreš* preceded an expected teacher. Although the *dōreš* cannot be identified conclusively, he may have been Ezra. The teacher was a later figure, perhaps identical with the teacher of I,11.

VI,11	*Doreš*	Teacher (Messiah?)
XIX,35-XX,1	Teacher	Messiah
XX,13-14	Teacher	End of Men of War (Messiah?)

Clearly, the last two passages reflect a different understanding of the teacher from that of VI,11, so that the identification of the teacher in VI,11 with the messiah in the other passages is invalid. There is, of course, a way to preserve the order of the material and to understand it as it now stands in CD. The *dōreš* is the earlier historical figure; the Teacher, a later one, perhaps anticipated as the messiah. Davies suggests that this Teacher had claimed to be the Teacher of VI,11, the messiah, but thinks that this view may have been modified after his death.[108] MS B seems to anticipate another messianic figure.

How do these passages relate to CD I,11? Although a teacher is mentioned, neither a *dōreš* of the past nor a future messiah play any role. The teacher of I,11 is apparently a figure of the past, but how distant his existence was chronologically from the time of the final redaction of CD and what his relationship is to other passages mentioning a teacher remain unanswered questions.

The last two references to a teacher are found in the concluding unit of CD, in XX,28 and XX,32. The teacher appears in statements that frame a confession.

Statement	All who have held fast to the commandments of God, going in and out according to the laws, and have obeyed the Teacher, and confessed before God.
Confession	For we have done evil, both we and our ancestors in our trespassing the laws of the covenant. Righteousness and truth are your judgment over us.
Statement	And they obey(ed) the Teacher of Righteousness and do not apostasize away from the laws of the covenant when they hear them.

In the introductory and concluding statements, 'holding fast to the commandments of God', 'following the law', and 'obeying the Teacher' are three ways of expressing faithfulness. Denis and Murphy-O'Connor are probably correct in maintaining that the Teacher in this section is either God or God's legislator, i.e. Moses (cf. XV,3, 9, 12; XVI,2, 5).[109]

In conclusion, what has this analysis contributed to understanding the expression מורה צדק in CD? The structural-thematic approach to the relevant passages illustrates clearly that the various references to a 'teacher' are by no means identical and, therefore, need not refer to the same person. (1) In a few passages, God is implicitly or explicitly the teacher: II,12; III,13-14; VI,3; VII,4; possibly also XX,4, 28, 32. This seems to be a fundamental ideological element in CD—based partly on or related to Isaianic traditions like 30.20 and 8.14. (2) In I,11, VI,11; XIX,35–XX,1; XX,13-14, the expression 'teacher' may refer to a historical figure but not to a clearly identifiable one.

Davies has raised the question whether reference to a human teacher of righteousness could be secondary to an original pre-Qumranic *Admonition*.[110] This question can only be answered tentatively, since there are no thoroughly convincing criteria for making such a decision. Where the expression מורה צדק or its equivalent may seem to be an afterthought from *our* perspective, one may entertain the possibility of secondary interpolation. This applies solely to I,11, where the mention of מורה צדק interrupts the flow of the series of verbs whose subject is God. The transition from God's activity to that of the Teacher, which functions essentially as an extension of God's activity, is certainly abrupt. Even if it should be secondary, a matter which is less clear than the secondary insertion of chronological information in ll. 5-6, the reference to the Teacher provides a counterpart to the Liar in the midrash in ll. 13-18a. According to the present form of col. I, the Teacher and the Liar are figures of the past. Unlike in 1QpHab and 4QpPs 37, the unfaithful of CD I are not accused of not having obeyed the Teacher but of having been misled by the Liar. If our translation of the verb עשה with a past tense is correct, the Teacher instructed last generations about God's past dealings with the Liar and the unfaithful. The Liar and the unfaithful seem to be anterior to or relatively contemporary with the Teacher. Even if one should consider them to be contemporary, there is still no information about a direct confrontation between them.

The reference to 'the coming of the Teacher of Righteousness at the end of days' in VI,11 seems to intend a figure of the future. This depends, of course on, when one dates the end of days. If the writer or reader viewed himself as living already in the last days, this figure might be considered a relative contemporary. Elsewhere in CD, he is clearly a figure of the past (I,1; XX,1, 14). The midrash preceding VI,11 knows a *dōreš hattōrâ*, an expositor of the law, who predated an expected teacher. One cannot determine how distant the *dōreš* was chronologically from the Teacher, based on the sparse information given in col. VI. Two other passages are formulated similarly. In the explanation of Ezek. 44.15 in IV,3-4, the sons of Zadok are identified as the chosen of Israel, those called by the name, who will stand (arise) at the end of days. The sons of Zadok would seem to be a group of the writer's time, perhaps his own group, or one of his relative future. V,5 speaks of a law that remained hidden until the emergence of Zadok. While this Zadok cannot be absolutely dated, the text indicates that he must be a figure later than David. This inference rests on the statement that David did not know about the law of creation permitting only one wife. David could not have known this law, since it was hidden until the time of Zadok (V,2-6). While IV,3 speaks of the sons of Zadok as a group of the end of days and V,5 seems to be concerned with a figure after David who revealed an older, hidden law, neither of the two passages knows of a *dōreš* who preceded Zadok or the Zadokites.

In I,10, the remnant is said to have discerned its guilt and sought God (דרשוהו). Because of their searching for him, God gave them a Teacher of Righteousness. Therefore, I,10 resembles VI,6, which says that the princes, who had emigrated to Damascus, searched for or inquired of God/the *tōrâ* (דרשוהו). This group is supposed to have inquired of the law with the help of the Staff, who is identified as the *dōreš hattōrâ*. This figure will be followed by the Teacher of the last days. In respect of the question of the identities of these figures, these similar formulations are not helpful. Nevertheless, I,6 and V,20 do seem to associate the emergence of the remnant with the exile. V,20 speaks only of the destruction of the land, which could be a reference to the exile. I,6 refers to God's delivering up the unfaithful into the hands of Nebuchadnezzar. The two passages differ significantly, because the chronological information of I,5-6 seems to telescope the emergence of the remnant and the Teacher into the time 390 and twenty years respectively after the exile.

While CD presents neither a systematic doctrine about a historical Teacher of Righteousness nor detailed information about his life, his beliefs, and his relationship to the remnant group that he instructed and the Liar, it does provide information that is useful for understanding the historical perspective of the writer or compiler. In I,11 reference is made to a Teacher that God gave to a remnant 410 years after the exile. XIX,35–XX,1 and XX,13-14 apparently refer to this person's death. XX,28 and 32 continue to speak of the Teacher, that is, his instructions, as authoritative for the writer's generation. The chronological information in I,5-6 indicates that the Teacher was a figure of the post-exilic period. If one may take the reference to 390 and twenty years literally, he joined a remnant group around the beginning of the second century BCE. The writer represents an even later perspective at some time after the Teacher's death.

b. *The Liar*

References to the enemies of the Qumran community and its teacher have also played a role in discussions of the community's history. Since statements about *a* (*the*) teacher turned out to be less transparent than is often claimed, and, consequently, become problematic for use in historical reconstructions, passages concerning enemies become that much more significant—if they do in fact preserve information that is specifically relevant to episodes in a Qumran history.

Several passages may be eliminated initially from the discussion of Qumran's enemies either because they refer generally to evil[111] or because they refer unquestionably to the wicked ones of Israel's distant past.[112] Our analysis of CD indicates that evil is an integral element of human existence, including the *Heilsgeschichte* of Israel for the writer(s) of CD. CD's message is historical in the sense that obedience and disobedience to God's covenant (ברית אל) are depicted as forms of behavior that persist from the fall of the Watchers to the sins of the kings (II,16–III,12). At the same time, CD's message is typological, allowing its audience to simplify reality and understand it as a history of obedience and apostasy—as a struggle between those who choose to do their teacher's/God's will, associated with repentance, and those who choose rather to do their own will, associated with the failure to repent. This pattern can be found in Israel's past as well as in her present situation. Used as a rhetorical device, this patterning enables the audience to envision the future as a *heilsgeschichtliche* continuation or repetition of the past, which would come to an end with the coming of the messiah(s)[113] or God's appearance to Israel.[114]

A few passages referring to evil ones are thought to be more specifically related to the history of the Qumran community, i.e. the struggle between the Teacher of Righteousness, the Wicked Priest, and their respective communities. Scholars have often looked for this conflict, which is documented in some of the pesharim,[115] and also in CD. The Teacher never appears in conflict with the Wicked Priest or any other individual in CD. The Wicked Priest is not even mentioned in this document. In spite of that absence, there are several references to the Liar (איש הלצון, I,14;cf. XX,10-11, אנשי הלצון; הצו, IV,19; מטיף, IV,19; מטיף כזב, VIII,13; איש הכזב, XX,14-15) that are often viewed in light of the conflict between the Teacher and the Wicked Priest.

The first reference to the figure known as the Liar is found in col. I, which literary analysis has shown to be composite.[116] It is embedded in a midrashic section I,13-18a.[117] In the remainder of col. I, reference is consistently made to a plurality with which God is angry rather than to the Liar (I,13). The superscription introduces the following lines as a statement about God's *rîb* with all flesh (כל בשר) and all his despisers (כל מנאציו), but not with a specific evil person. As determined from a study of passages dealing with *a* (*the*) teacher, col. I deals with the divine mercy that follows an admission of guilt: 'and they realized (after/because of the exile?) that they were guilty ones' (I,8-9).[118] Recognizing their sincere contrition, God 'raised up for them a teacher of righteousness to guide them' (I,10-11). This teacher informed them of what God had done[119] with a last generation, with a congregation of traitors (I,11-12).

This section, I,1-12, is followed by a stylistically distinctive passage (I,13-18a), that associates this congregation of the past with the Liar (see the discussion of *dōr 'aharōn* above in section C.1a). Using a nominal sentence הם סרי דרך, a redactor has made an identification of the 'traitors' with 'those who turn (have turned) from the way' (סרי דרך). This statement is followed by the explanatory phrase 'This is the time about which it was written' (in Hosea): 'Like a stubborn heifer, so Israel is stubborn' (4.16). Thus ll. 1-12 and 13-14a concern the apostasy of a group about which *a* teacher of righteousness had instructed the penitent remnant. The verb עשה in l. 12 refers to God's historical dealing with this congregation of apostates, thereby reiterating the topic of a *rîb* introduced already in l. 2. The equation of the עדת בוגדים with the סרי דרך suggests the verbal connection of כפרה with ישראל from Hos. 4.16 also. The phrase הם סרי דרך itself makes the further equation of the congregation of traitors (עדת בוגדים) with the people of Israel, thus echoing what was said in l. 3: '(God) hid his face from Israel'. God's hiding his face is reflected in the more aggressive images of the curses of the covenant and destruction by the sword (1.17).

Following the citation from Hosea, ll. 14-18 introduce a new twist to the theme of Israel's guilt and apostasy. It is directly associated with the activity of the Liar (איש הלצון) who is said to have preached waters of lie(s) הטיף לישראל מימי כזב to Israel, thus causing Israel to stray from the way. A more concrete description of the activity of the one who has misled Israel at some time in the past is not forthcoming.

In spite of the intrusive interlude concerning the Liar, ll. 18-20 take up the theme of the 'congregation' again, accusing them of having sought smooth things and chosen illusions... of having justified the wicked and condemned the righteous, and of having transgressed *a* covenant (cf. Isa. 30.10-11). As in ll. 3 (במועלם... עזבוהו) and 14 (בעמוד... הטיף), a past action is related by means of an infinitive construct בעבור followed by the relative particle אשר and the finite verbs דרשו, ויבחרו, ויצפו, ויבחרו, ויצדיקו, וירשיעו, and ויעבירו.

In sum, several points must be made about the statements concerning the Liar in CD I,14ff. First of all, nothing is said about this figure that would help the historian to identify him with a known person of Second Temple Judaism. He is accused of preaching lies and misleading Israel—deviation from an established theological norm rather than recognizable political or military activity. 'Pouring out waters of lies' seems to be an expression culled from Mic. 2.6. Secondly, the Liar's crime is one against Israel, not unequivocally one against a remnant group within Israel. It is impossible to know precisely who is meant by reference to Israel, unless it is the nation at large. Finally, the Liar's deceptions are placed at some indeterminable time in the past.

The superscriptions in I,1-2 suggest that the material running from I,1-18(II,1) is meant to explain the reason for God's anger against 'all flesh' (l. 2), 'his despisers' (l. 2), 'the congregation of traitors' (l. 12), and 'the Seekers after Smooth Things' (l. 18) in Israel to those who know righteousness. The Liar functions above all as the catalyst for the unacceptable behavior of the wicked, but his identity is not the concern of the author of CD I. He (they) is (are) contrasted with those who know righteousness and their teacher of righteousness with the traitors and the Liar to produce a theological lesson. The writer (redactor) of cols. I and XX may or may not have known the identity of the Liar.

With II,2 a new admonition addressed to those who are entering or have entered the covenant begins concerning the ways of the wicked. The expression סררי דרך (II,6) makes a catchword connection with the previous admonition and midrash (I,13-14). Unlike the historical perspective of I,1–II,1, this second admonition points out that God did not choose them (לא בחר אל בהם מקדם) from the beginning of the world. In fact, God knew in his omniscience of their future evil deeds even before they came into existence. There are parallels with IQS III,14ff., but Davies points out that IQS III,14ff. is dualistic, evil being attributed to the spirit (angel) of darkness, whereas God is the cause of evil in CD II,13.[120] This passage states that God leads those astray whom he hates. This is a distinctly different understanding of the cause of evil from that presented in I,13 where the Liar is held responsible for leading many astray.

The subsequent admonition running from II,14 to at least III,12 preserves a historical survey of the many throughout history who have disobeyed God's commandments and of the few who have been faithful. The listeners or readers are encouraged to pay attention in order to understand God's deeds and in order that they might choose what God desires and hate what he hates. By means of this survey, which pits the disobedient against the obedient, the listeners are urged to view themselves as successors of the latter—Abraham, Isaac, Jacob, and later ones who held fast to the commandments of

God (III,7). They are encouraged to see themselves as ones who are obedient to their Creator and their teacher (III,7). They are also associated with the 'sure house' that God had built. This seems to be a post-exilic perspective. Viewed chronologically, the audience appears to have lived between the time of God's establishing a 'sure house' and the end-time when the sons of Zadok, the chosen ones of Israel, will arise. A more exact determination of the period in which the audience lived—from the author's perspective—cannot be made, since no reference is made to recognizable contemporary events and persons. (The chronological information in col. I is discussed below in section 3.)

With IV,10 a new idea appears. The audience is told that a time will come when no one can join the house of Judah—the community of believers. In this period Belial will be unleashed on Israel as Isa. 24.17 had predicted. As a historical example of Belial's activity, 'Zaw' (הצו) and those who follow him, 'the builders of the wall' (בוני החיץ) are mentioned. Then the author identifies הצו with המטיף, the Liar (cf. Mic. 2.6). The word המטיף appears in Hos. 5.11b. Thus the midrashic passage seems to have some connection with I,13-18, but it is just as unspecific about the identity of these figures as is the latter.[121] In any case, 'Zaw' and his followers are accused of wrong behavior—marrying two wives at a time, defiling the temple, and marrying inside of established family lines. IV,17-18 presents these actions as nets of Belial. It mentions a third net, riches, which is not explicated further in col. V. In order to underscore the fact that 'Zaw' and 'the builders of the wall' are manifestations of the dominion of Belial, the author mentions the non-biblical episode concerning the opposition of the Prince of Lights, Moses, and Aaron to Belial, Jannes, and his brother. Neither 'Zaw', 'the Preacher', nor 'the builders of the wall' are described more concretely.

In VIII,12-13 (cf. XIX,24-26), 'the builders of the wall' are said not to understand the meaning of Deut. 32.33, which refers to the ways of the kings of the peoples. They failed to understand this, because they were misled by the Windy One, the one who preaches a lie. In XX,10 reference is made to the judgment of 'the men of scorn' (אנשי הלצון), who slandered the statutes of righteousness and rejected the covenant. Neither 'the builders of the wall' nor 'the men of scorn' are associated with public events of any historical period. Instead, they are essentially accused of crimes against God's law and covenant.

Davies believes that all references to individual enemies of the community derive from at least one Qumranic redaction of the *Admonition*.[122] Mention of the Liar represents a Qumran interest, according to this view, as does concern with the Teacher. While the Teacher and the Liar are juxtaposed in col. I, it is instructive that they are never clearly opposed to each other in CD as the Teacher and the Wicked Priest are in 1QpHab. There is no evidence of any personal confrontation. In conclusion, the real problem for the reconstruction of the history of the Qumran community is the concreteness of statements made about the individual figures. Our analysis of statements referring to a teacher in CD demonstrated that they were neither in total agreement with each other nor were they specific enough for use in a historical analysis (see section 1.a above). This applies to the Liar, 'the builders of the wall', and 'the men of scorn' as well. Both the Teacher and the Liar are presented as figures of the past from the perspective of the writer. XX,13-15 suggests that both figures were contemporaneous. The Teacher seems to have died even before the activities of the Liar and his adherents ceased. Stegemann believes that CD's statements about the enemies of the (Qumran) community can be correctly understood only on the basis of statements about individual characters in the pesharim (see below Chapter 6).[123]

2. *Damascus*

Before the association of CD with Khirbet Qumran and the Qumran community, the name 'Damascus' in CD was almost unanimously construed as a literal reference to the city of Damascus and its general region. Since the discovery of fragments of CD in the caves of Qumran, this strictly literal interpretation of the name Damascus has had to make way for symbolic understandings. Davies has cited three current approaches to the interpretation of 'Damascus':[124] (1) 'Damascus' refers to Qumran's sister communities located in the region of Damascus; (2) it may refer to a Damascan community that sought refuge at Khirbet Qumran; and (3) 'Damascus' may be a symbol for a place of refuge. Stegemann thinks it refers in a transferred sense to the Judaean desert;[125] Cross, to Qumran.[126] Murphy-O'Connor and Davies interpret it as an allusion to Babylon.[127]

The last-named scholar has reiterated the often overlooked fact that the term 'Damascus' is restricted in the Qumran documents to

CD alone and that it requires an exegetical solution in that context before its integration into a historical reconstruction using other Qumran texts.[128]

'Damascus' (דמשק) is found in six passages.

VI,5	היוצאים מארץ יהודה ויגורו בארץ דמשק
VI,19	הברית החדשה בארץ דמשק
VII,15	כיון צלמיכם מאהלי דמשק
VII,19	דורש התורה הבא דמשק
XIX,33-34	בברית החדשה בארץ דמשק
XX,12	בברית ואמנה אשר קימו בארץ דמשק

A close reading of CD indicates that the references to 'Damascus' are based on a scriptural citation of Amos 5.26-27 found in VII,14-15.

In order to understand the use of the term 'Damascus' in CD, one should probably turn first to VII,15. The midrash in ll. 13-20, which consists of explicit quotations from Isa. 7.17, Amos 5.26, 9.11, and Num. 24.17, functions as a tissue of proof-texts for the generalizing statement in l. 9: 'when God comes to visit (punishment) upon the land, the recompense of the godless will come'. The threatened destruction of the wicked is viewed as having been foretold in Isa. 7.17. Reference is then made to the steadfast ones who escaped to the land of the north. This statement would remind the reader of Amos 5.26. Then the expression ספר התורה is associated with סוכת דוד in Amos 9.11. Subsequently, the 'Star'='Seeker of the Law' who came to Damascus is mentioned. Since the 'Star' does not derive from the foregoing, it is demonstrated by Num. 24.17, which says 'a Star will come out of Jacob'.[129]

Another feature of this midrashic technique deserves special attention: ספרי התורה is identified with סוכת המלך; המלך, with הקהל. Thus there are two ways to construe the central point of this passage. (1) The books of the Law and the Prophets are exiled beyond the tents of Damascus. (2) But option (1) is complicated by the identification of המלך with הקהל. The midrashist seems to want to associate, perhaps even identify, the congregation with the books of the Law and the Prophets.[130] In any case, the midrash mentions no return to Judaea, only the exiling of scripture/a congregation beyond the tents of Damascus at some time in the past.

As noted above in section 1.a, it is important to determine the temporal orientation of the midrash in order to clarify particular elements such as 'Damascus'. The midrash takes up the elements in the citation one by one and identifies them. The independent pronouns function in a 'this is that' fashion. That is, they act as a copula. But the temporal aspect of the identifications, whether past, present, or future, is not obvious from the information presented in the midrash and has to be determined by the larger context in which the midrash is embedded.

The midrash in VII,14-21 is certainly meant to explain to the writer's audience that God will deal with present unfaithfulness as he had once dealt with it in the past, when the faithful escaped to the land of the north (VII,10-12). The promised divine destruction is likened to the time when Ephraim departed from Judaea (Isa. 7.17). At that time the unfaithful were delivered up to the sword, while the faithful escaped to the land of the north.

ll. 13-14 וכל הנסוגים הוסגרו לחרב ומחזיקים
נמלטו לארץ צפון

The reference to this past escape to the land of the north is then proof-texted with Amos 5.27, which refers to an exile beyond Damascus. An additional section of the midrash, that concerning the Star, the *dōreš hattōrâ*, locates him in Damascus (cf. VI,5). It is interesting that the midrashist never finds it necessary to give Damascus, the land of the north, an additional interpretation. The past perspective set by ll. 13-14 is picked up again in VII,21–VIII,1 after the conclusion of the midrash.

l. 21 אלה מלטו בקץ הפקודה הראשון

In VIII,2 the essential validity of God's judgment on past, present, and potential future traitors is echoed (cf. VII,10).

Along with the almost identical statement in VII,13, the one in VII,21–VIII,1 to the effect that the unfaithful were delivered up to the sword forms a narrative past framework against which to understand the individual elements of the midrash. While MS A (VII,21–VIII,1) unequivocally presents a past perspective (מלטו), MS B (XIX,10) preserves a future one (ימלטו). Nevertheless, the point of MSS A and B is essentially the same: the evil ones will be punished and the faithful will be saved at the time of the divine visitation. The means for making this point differ significantly. It is not necessary, however, to delve into the hypotheses concerning the layout of the original text and its transformation in MSS A and B, since the issue in the present discussion is the correct understanding of the place name

Damascus.[131] Neither the escape to the land of the north nor Damascus is mentioned in XIX,5-14 (MS B).

In a stylistically similar context (VI,3-10, esp. l. 5), that is, one in which the midrashic method of taking up specific elements of a citation one by one and identifying them, one finds another reference to 'Damascus'.

l. 5 שבי ישראל היוצאים מארץ
יהודה ויגורו בארץ דמשק

As in VII,10-21, this midrash is also framed by a narrative past perspective, suggesting that the third person, independent pronouns functioning as copulas, should again be understood as referring to entities of the past. This applies also to the participle whose temporal aspect is incontrovertibly determined by היוצאים following the verb ויגורו. The entire phrase כמצאת...החדשה (as well as בארץ...דמשק) may be secondary to the original midrash, perhaps an explanatory interpolation based on VII,15 and 19.

In VI,18-19, 'Damascus' appears as the location of the 'new covenant'. The readers of CD are urged to obey the laws of the sabbath, the festivals, and the day of fasting according to the finding (=interpretation) of the members of the 'new covenant' in Damascus. Reference to legal material fits well into the context of VI,14–VIII,8. Stylistically, the series of infinitive commands is continued by the phrase לשמר את יום...יום התענית. Nevertheless, the phrase כמצאת...דמשק gives the impression of being an afterthought.

Let us summarize our findings in regard to 'Damascus' to this point. VII,14-15, 18, VI,5, and VI,18-19 do seem to have a literal exile to Damascus in mind. In any case, this name is never interpreted otherwise in CD. This event, at least in its present context, lies at some unspecified time in the past. Only VI,19 refers to this exile as the 'new covenant' (ברית החדשה).

The 'new covenant' is mentioned again in XIX,33. The entire phrase from כן to מים החיים refers to those who had abandoned the well of living water (cf. VI,9; III,16). These will not be reckoned in the council of people. The use of כן (l. 28) appeals to the foregoing statement to the effect that God despised the 'builders of the wall' and their adherents (ll. 31-32) and continues to despise everyone who rejects his commandments. From the perspective of the reader the 'builders of the wall' and the 'new covenant in Damascus' are entities of the past. The former is presumably chronologically anterior to the latter. The 'builders of the wall' had apostasized from the covenant of the fathers (l. 21, ברית אבות). Likewise, the 'new covenant' also had its apostates.[132]

The language of XX,11-12 is similar to that of XIX,33–XX,1. This passage is oriented to the past as is witnessed by the verbs דברו, ומאסו, and קימו. The phrase והוא ברית החדשה appears almost certainly to be a gloss insuring the identification with the covenant in Damascus. The supplemental reference to the Damascan covenant as the 'new one' would suggest that this expression had a special meaning for the Qumran scribes.

Davies has recently presented an innovative understanding of this gloss which deserves some attention. He views the original Damascus Document (=the *Admonition*) as a literary product of a Babylonian community that was later received and redacted in the Qumran community. Unlike most analysts of CD, he considers some of the passages which refer to Damascus as secondary and associates them with the Qumranic redaction: VI,18-19; VII,14–VIII,1; XX,12. He maintains that references to a covenant in Damascus (e.g. VI,5) did not appear in the original document. Rather, reference to the 'new Damascan covenant' comes from the literary activity of a later community. The use of the word 'new' (חדשה) to modify the word 'covenant' (ברית) signifies for Davies (1) a historically later community that adhered to the Teacher of Righteousness and his instructions=Qumran community, and (2) a qualitative contrast with the earlier Damascan community.[133]

This claim is based largely on Davies's understanding of the clause והוא ברית החדשה in XX,11-12. He treats this phrase correctly as a gloss on the word דמשק, but both his exegetical and historical inferences therefrom seem to stray from the textual evidence. As argued above, the reference to 'going out to' or 'being exiled in' Damascus in VII,14-15, 18 provides a scriptural foundation for other references to 'Damascus' in CD. In the midrashic section VII,14-20, the modifying adjective 'new' is absent. Elsewhere in CD (e.g. V,18-19; XIX,33-34; XX,11-12), reference is made to the 'new covenant' in Damascus, and this is probably associated with the event mentioned in VII,14-20. While the gloss in XX,11-12 is certainly secondary, it is not obviously polemical in the sense that Davies claims. A scribe wanted simply to harmonize this reference to the Damascan covenant with others in CD, not to distinguish a parent from an offspring (=Qumran) community.

What is the reason for using the word 'new' to modify the word 'covenant' in CD, if Davies's historical explanation should be incorrect? First of all, within the context of CD itself covenants are mentioned with the implicit qualification that the most recent remnant or covenant community is in some sense a genealogical continuation of an older covenant as well as a refinement or improvement of it. Secondly, the 'new covenant' terminology is implicitly associated with that found in Jer. 31.31-34, the only Old Testament prophetic book that explicitly speaks of a 'new covenant'.

> Behold the days are coming, says the Lord, when I will make a new covenant with the house of Israel and the house of Judah, not like the covenant which I made with their fathers when I took them by the hand to bring them out of the land of Egypt, my covenant which they broke, though I was their husband, says the Lord. But this is the covenant which I will make with the house of Israel after those days, says the Lord: I will put my law within them and I will write it upon their hearts; and I will be their God, and they shall be my people. And no longer shall each man teach his neighbor and each his brother, saying, 'Know the Lord', for they shall all know me, from the least of them to the greatest, says the Lord; for I will forgive their iniquity, and I will remember their sin no more.

The association of CD with Jeremiah, although not directly made with 31.31-34, is made explicitly in VIII,20-21: 'This is the word which Jeremiah spoke to Baruch the son of Neraiah and Elisha and to Gehazi his servant'. Davies perceives no explicit connection with the preceding and following material in CD, and, therefore, considers VIII,20 to be an independent statement.[134] Because of this and because of its absence from MS B, he refused to recognize the association of the passage in Jeremiah with CD's 'new covenant'. Even if VIII,20, where Jeremiah is mentioned, and VIII,21 the reference to the 'new covenant' in the land of Damascus, are never clearly explained in CD, they are in fact contextually juxtaposed, and this phenomenon would suggest a possible dependence of passages in CD concerning the 'new covenant' on Jer. 31.31-34 or traditions arising from it. More than this cannot be said.

One of the consistently recurring features of the language of CD is its various references to covenants. Sometimes this is implicit as in II,16–III,12, where a long list of groups that did not adhere to God's covenant or his commandments is drawn up, e.g. the Watchers, their children, all flesh, Noah's children, Jacob's children in Egypt, in the desert, and Israel's kings and warriors. In III,10-11 this long list is balanced with a list of persons who had been faithful, the first covenant members (הברית הראשנים). Noah, Abraham, Isaac, Jacob, and other unnamed faithful ones are designated both as a remnant (נותרו) and as eternal members of God's covenant for Israel (בריתו... עד עולם) in ll.12-13. In other passages the covenant of the first ones (I,4, 16, 18, 20; III,4 10-11, 13) or of the fathers (VIII,18=XIX,31) is mentioned. Genealogically, the 'new covenant' in the land of Damascus (VI,18-19; XIX,33-34; XX,11-12) is a continuation of God's covenant with the faithful ones. It is chronologically distinct from the covenant of the first ones or of the fathers (ll. 28, 29, 31). No information is given in CD that would help date the 'new covenant' in Damascus. XIX,33–XX,1, which speaks of disobedience to the Damascus covenant, suggests that a later perspective is present. The reference to 'the congregation of the men of perfect holiness' (XX,2) *may* represent an even later perspective. It would go beyond the evidence to attempt to date the emergence of the Damascan community. Outside of CD, nothing is recorded about this group.

3. *Chronology*

Together with the problem of understanding references to the Teacher of Righteousness, the Liar and other enemies, and Damascus, the chronological elements have always played a central role in discussions of CD's significance for reconstructing the history of the Qumran community. Unlike the pesharim and 1QH, CD presents chronological information related to the origin of the community and to its reception of a teacher (I,3-11).

> (3) When they rebelled (all flesh), by forsaking him (God), he hid his face fom Israel and from his (its) temple. (4) He delivered them up to the sword. But when he remembered a covenant of the first-ones, he allowed a remnant to remain (5) for Israel and he did not deliver them up to destruction. And in the Age of Wrath, three hundred (6) ninety years after his delivering them into the hand of Nebuchadnezzar the king of Babylon, (7) he visited them and caused a root of planting to grow up from Israel and from Aaron in order to inherit (8) his land and to grow fat on the good of his land. And they discerned their guilt, and knew that (9) they were guilty people and like blind ones groping for the way (10) twenty years. And he (God) discerned their works that they sought him with a

> perfect heart (11) and he raised up a teacher of righteousness for them to guide them in the way of his (God's) heart.

The references to the 390 years, the Age of Wrath (קץ חרון), and the twenty years have been hotly debated.

As Davies's review of research on this issue demonstrates, there was no accepted consensus on understanding the chronological notes in CD I before this document was associated with Qumran and the Dead Sea Scrolls.[135] Its first editor, Schechter, although skeptical of the historical reliability of these notes, offered four possible ways of understanding them: (1) they are literal and reliable; (2) they are symbolic; (3) the reference to the 390 years/eight jubilees is a calculation of the eschaton; or (4) they are an inaccurate guess without literal or symbolic value.[136]

If one takes the chronological information in I,3-11 literally, the Age of Wrath would refer to 390 years after the exile (597/586 BCE). At the end of this period (197/186 BCE or later), the community arose. Twenty years later (c. 177/166 BCE or later), God gave the community a teacher.[137] Despite statements to the effect that the 390 years is not historically reliable and the twenty years only approximately accurate, the scholars who comprise the prevailing consensus in fact treat this chronological information as historically accurate data. The translation of the preposition ל in l. 6 as 'after' was called into question and interpreted as 'during'. For example, Ginzberg thought the 390 years culminated in events associated with the year 721 BCE.[138] Rabinowitz viewed the 390 years as ending with the Babylonian exile (597/587 BCE).[139] The views of these two scholars remain a minority report. But they too, like scholars translating ל with 'after', take the chronological information more or less at face value.

Before appropriating this information for purposes of historical reconstruction, one must first understand it within its literary context. Although he viewed the chronological notes in CD I as a accurate calculation, R.H. Charles put the reference to 390 years within brackets, indicating that he thought it was secondary to the original document.[140] Stegemann also concluded that both the references to the 390 and the twenty years were secondary.[141] Murphy-O'Connor, who viewed CD I as a later addition to the Missionary Document, raised neither the question of their originality nor that of their reliability.[142] Both are assumed. Both Stegemann and Murphy-O'Connor fail to recognize how the interpolation of chronological information into col. I would modify the meaning of the original text. This possible secondary data may or may not be reliable, but an understanding of its redactional function within CD precedes its use in historical reconstruction.

Davies has recently reemphasized the secondary nature of the chronological information in I,5-6, 10.[143] He views this material as secondary based on metrical considerations. While metrical considerations are not entirely convincing as an independent argument, taken together with stylistic considerations, they strongly suggest that these chronological notes do function as glosses. Unlike other scholars, Davies questions their usefulness for historical purposes.[144]

Non-verbal temporal formulations of two related kinds can be found in CD: (1)(a) there are several references to an age whose specific chronological parameters are never mentioned, e.g. the Age of Wrath[145] or the end of days;[146] (b) there are a few references to former and latter generations;[147] (2) there are temporal phrases indicating duration, but whose actual specification is never clearly spelled out, e.g. 'from event X to event Y',[148] or partially durative formulations.[149]

These non-specific references to an evil age, to years, to the end of days, to earlier and later generations as well as to durative phrases formulated in the form 'from event X' or 'from event X to event Y' dominate the original temporal language of CD. The presence of such equivocal formulations might have encouraged more precise calculations of the Age of Wrath, which were occasionally incorporated into the body of the document. Thus it seems that the mention of the 390 years in association with the Babylonian exile (I,5-6), the following twenty years (I,10), and the approx. forty years (XX,15) do in fact serve to elucidate the temporal dimension of the text.

Specific chronological calculations like 390, twenty, and forty years are restricted in CD to cols. I and XX. The reference to the approx. forty years in XX,13-14 (כשנים ארבעים) functions in its context as a calculation of the Age of Wrath (קץ חרון), when God became angry with Israel. It also clarifies the almost identical formulation in XIX,35–XX,1 concerning the period from the 'death' or 'gathering' of the teacher until the coming of the messiah from Aaron and Israel. In I,5-6 the phrase from וקץ to פקדם is located between לכלה and ויצמח, serving as a calculation associated with the Age of Wrath.

Other considerations induce one to agree with Davies and others who claim that the chronological information in I,5-6 is secondary. The personal name Nebuchadnezzar appears to have been introduced here in order to focus the context on the Babylonian exile. In no other passage in CD and the Dead Sea Scrolls is Nebuchadnezzar again mentioned. Furthermore, the infinitive construct is peculiar usage as witnessed by the immense debate that it has aroused. Nowhere else in CD is it used with the preposition ל and the masculine singular pronominal suffix. Therefore, on the basis of general stylistic considerations, specifying chronological notes seem to be secondary to more vague temporal formulations in CD.

It is not sufficient merely to claim that specific chronological notes are secondary. The crucial issue is after all their reliability. As Schechter noted even before the Qumran finds, the chronological information in CD may be based on calculations of the eschaton as a period of 490 years or ten jubilees as in Daniel 9.[150] Schechter even suggested that the 390 years may be a mistake for 490 years. Others have recognized that this is a possibility, but have maintained that there is no slip of the pen in this passage. According to the thesis of a calculation, the scheme of 490 years allows for 390 years after the exile as the date of the community's emergence, twenty years later as the time of its reception of a teacher, forty years of activity of the teacher, and forty years of waiting for the messiah after the death of the teacher. The forty years when the teacher was presumably active is hypothetical, finding no support in any documentary source. Nevertheless, the chronological information in CD does seem to be derived from some sort of calculation.

Despite the use of concrete temporal references in CD I and XX, this information is suspect for historical reconstruction. It is rooted in biblical passages and not in external historical evidence. The reference to 390 years appears to be based on Ezek. 4.5.

> (4) Then lie upon your left side, and I will lay the punishment of the house of Israel upon you; for the number of the days that you lie upon it, you shall bear their punishment. (5) For I assign to you a number of days, three hundred and ninety days, equal to the number of the years of their punishment; so long shall you bear the punishment of the house of Israel. And when you have completed these, you shall lie down a second time, but on your right side, and bear the punishment of the house of Judah; forty days I assign you, a day for each year.

The reference to forty years in XX,15 could derive from this passage, but Deut. 2.14 may have also been in the mind of the redactor.

> And the time from our leaving Kadesh-barnea until we crossed the brook Zered was thirty-eight years, until the entire generation, that is, the men of war, had perished from the camp, as the Lord had sworn to them.

The reference to the 390 and forty years are essentially symbolic in Ezekiel and Deuteronomy and are perhaps understood symbolically in CD. There is absolutely no empirical evidence for the duration of the teacher's activity. It is not clear what the source is for the reference to twenty years. One could say minimally that the chronological notes do date the community's self-conscious foundation at a considerable distance from the time of the exile—in the early second century BCE. To claim more than that exceeds the evidence. One can only concur with Davies, Knibb, and others who draw our attention to the fact that there is no external evidence that would support more precise historical use of this information.[151]

Conclusion

Investigation of CD indicates that it is a composite theological document, preserving both narrative and legal material. In the narrative section, there are three kinds of information that have usually been viewed as relevant to the history of the Qumran community. These are references to a Teacher of Righteousness, a Liar, the New Covenant in Damascus, and chronological notes.

The expression 'Teacher of Righteousness' proved difficult to interpret, because it referred sometimes to God (II,12; III,13-14; VI,3; VII,4; XX,4, 28, 32) and sometimes to a past historical (I,11; XIX,35–XX,1,13-14) or a future historical figure (VI,4). A structural-thematic analysis of the latter passages in which a 'teacher' appears revealed that this figure represented the hope for divine salvation in CD. A key biblical model for developing language about the Teacher is found in Isa. 30.16-19.

Clearly, CD does not present a systematic and detailed picture of the Teacher, but a few passages do refer to a figure of the writer's past. In I,11 the Teacher is discussed as God's messenger, who will instruct last generations about God's dealings with a *dōr 'aharōn*, a congregation of traitors. These traitors are identified with the Liar and those whom he misled. XIX,35–XX,1 and XX,13-14 refer to the death of the Teacher. XX,14 deals with the destruction of the men of war who turned away with the Liar. XIX,33-34 refers to those who apostasized from the 'new covenant' in Damascus. The reference to the forty-year period from the Teacher's 'death' to the destruction of the Liar's men suggests the relative contemporaneity of both. While one cannot speak of a direct confrontation between the Teacher and the Liar in col. I (as seems to be the case in 1QpHab and 4QpPs 37), the only other place in CD where chronological information is given, they seem to be contemporaneous here as well. One can infer from the chronological glosses dating the origin of the community 390 years after the exile and the Teacher twenty years later that the Liar also existed at about this time. If the chronology is taken literally, the writer is thinking of the (his) community's conscious emergence in the early second century BCE. However, the information presented about the Teacher's existence, his role as revealer of God's plan for the unfaithful, and his death does not allow one to identify him with personalities of known Jewish history of this period. There seems to be no other documentary evidence, Qumranic or otherwise, that would verify this chronological information.

Passages mentioning 'the Liar' were also investigated. Like references to 'a teacher', references to this figure turned out to be unyielding for the historian's use. Using theological rather than historical language, CD speaks of 'the Liar' as one who has preached lies and misled Israel. This characterization is grounded above all in traditional, biblical language—Mic. 2.6. 'Zaw' is based on Hos. 5.11b. Since 'the Liar' is never clearly confronted with the Teacher, the historian must remain in the dark about the details of their conflict. In col. I the Teacher and the Liar are implicitly associated by the interpolation of material concerning each. But this material is itself unyielding for the historian.

Six passages mentioning 'Damascus' were also investigated—VI,5; VI,18-19; VIII,14-15; VIII,18; XIX,33-34; XX,11-12. As was the case with the Teacher and the Liar, the references to Damascus in CD derive from biblical ideals and images. The reference to an exile in VII,14-15 is based upon the language of Amos 5.26-27. 'Damascus' is interesting for the author(s) of CD, because it provides a locality for the 'new covenant' (cf. Jer. 31.31). VII,14-15, 18, VI,5, and VI,18-19 seem to have had a literal exile to Damascus in mind. It is not clear whether Damascus also carried a symbolic meaning for the writer of CD. In any case, the emergence of the Damascan covenant was an event of the past but one that cannot be dated with any confidence.

The references to the Teacher of Righteousness, the Liar, the 'new covenant' in Damascus, and the chronological notes are particular elements that help to concretize and historicize the general theological message of CD. The basic message is that God has become angry with the disobedient at different times before and during Israel's history, has established remnants of chosen ones, and plans to destroy the disobedient and preserve the obedient. In col. I, the contrite and obedient are represented by the remnant whom a Teacher of Righteousness will instruct about God's dealings with traitors. These traitors are represented by the Liar and those misled by him. Without the chronological notes which were determined to be secondary and of questionable historical value, it is virtually impossible to place these figures in a relatively restricted historical context. The inclusion of these two notes, cross-referenced against Nebuchadnezzar's exile, associates the remnant, the Teacher, and the Liar with the early second century BCE. Outside of a few references to a Damascan community (e.g. VI,5,19; VII,13,15,19; VIII,21; XIX,34; XX,12), there are no clues in CD to the original provenance of the remnant mentioned in I,4-12. The writer, whose own group is possibly a historical descendant of the 'new covenant' in Damascus, seems to live at some indeterminable chronological distance from the time of the original remnant, the Teacher, and the Liar and apparently belongs to a group called the Men of Perfect Holiness (XX,2).

Chapter 6

THE PESHARIM AND THE HISTORY OF THE QUMRAN COMMUNITY

A. *General Observations*

A perusal of the literature written about Qumran's pesharim since the publication of 1QpHab in 1950[1] indicates that the pesharim have been widely understood as Qumranic interpretation or commentaries on oracular writings, referring to episodes in the history of the Qumran community by means of a coded language. By coded language is meant that the pesharim use designations such as the Teacher of Righteousness (מורה הצדקה), the Priest (הכוהן), the Men of Truth (אנשי האמת), the Doers of the Law (עושי התורה), the Poor (הפתאים), Lebanon (הלבנון), the Council of the *Yaḥad* (עצת היחד), the Returnees from the Wilderness (שבי המדבר), the Wicked Priest (הכוהן הרשע), the Liar (איש הכזב), the Traitors (הבוגדים), Those Violent to the Covenant (עריצי הברית), the Seekers after Smooth Things (דורשי החלקות), the Last Priests of Jerusalem (כוהני ירושלם האחרנים), the Evil Ones of Ephraim and Manasseh (רשעי אפרים ומנשה), the Evil Ones of Israel (רשעי ישראל), the Kittim (הכתיים), the Rulers of the Kittim (מושלי הכתיים), the Kings of Yavan (מלכי יון), the Lion of Wrath (כפיר החרון), and the House of Peleg (בית פלג). The Teacher of Righteousness, the Liar, the Traitors, and the Seekers after Smooth Things are known already from CD (see especially MS A col. I and MS B cols. XIX–XX). The names of two Seleucid monarchs are mentioned in 4QpNah I,2-3 and apparently require no decoding: these are Demetrius (דמי[טרום]) and Antiochus (אנתיכום). The House of Absalom (בית אבשלום) is sometimes thought to be a personal name referring to a known figure of Jewish history.

According to the current understanding of the pesharim, one must first crack the code in order to grasp what the pesharim are cryptically saying about Qumran history. Nevertheless, when one searches the secondary literature for concrete arguments justifying the use of statements in the pesharim to reconstruct historical episodes involving members of the Qumran community and their enemies, one comes away rather perplexed, for a defense of this central assumption—that the pesher is a source of historical information about a particular historical community—can hardly be found. That is perhaps in part due to the fact that the assumption has seldom been viewed as such and has consequently not been called into question.

In recent years several discussions of the pesharim have begun to hint at a move away from emphasis on the historical intention and reference of the pesharim. William H. Brownlee's *The Midrash Pesher of Habakkuk* deals only obliquely with the issue of interpreting the pesharim historically.[2] In her work on the pesharim, Maurya Horgan mentions some reservations about pursuing the historical discussion.[3] In his article on the redefinition of the genre 'Qumran Pesher', George Brooke steers rather obviously away from historical interests and associates the pesher with the broader category of midrash.[4] In a recent study of the Damascus Document, Philip R. Davies has also expressed his skepticism about the historical reliability of the information in the pesharim and about the appropriateness of its use as evidence in reconstructions of the history of the Qumran history.[5] This avoidance, and often the suspicion, of the application of a historical hermeneutic to the pesharim suggests a healthy return to fundamental questions about their genre, language, and setting.

B. *The Pesher as Literary Type*

Whereas CD demonstrates a complexity of structure due to its apparent use of a variety of material, both biblical and non-biblical, and its unusual transitions from one section to another, the structure of the three pesharim that are used in the reconstructions of the history of the Qumran community—1QpHab, 4QpPs 37, and 4QpNah—is relatively simple. These pesharim consist of continuous quotations of a biblical book, each lemma cited before a following explanatory section. They are, therefore, called continuous pesharim.[6] This approach contrasts with the compilation of quotations from a variety of biblical sources, which are grouped around a central idea, e.g. 4QTest, 4QFlor. These are called thematic pesharim. As in the continuous pesharim, in the thematic pesharim each quotation is followed by an intepretive section. The pesharist of 4QpIsa[c] chooses several passages within the book of Isaiah as well as citations from other prophetic books, e.g. Isa. 8.7-8; 9.11a-e, 13-16, 17-20; 10.12-13b, 13c-19a, 19, 20-22b, 22a-b, 22b-23, 24; 14.8, 26-27, 28-30; 19.9b-12; 29.10-11, 15-16, 18-23; Zech. 11.11; Isa. 30.1-5, 23, 15-18; Hos. 6.9a(?); Isa. 30.19-21; 31.1. This pesher may have preserved a running commentary on the entire book of Isaiah, but the relatively few surviving fragments can only circumstantially support this view.[7]

The typical structure of a continuous pesher is quite simple,[8] as the following example illustrates:

I. Quotation: Hab. 1.10a
AND AT KINGS THEY SCOFF, AND PRINCES ARE TO THEM A LAUGHING MATTER (1QpHab III,17)

II. Interpretation
A. Introductory Formula:
The interpretation of it is (1QpHab IV,1)
B. Explanation
that they mock great ones, and they despise honored ones; kings and princes they mock, and they scoff at a great people (1QpHab IV,1-3)

After the citation, the introductory formula פשרו is used, but variations of this formula are also possible: פשר על, פשר אשר, פשר הדבר על, (pronoun +) פשר אשר. Occasionally, as is the case in 1QpHab, the forward progression of the quotation and the interpretation of the book is halted and part of previously cited material may be taken up again. In that case, this reiteration is introduced by the formula ואשר אמר or a variation of it: כי הוא אשר אמר (III,2, 13-14), כי המה (IX,7; X,1-2). This procedure allows the pesharist to provide transitions and to add new information. 1QpHab I,16–II,10 preserves a similar phenomenon, which presents a three-layered interpretation of Hab. 1.5. After the citation, the interpretive material is introduced first by פשר הדבר על הבוגדים (II,1-2), then by ועל הבוגדים בברית החדשה (II,3), and finally by וכן פשר הדבר על כול הבוגדים לאחרית הימים (II,5).

The pesher's basic structure is known already from the Bible.[9] The stories about Joseph's dream-interpretation in Gen. 40–41 illustrate this sufficiently. Before interpreting the chief butler's and chief baker's dreams, Joseph points out that interpretations (פתרנים) belong to God, but he asks to hear the dreams. The chief butler and the chief baker report their dreams/visions in which several objects appear. In each case, the dream is reported. Then Joseph utters the formula 'this is its interpretation' (זה פתרנו). This is followed by the interpretation of the objects as symbols of information known only to God.

In Genesis 41, the Pharaoh reports his dream to Joseph, who explains it as God's way of informing Pharaoh of what he is about to do. No formula is used to introduce the dream's interpretation. Then Joseph addresses himself to the identification of the objects in Pharaoh's dream and to explaining their meaning.

These reports of dreams and their interpretations in Genesis bear a general resemblance to the Qumran pesharim. The dream is comparable to the quoted biblical verse or fraction of a verse. This may be followed by a formula introducing the interpretation itself— זה פתרנו (Qumran, פשרו). The actual interpretation then follows. In Gen. 40.20-23 the fulfillment of Joseph's interpretation is reported. In Gen. 41.47–47.26, the subject of Pharaoh's dream comes to pass.

The book of Daniel also preserves several sections that are similar to the structure of the pesharim. Just as Joseph gave the interpretation of dreams at Pharaoh's court, the young Israelite youth Daniel can also give interpretations at the Babylonian courts. He is even required to give the dream on one occasion (2.17-45). When summoned to tell King Nebuchadnezzar his dream and its interpretation, Daniel echoes the words of Joseph to Pharaoh. He says that the dream is a mystery (רז) from God about the future (להוא באחרית יומיא). After telling the king the dream, Daniel says 'this is the dream and its interpretation (פשרה) we will relate' (2.36). In a general sense, pesher interpretation can be found throughout Daniel. Daniel 5 and 9 present interpretations of written messages.

Daniel 5 narrates the appearance of a human hand writing on the wall of King Belshazzar's palace. The Chaldean Daniel is then called in to read and interpret this writing. He reads the inscription as follows: *menē'*, *menē'*, *tekēl*, and *parsîn*. Each word is then explained as a prophecy about the future of the king's dominion. *Menē'* means that God has numbered the days of the king's dominion and has brought it to an end; *tekēl* means that the king has been weighed in the balance and found wanting; *perēs* means that the kingdom is divided and given to the Medes and Persians.

In ch. 9, Daniel finds a reference to the fulfillment of the vision of chs. 7–8 in the book of Jeremiah (25.11-12; 29.10), according to which seventy years will pass before the end of the desolation of Jerusalem. Dan. 9.24 takes up the seventy years of Jeremiah and interprets it as seventy weeks of years (7+62+1)=490 years. While both Daniel 5 and 9 present pesher interpretations of written texts, only the latter preserves the interpretation of prophetic texts from the Bible.

Joseph and Daniel understand dreams and visions as divine messages about something that will happen in the future. In the case of the dreams of the kings of the eastern Diaspora and the visions of Daniel, the divine messages concern God's absolute control over human kingdoms. The divine messages as well as their interpretations come from God, but are reported by human and angelic agents.

The dreams/visions and interpretations of Genesis and Daniel bear a remarkable resemblance to the continuous pesharim. The former are to be understood not as texts originally, but rather as experiences that are verbalized. They become texts once they are written down. Only the interpretations in Daniel 5 and 9, especially the latter, clarify written material. In the textual form, the dreams and visions may be interpreted in the same way as texts like Habakkuk, Psalm 37, and Nahum are. The interpretative procedure is essentially the same. Elements within the text are taken up one by one, identified, and then explained.

A few significant differences do exist, however, between the interpretation of dreams and visions in the Bible and the pesher-interpretation from Qumran. First of all, the pesharim lack the fictive historical setting provided in the narrative framework of Gen. 40–41 and Daniel. Although difficulties arise in determining the historical setting against which to interpret the pesharim, Qumran scholars usually understand them as referring to the history of the Qumran community. This view rests on the belief that the persons and events alluded to in the pesharim were characters involved in the history of the Qumran community, e.g. the Teacher, the Wicked Priest, and the Liar.[10] Thus according to the prevailing consensus, the biblical texts interpreted in the Qumran pesharim are treated as divine messages, like the dreams and visions of Genesis and Daniel, whose fulfillment has largely occurred in the life of the Qumran community. Several passages are thought to refer to the last days or the end-time.[11]

Certainly, the pesharim preserve statements alluding to figures and events of history. This is clearest in 4QpNah, which mentions known Seleucid rulers, allowing one to speak with certainty about a particular historical context. One can safely assume that 1QpHab and 4QpPs37 are concerned with historical persons and events, but the crucial issue is whether the preserved information allows one to make specific identifications. In order to understand this information, attention must be given to the specific texts that are thought to bear on the history of the Qumran community.

C. *The Pesharim and Qumran History*

1. *Methodological Considerations*

One of the best methodological discussions of the literary evidence from Qumran is that of Hartmut Stegemann. He makes the pesharim his central witnesses for the history of the Qumran community, recognizing that this body of evidence preserves several categories of information potentially relevant and useful for the historian. He tries first of all to determine which topics found in the pesharim might yield the best and most reliable data about the historical period in question and the historical events themselves. He entertains the possibility that one could begin with statements about non-Jewish rulers, military leaders, and troop movements, because this category of statements would possibly be corroborated or discounted by ancient authors who recorded such things. It might even supplement the reports of the ancient authors. Because the information in the pesharim is susceptible to a variety of interpretations, he rejects this category as the best possible starting-point. Concurring with his colleague Jeremias, Stegemann says that such non-Jewish entities are never associated with the beginnings of the Qumran community. In this case, he is speaking about the Kittim, which he understands as the Romans.[12] Then he turns to statements about the Teacher of Righteousness, who would seem to be the best documented candidate and would serve as a good starting-point for the historical discussion. This possibility is also rejected, because of the variety of conflicting and controversial identifications of the Teacher represented in the secondary literature at the time of Stegemann's writing.[13] In addition, Stegemann doubts that the Teacher had founded the community as Jeremias had claimed.[14] He also rejects attempts to arrange the Qumran texts according to their presumed dates of composition and to use these hypothetical chronological pegs as a framework against which to reconstruct a series of historical episodes found in the texts themselves.[15] Finally, he argues against the mixing of several thematic fields, e.g. the community's opponents, the Teacher, rules of conduct, the eschatological community of salvation, and foreigners.[16] For the sake of clarity and power of conviction, he says, one requires one basic thematic field in which all the elements are historically related and whose chronological relationship can be determined. Applying this criterion, he restricts his search to statements made about the inner-Jewish enemies of the Qumran community and the polemics involving them.[17]

Stegemann is aware that some of the polemical statements about the community's enemies may be distorted and may, for that reason, not be used in the historical reconstruction. An additional problem, he points out, is the presence both of earlier and later statements about different enemies, the later depictions being potentially inaccurate understandings of earlier ones.[18] This applies above all to the statements about enemies in CD.

Despite his own methodological warning, Stegemann argues that certain stereotypical statements about the community's opponents that recur in formally and chronologically distinct texts are valuable for their depictions of episodes of Qumran history.[19] Because particular persons are painted with such striking traits, he says, they must be historical individuals associated with Qumran history.[20] Since the community's origins are entangled in controversy, polemical statements about the enemies of the Qumran community and its Teacher provide the most ideal category of evidence.[21]

The best evidence about these enemies is found in some of the pesharim. Not all of the pesharim, however, are historically useful.[22] For example, he eliminates pesharim on Micah, Zephaniah, Psalm 68, and several on Isaiah (1Q14-16; 3Q4; 4QpIsa^{a-d}), because they offer little historical information. He excludes 4QpHos, because he is not sure of its historical stance, that is, whether it concerns the Qumran community in particular or the larger Jewish community.

The pesharim that have played a dominant role in historical reconstructions are 1QpHab, 4QpPs 37, and 4QpNah. These interpretive texts are connected by a common genre and terminology, which is thought to allude to the history of the Qumran community.[23] While this terminology is not used with complete consistency from one pesher to another, sufficient overlap does exist to indicate the shared interests of the different pesharim. Stegemann has pointed out that 4QpNah evidences a different terminology, perhaps because of the particular language of the biblical book, or because of the special interests of the pesharist, or because of the poor condition of the extant text. He suggests cautiously that the lost sections of it may have resembled 1QpHab and 4QpPs 37 more closely.[24]

Stegemann observes that the overlap in terminology is crucial for understanding the shared historical context to which the pesharists are referring.[25] He points out, for example, that the Teacher of Righteousness and the Wicked Priest, the Liar and the Ones Doing Violence to the Covenant appear in 1QpHab and 4QpPs 37. These four subjects do not appear even once in 4QpNah. On the other hand, the Seekers after Smooth Things, who play an important role in 4QpNah, are not mentioned in 1QpHab and 4QpPs 37. Furthermore, 1QpHab and 4QpNah share an interest in the Kittim, a term not found in 4QpPs 37. Similarly, 4QpPs 37 and 4QpNah are associated by the presence of the terms Ephraim and Manasseh, which do not appear in 1QpHab.

Stegemann justifies the use of the pesharim in historical reconstructions as follows: because the pesharim offer the most detailed and differentiated information about the Qumran community and its historical environment, they are correctly placed at the center of the discussion about the history of the Qumran community.[26]

2. *The Pesharim*

In order to understand the language of the pesharim about the Qumran community and its enemies as well as the chronological framework for their conflict, 1QpHab, 4QpPs 37, and 4QpNah will be investigated in their own individual literary contexts.

a. *1QpHab*

Several passages that are presumably relevant to the historical question require attention—1QpHab I,16-II,10; V,8-12; VI,12–VII,2; VII,3-5; VII,17–VIII,3; VIII,3-13; X,6-13; XI,2-8, 8-15, 17–XII,6; XII,12.

1QpHab I,16–II,10 has played an important role in the historical discussion because of its mention of the Liar, the Teacher, and the Priest. The first two are known from CD. The Priest is not mentioned in CD.

(1) [פשר הדבר על] הבוגדים עם איש
(2) הכזב כי לו[א שמעו אל דברי] מורה הצדק[ה] מפיא
(3) אל ועל הבוג[דים בברית] החדשה [כי]א [לו]א
(4) האמינו בברית אל [ויחללו] את ש[ם ק]ודשו
(5) וכן פשר הדבר [על כול הבו]גדים לאחרית
(6) הימים המה ערי[צי הבר]ית אשר לוא יאמינוא
(7) בשומעם את כול הב[אות על] הדור האחרון מפי
(8) הכוהן אשר נתן אל ב[לבו בינ]ה לפשר [א]ת כול
(9) דברי עבדיו הנביאים [אשר ב]ידם ספר אל את
(10) כול הבאות על עמו ו[ארצו][27]

This unit may be characterized as an extended pesher on the word בוגדים in the lemma which is restored from Hab. 1.5. The pesher itself treats the Hebrew word in the MT בגוים as בוגדים, agreeing with an emendation of the MT based on the Greek οἱ καταφρονηταί. The peculiarity of this unit is the presence of formulae within the larger unit indicating subsections or additional interpretations. These formulae are [פשר הדבר על] הבוגדים (l. 1), ועל הבוג[דים בברית] החדשה (l. 3), and וכן פשר הדבר [על כול הבו]גדים לאחרית הימים (l. 6). All these subsections deal, therefore, with 'the traitors' (הבוגדים). What does each section say about these 'traitors'? Of what are they accused concretely? Are they figures of the past, or of the present, or of the future?

The first group of 'traitors' is associated with the Liar, who is also mentioned in CD, and are accused of having disobeyed the words of מורה הצדקה from the mouth of God (II,1-3). The text provides no clues as to which specific acts of disobedience are meant. From the context of CD I,12-15, it is known that the Liar and the 'traitors' were associated. In that context, the Liar is accused generally of preaching lies and misleading Israel at some undefined period of the past, not of disobeying or inciting others to disobey the words of the Teacher. Nothing more concrete is known about the activities of the Liar and his adherents from CD.

In the second subsection, the 'traitors' of the 'new covenant' are mentioned (II,1-3). They are accused of not having believed in God's covenant. The purpose of this second reference to 'traitors' seems to have been to distinguish them from those who were not obedient to the Teacher of Righteousness. In essence, both groups of 'traitors' have rejected God. The initial group of 'traitors' is depicted as following the Liar and opposing the Teacher. This opposition is not explicitly stated concerning the second group of 'traitors', but perhaps it would have been assumed. The only verbal sign of a possible distinction between the first and second group of 'traitors' is the association of the latter with the 'new covenant'. By using the word החדשה the pesharist explicitly contrasts 'more recent traitors' with 'earlier' ones, at the same time suggesting that a typological, perhaps even a historical, connection exists between the earlier and later covenants. The 'traitors' are accused in theological language of not believing, an affront to God. Therefore, one must be cautious not to read more into this generalizing statement than the statement itself actually allows. For the modern reader, there is no recognizable allusion to known historical persons or groups.

In the third subsection, reference is made to the 'traitors' of the end-time (II,5-10). Several statements are made about this third group of 'traitors'. First of all, they are identified as Ones Doing Violence to the Covenant (II,6). This would seem to be a reference to violence against the 'new covenant'. Then it is said that they do not or will not believe when they hear from the divinely inspired Priest about future events concerning the last generation. In this context, the 'traitors' are specifically accused of not accepting the Priest's interpretation of the prophetic books (II,8-9), which are understood as oracles about the future of God's people and land (II,9-10).

With the mention of the 'traitors' of the end-time, a chronological equation seems to become recognizable about 'traitors' throughout history. The first two subsections seem to deal with 'traitors' of the past. The earliest group seems to have been contemporaneous with the Teacher of Righteousness. Three elements in the third subsection suggest that it might be concerned with traitors of a later time. First of all, the pesharist has used an imperfect form, לוא יאמינו, in this subsection in contrast to the perfects of the first two subsections (II,2 [restored], 4). Secondly, he uses the temporal expression לאחרית הימים, which refers to his time or the future, whereas he does not do this in the first two subsections. Finally, he says that the traitors do/will not believe the Priest. In the first subsection, they did not obey the words of the Teacher; in the second, they did not believe in God's covenant, the new one. Is the Priest a later figure, distinct from the Teacher mentioned in the first subsection?

Stegemann poses the issue clearly: is 1QpHab II,2-10 presenting three distinctive groups of *bōgᵉdîm* or one according to three different aspects?[28] He points out that the perfect form לוא שמעו in

l. 2 does not unequivocally indicate a past action. Nevertheless, he continues, since V,9-12 knows the Liar as a figure of the past, the writer must have included the past aspect. Stegemann emphasizes, however, that the issue for the pesharist is the contemporary opposition to the Teacher.[29]

For Stegemann, the second group of *bōgᵉdîm* is depicted as having rejected the community rather than the Teacher.[30] He identifies the Teacher's followers with the Qumran community. The traitors of this subsection were, according to him, either traitors from the 'new covenant' in the sense of having once belonged to it or traitors who never did belong to it. A traitor is one who actively decides not to believe the words of God through the Teacher.

It seems, however, that one need not draw the conclusion that the first subsection deals with the immediate contemporaries of the Teacher and the Liar, while the second deals with two later, opposing groups adhering to the instructions of the Teacher and the Liar respectively. Both subsections seem to be concerned with disobedience to the Teacher in the past. Elliger points out that the first subsection presents apostasy in personal terms as rejection of the Teacher; the second presents it objectively as an affront to God's 'new covenant'.[31]

What is the relationship of the third subsection to that of the first two, which are concerned with disobeying the Teacher in the past? The pesharist clearly views the Teacher as an important authority figure who lived at some earlier time. It is impossible to determine the chronological relationship between the Teacher and the pesharist more precisely. The pesharist is apparently comparing the contemporary traitors who do/will not believe God's message as proclaimed by the Teacher with those of the past.[32] This message concerns that which is about to happen to the last generation. In II,7-8 another figure is introduced. This is the Priest who seems to be a figure later than the Teacher, but 4QpPs 37 III,15 and IV,5-6 identify him with the Teacher of Righteousness.[33] There are no other passages in the pesharim, CD, and 1QH that support a distinction between the Teacher of Righteousness and the Priest. The reference to the Priest in this subsection seems to be a cultic designation for the Teacher, who in his role as teacher assumes a prophetic and pedagogical role. The clue to understanding the time of the Priest in relationship to the *bōgᵉdîm* of the end of days seems to lie partly in the sentence modifying the reference to the Priest: 'in whose heart God gave insight to interpret' (II,8). The use of the perfect form of the verb נתן would seem to indicate that the Priest already exists or existed previously. The phrase 'out of the Priest's mouth' (ll. 7-8) parallels the phrase 'out of the mouth of God' (ll. 2-3). The former would seem to refer to the Teacher's legitimization. His message comes ultimately from God. The Priest who should be identified with the Teacher—based on 4QpPs 37 III,15—also enjoys divine sanction. Those who will not accept his understanding of the prophets could have been both his contemporaries and subsequent 'traitors'.

In isolation from the third subsection, one might construe the perfect forms in ll. 2 and 4 simply as characterizing the disobedience and disbelief of the Liar and his adherents, rather than referring to the time when they did not believe. If one reads them in light of the temporal information provided in the third subsection, they do seem to refer to a past relative to the time indicated by the imperfect form לוא יאמינו and the expression לאחרית הימים. Thus the *bōgᵉdîm* of the third subsection would seem to stand in contrast to the men of truth, the doers of the *tōrâ* (VII,10-12), who will not tire in the service of truth when the last age is extended. The temporal aspect of the verb forms in VII,7 and 9-13 are consistent with that of II,6.

The pesharist is concerned, therefore, with two temporally distinct groups of traitors, not three—those traitors who disobeyed and disbelieved the Teacher in the past, associating themselves with the Liar and apostasizing from the 'new covenant' (subsections one and two) and potential traitors of the time of the pesharist and the future. The verbs in ll. 2, 4 and 6 do, of course, characterize the traitors, but they do even more than this. They set up a chronological equation concerning traitors of the past and those of the writer's contemporary situation. Both groups of traitors lived in the *dōr 'aharōn*.

Turning to the larger context of the Qumran documentation, one finds in CD I,11-15 an approximate parallel to what is said about the Priest and the 'traitors' of the end-time. This passage says that God raised up a Teacher and (he) made known to last generations what he (God) had done in the last generation with a congregation of 'traitors'. These 'traitors' are then identified as Those Who Turn(ed) from the Way. Then Hos. 4.16 is cited as a proof-text relating to the notion of disobedience. Thus Hosea, according to the correct interpretation=the perspective of the compiler of CD I, is thought to refer to the last evil and rebellious generation. The idea of rebellion כפרה סורירה סרר ישראל (l. 13-14) is echoed in the expressions סרי דרך

and סרר ישראל (ll. 13-14). This rebellion is associated with the emergence of the Liar who preached lies to Israel.

There are obvious parallels between this passage and 1QpHab II,5-10. 1QpHab II,5-10 concerns the Priest; CD I,11-15, the Teacher. Both know the Teacher as a figure of the past. The Priest is also a figure of the past, according to 1QpHab II, 8. Language about the Priest in 1QpHab resembles that in CD I,11-12 about the Teacher: 'and he (God/a Teacher?) *made known* to last generations what he (God) had done with a last congregation of 'traitors'. As was pointed out in Chapter 5, several analysts have translated the perfect form עשה as a future tense, 'will, would do'.[33] Under the influence of the statement in 1QpHab II,7-10, which speaks of the Priest's interpretation of the prophetic books as divine oracles about the future, about a last generation, one might be tempted to harmonize the latter's statement with that in CD I,11-12 and treat עשה as an imperfect. The larger context of CD I militates against rendering עשה in this way. In I,14, the use of the infinitive construct בעמוד and the perfect form הטיף indicates that the Liar was a figure of the past. In 1QpHab II,1-2 the Teacher and the Liar are clearly contemporaries. If the perspective of 1QpHab should apply to CD I, then both would belong to Israel's past.[34]

Above, in Chapter 5, the expression *dōr 'aharōn* was discussed in the context of CD I. It was determined that the last generation was a period of time to which the Liar and his adherents belonged. 1QpHab VII,2-13 suggested that this period was one about which the Teacher had spoken but whose completion was not yet recognizable in the time of the pesharist and his audience, the Men of Truth, the doers of the *tōrâ*. Thus the *dōr 'aharōn* was an extensive period, just how extensive is impossible to know, running from some time in the past into the immediate future.

If the ideology of CD should parallel that of 1QpHab II,3-5, one would expect to find references in the former to a 'new covenant'. In XIX,33-35, the 'new covenant' in Damascus is presented as an entity of the past. Among its ranks 'traitors' were also found.

Does CD preserve anything comparable to the third subsection in 1QpHab concerning the 'traitors' who do/will not believe the Priest? Two observations suggest that this may be the case. First, immediately following the reference to the 'new covenant' in Damascus and its 'traitors', a new community and its potential 'traitors' are mentioned (XX,1-2): 'this is also the judgment on all those who enter the

Congregation of Perfectly Holy Ones'. Clearly, the Priest of 1QpHab is not mentioned, but one circumstance may associate this figure with the Community of Perfectly Holy Ones. In III,21–IV,2, Ezek. 44.15 is quoted concerning the Priests, the Levites, and the Sons of Zadok. The Priests are identified in the midrash with שבי ישראל. The Levites are their adherents. The Sons of Zadok are identified as the Chosen Ones of Israel at the end-time. All three designations refer to a 'priestly' community. The reference to the Priests and the Levites would seem to allude to a community of the past. The Sons of Zadok are a community that belongs to the present or the future, depending upon one's understanding of העמדים באחרית הימים.

Is there perhaps a correspondence with the Priest and the 'traitors' mentioned in 1QpHab II,5-8?

> 1QpHab II,5-8:
> (5) This also concerns the 'traitors' at the end (6)-time. They are Ones Doing Violence to the Covenant, who do not/ will not believe, (7) when they hear all which is coming on the last generation out of the mouth of (8) the Priest, in whose heart God placed insight.
>
> CD IV,2-4:
> (2) The Priests are the Returnees of Israel, who (3) left the land of Judah; and the Levites are those who joined them. And the Sons of Zadok are the Chosen Ones (4) of Israel. . ., who are/will stand at the end-time.

Should the Sons of Zadok be identified or associated with the Priest of 1QpHab and his community, which is not mentioned, but which may be assumed? If there were 'traitors', who do/will not believe the Teacher's/Priest's interpretation of the prophets, there was probably also a group of loyal followers. The circumstances that both the Sons of Zadok, genealogically a priestly community, and the Priest belong to the end-time would at least suggest that the CD and 1QpHab both reflect post-Teacher and Liar perspectives, which are in general agreement about salvation for the faithful and judgment for traitors.

Is there any other textual support for the progression from the 'new covenant' to a later community? The key to answering this question may lie in CD (MS B) cols. XIX,32–XX,2.

(32) וכמשפט הזה לכל המאס במצות אל
(33) ויעזבם ויפנו בשרירות לבם כן כל האנשים אשר באו בברית

(34) החרשה בארץ דמשק ושבו ויבגדו ויסורו מבאר מים החיים
(35) לא יחשבו בסוד עם ובכתבם לא יכתבום יום האסף
(1) מורה היחיד עד עמוד משיח מאחרון ומישראל וכן המשפט
(2) לכל באי עדת אנשי תמים הקדש

In this passage, which resembles 1QpHab II,1-10, judgment is pronounced upon those who reject God's commandments and those who have apostasized from the 'new covenant' in the land of Damascus. The traitors will not be recorded (in a book listing the names of the faithful) from the 'death' of the Teacher of the *Yaḥîd* until the emergence of a messiah from Aaron and Israel. The same judgment applies to those who enter the Congregation of the Men of Perfect Holiness and then apostasize.

A cursory reading of this passage might lead one to find three groups of traitors: those who reject God's commandments (XIX,32-33), those who have apostasized from the 'new covenant' (ll. 33-34), both of the past, and those who apostasize from the Congregation of the Men of Perfect Holiness (XX,1-2), apparently a reference to the writer's group. According to this understanding, the writer is concerned with three chronologically distinct groups: the unfaithful of an earlier covenant, those of a 'new' or later covenant, and those of the writer's time, an even later group.

This chronological equation is possible on the face of it. Read in light of 1QpHab II,1-10, however, it seems to be only partly correct. One need not construe those who reject God's law and those who apostasized from the 'new covenant' as two distinctive groups. כן is used in this passage to add information characterizing the nature of and the judgment on the unfaithful. This use resembles that of על in 1QpHab II,2-3 and כן in II,5. It is difficult to determine any chronological equation with certainty. The participle plus the definite article המאס in CD XIX,32 seems to intend the general act of rejecting God's law. In l. 33, the phrase ויעזבם ויפנו בשרירות לבם speaks clearly of apostasy in the past. Those traitors will not be recorded. In XX,1-2 no temporal aspect is clearly stated, but one has the impression that the Congregation of the Men of Perfect Holiness lived in the period after the Teacher's death and before the coming of the messiah. The writer's intention in the passage is to liken the judgment on the unfaithful in his time to that on the unfaithful of the past (cf. 1QpHab II,1-4 and CD XIX,32-35; 1QpHab II,5-10 and CD XX,1-2).

This relatively extensive analysis of 1QpHab I,16–II,10, and of CD I, III,21–IV,4 and XIX,32–XX,2, because of their similar interests and language, was undertaken in order to increase our understanding of the meaning of certain terms within their literary contexts, e.g. the Teacher, the Priest, and the 'traitors'. In that sense, it serves as a prolegomenon to the question about the historical import of 1QpHab I,16–II,10. While one cannot deny the possibility in principle that the pesharist could have named the Teacher, or the Priest of the end-time, or any number of 'traitors', this is precisely what he failed to do. Instead, he offers an extended pesher dealing with the themes of obedience and disobedience under the guise of sobriquets. Reference to individual figures by means of such designations does suggest that the pesharist is concerned with historical persons and situations. The characters involved in this progression are in fact dated in a relative chronological order, earlier and later, but since none of them are named and clearly associated with events of public history, the historian is unable to integrate this information into an already known or even in part empirically reconstructed history. Methodologically, such an attempt would proceed far beyond the available evidence. Are other passages in 1QpHab any more concrete?

The next reference to the 'traitors' appears in V,8, the quotation of Hab. 1.13. In the pesher which follows the 'traitors' are identified with the House of Absalom and its partisans who did not aid the Teacher of Righteousness against the Liar. This passage is obviously alluding to a confrontation between the Teacher and the Liar, but the particular point is the indifference of the House of Absalom during this conflict. Who is the House of Absalom? A controversy surrounds the interpretation of this expression. One group identifies the House of Absalom with a known, historical figure and his family in the Second Temple period.[35] Another treats the name Absalom as symbolic.[36] Certainly, the use of personal names in 4QpNah I,2-3 does show that the authors of the Qumran texts could speak of historical persons directly. That is, however, not a positive argument for the interpretation of Absalom as a personal name in 1QpHab V,10. The context of 1QpHab V,8-12 suggests that the name Absalom is in fact used as a traditional, symbolic reference applied to a group not an individual. The antecedent to the House of Absalom and their council are the *bōgᵉdîm* in the quotation of Hab. 1.13b. In 1QpHab II,2-3, as in this passage, the *bōgᵉdîm* are associated with the Liar, who rejected the Law. V,10-12 seems to add to the information concerning the Liar and his adherents in II,2-3 (cf. X,5-13; XI,1). Brownlee has pointed out that the silence of the House of Absalom reminds one of Absalom's (Tamar's) silence before he slew his brother (2 Sam. 13.22).[37] Teicher claimed that the House of Absalom was suggested to the pesharist by the verb *haḥarîšî* in 2 Sam. 13.20 (cf. *taḥarîš* in V, 8).[38] In 2 Sam. 13.20, Absalom tells Tamar not to report the incident involving Amnon. Then she returned to dwell in the house of her brother Absalom. In this story, Absalom is characterized as one who remained silent, when he should have acted. This is precisely the transgression of Absalom in V,8-12. 2 Sam. 13.20–18.18 depicts Absalom not only as the silent one, but clearly as a traitor to his father. Thus the House of Absalom in 1QpHab V,10 provides a concrete, symbolic example of the traitors mentioned in the quotation of Hab. 1.13b.

In V, 8-10, there is no clue to the nature of the specific conflict in question nor to any of the motivations for it. The Liar is accused generally of 'having rejected the Law in the midst of their congregation'. The House of Absalom is accused simply of silence during the conflict between the Teacher and the Liar. Nothing is said specifically about the identities of the members of this House nor of its party affiliation nor of the time-frame in which the conflict occurred.

In VI,12-16, Hab. 2.1-2 is quoted. In VII,1-2, the reader is told that God's word to Habakkuk concerned the last generation, but God did not reveal to him anything about the completion of the age (גמר הקץ). In order to point out who did know about the end of the age, that is, about the correct interpretation of Habakkuk's oracles, the pesharist takes up Hab. 2.2 again and interprets it as referring to the Teacher of Righteousness, to whom God had announced all the mysteries of the prophetic words. This is an obvious cross-reference to 1QpHab II,2, which says more or less the same thing about the Teacher. Nothing is reported about the substance of conflict with the Liar or the Wicked Priest. As for the identity of the Teacher, one can only draw the conclusion that he was a person living after the time of the prophet Habakkuk. Since insufficient information is given, even the best historian can only very tentatively postulate the identity of this person.

In VII,5-8, Hab. 2.3 is quoted. It refers back to the notion of the completion of the age. VII,7 states that the last age would exceed the proclamations made by the prophets. This is a peculiar statement.

Should one get the impression that the Teacher himself is speaking? It is not clear. The remainder of Hab. 2.3 is quoted and interpreted as referring to the 'Men of Truth, Those Doing the Law', whose hands do not tire in the service of Truth—even when the final age may last longer than was anticipated. In VII,17-VIII,3, Hab. 2.4 is interpreted again as concerning Those Doing the Law in the House of Judah. It is said that God will save them from the impending judgment because of their faithfulness to the Teacher of Righteousness. These passages provide no concrete information either on the precise age or period when the Doers of the Law lived nor on the identity of their Teacher. The reference to the faithfulness of the Doers of the Law to the Teacher of Righteousness does suggest that the former lived after the Teacher.

With the pericope VIII,3-13, the Wicked Priest is introduced into 1QpHab. He is said to have been called by the name of Truth when he arose, but as he reigned over Israel (משל בישראל) he became puffed up with pride, forsaking God and acting treacherously against the statutes (ll. 9-10). He is also accused chiefly of a love of wealth (הון, ll. 11-12). Moreover, he is depicted as a renegade from the ranks of God's faithful. Scholars sometimes see in this description of the Wicked Priest an allusion to a known Jewish high priest of the second century BCE. Stegemann, for example, is confident that a high priest is intended and comes to the conclusion that this priest was Jonathan Maccabeus.

Stegemann presents an extensive discussion laying out the components of his argumentation. First of all, he points out several other references to the Wicked Priest in 1QpHab (IX,9-12; IX,16–X,1; X,3-5; XI,4-8; XII,2-10) and 4QpPs 37 IV,8-10.[39] 1QpHab IX,9-12 speaks of the divine punishment of the Wicked Priest because of his actions against the Teacher of Righteousness and God's chosen ones. IX,16 refers to the Priest (הכוהן). X,3-5 speaks of the divine judgment on the Wicked Priest in the midst of many peoples (cf. XI,12-16). XI,2-8, which is discussed below, deals apparently with a confrontation between the Wicked Priest and the Teacher of Righteousness on a Day of Atonement. XII,2-10 points out God's judgment on the Wicked Priest, who acted against the Poor. This group is then called Lebanon and identified as the Council of the *Yaḥad*. 4QpPs 37 IV,8-10 concerns God's judgment on the Wicked Priest by the violent ones of the nations, because he sought to kill the Righteous One (cf. 1QpHab IX,9-12; X,3-5; XI,2-8; XII,2-10).

Stegemann notes that the various statements about the Wicked Priest can be subsumed under three categories.[40] The first are those concerning his violence against the Teacher and his adherents (1QpHab [I,13f.], IX,9-12; XI,4-8; XII,2-10; 4QpPs 37 IV,8-10). The second are his cultic transgressions and non-observance of cultic prescriptions (1QpHab VIII,8-13, 16–IX,2; XI,12-16; XII,7-9). The final category deals with the divine punishment of the Wicked Priest for both kinds of transgressions (1QpHab VIII,16–IX,2; IX,9-12; X,3-5; X,12-16; XII,2-10; 4QpPs 37 IV,8-10).

The first and last categories, Stegemann observes, are applicable to the Liar along with his adherents and Manasseh.[41] Cultic transgressions and non-observance, the subject of the second category, apply only to the Wicked Priest. Stegemann considers that the Liar's rejection of or disdain for the Law might be construed as a general cultic transgression, but rules out this possibility. He distinguishes the Liar and the Wicked Priest. The former is always associated with false doctrine and the act of misleading. These characterizations are never used in reference to the Wicked Priest. Based on these observations, Stegemann maintains that they are two different figures.[42] This could be the case, but 4QpPs 37 IV,14-15 clouds the issue. In this passage, the Liar (א[י]ש הכזב) is said to have done something against God's chosen ones and sought to destroy (?). An almost identical statement is made about the Wicked Priest in 1QpHab XII,2-3 and the Liar in X,13. Thus it is not clear whether the two different characterizations, the Liar and the Wicked Priest, necessarily refer to two distinct figures. In any case, the chances of identifying either of the two lie with the Wicked Priest, who is called הכוהן and who is said to have ruled over Israel (משל בישראל).

Stegemann presents a lengthy list of Old Testament passages, where הכוהן is used as a titular designation for the high priest.[43] This title is typically used in conjunction with a personal name, e.g. Eli the (high) priest (1 Sam. 1.9), Simon son of Jonathan the (high) priest (Sir. 50.1). Even the prophet Ezekiel is called הכוהן (1.3), but Stegemann denies titular use in this case. He notes also that הכוהן can be used in a non-titular sense to refer to a functioning priest.[44] He mentions other designations for the high priest: הכוהן המשיח, the anointed (messianic) priest (Lev. 4.3, 5, 16), הכוהן הגדול, the highest ranking priest (Hag. 1.1, 12-14), and הכוהן הראש, the leading priest (2 Sam. 15.27). In Deuteronomy, הכוהן functions as a collective reflecting any individual who functions as priest.

Besides the titular reference to the Wicked Priest as הכוהן, Stegemann finds this use in the Qumran texts only for the Teacher of Righteousness (1QpHab II,8; 4QpPs 37 II,19; III,15).[45] Elsewhere the high priest is called the ר(ו)אש הכוהן in 1QM II,1; XV,4, XVI,13; XVIII,5; XIX,11. הכוהן can refer, of course, to any priest (1QS VI,3-4; CD XIII,2; 1QM VII,12; 1QSa II,19). Stegemann interprets הכוהן הראש as the title of the eschatological high priest in 1QSa II,12. He points out also that the Qumran texts never use the title הכוהן הגדול.[46]

Stegemann has shown that הכוהן can be interpreted as a reference to a high priest. He presents other evidence demonstrating that הכוהן need not refer to a high priest. Moreover, his examples of titular use from the Old Testament are accompanied by personal names. The major difficulty in identifying the Wicked Priest is the fact that this figure is never named in the Qumran texts, nor is it entirely clear that he was a high priest.

Stegemann's argument for the historical, high-priestly function of the Wicked Priest is supported by the statement in 1QpHab VIII,9-10 that he ruled over Israel. Since he has already determined that הכוהן could refer to a high priest and משל בישראל to a political activity, this Wicked Priest must have been both the highest religious and political leader of his people. But even before his reigning over Israel, he presumably held public office (עומדו, l. 9).[47]

In several passages, this high priest is further described by the modifying expression הרשע (1QpHab IX,9-12; XI,4-8; XII,2-10; 4QpPs 37 IV,7-10). As Stegemann explains, one has become accustomed to think the Priest was disqualified, as the expression הכוהן הרשע indicates, because of his treatment of the Teacher of Righteousness and his community.[48] 1QpHab VIII,8 presents a problem for this view, since neither the Teacher nor his community is mentioned.

Stegemann understands הרשע to refer to the illegitimacy of הכוהן. This priest was either guilty of grave cultic transgressions or he was unacceptable as high priest because of his family lineage.[49] Stegemann thinks he was probably disqualified because of his lineage and was therefore considered sinful in regard to his cultic activities.[50] This claim is, as he admits, speculative.[51]

In order to identify this figure, Stegemann turns to the determination of the broad chronological period when the Wicked (Illegitimate) Priest was active as the highest religious and political leader of the Jews.[52] In order to accomplish this, he appeals to the information presented in 4QpNah I,2-8. Lines 2-4 speak of Those Who Seek after Smooth Things, who encouraged the Seleucid king Demetrius III to come to Jerusalem. Line 5 refers to the Lion of Wrath. Lines 6-8 are concerned with the Lion's activity of 'hanging men up alive'. Stegemann identifies the Seekers after Smooth Things with the community of the Liar (cf. CD I,18) and the Lion of Wrath with Alexander Jannaeus. He associates the subject of 'hanging men up alive' with Josephus' report in *Ant*. 13.372-83 and *Bell*. 1.88-98. This report deals with the Pharisees, who sought to dethrone King Alexander Jannaeus with the help of the Seleucid Demetrius. In the Battle of Shechem c. 90 BCE, they defeated Jannai's troops. However, Jannai crucified 800 of these Pharisees—Seekers after Smooth Things. Since the Seekers after Smooth Things are associated with this battle, their existence is witnessed c. 90 BCE. The existence of this group would provide a *terminus ad quem* for the Liar's community in 90 BCE. In conjunction with the *terminus a quo* 200 BCE, established on palaeographical grounds, Stegemann maintains that the Wicked (Illegitimate) Priest, the Teacher of Righteousness, and the Liar were active between the years 200 and 90 BCE.

Having laid out the chronological background, Stegemann then proposes four criteria which a candidate must fulfill in order to fit the description of the Wicked (Illegitimate) Priest mentioned in pesharim.[53] (1) The expression הכוהן הרשע refers to the illegitimacy of this particular priest to function as high priest. This illegitimacy derives from his lineage or from his illegal appropriation of the high-priestly office. He is not accused of committing serious cultic transgressions. (2) His political role is described as משל, thus excluding the possibilities that he used the title 'king' and that there was a king or higher political representative in Israel at that time. (3) During the period when he was high priest the temple treasury was not robbed by non-Jews. (4) He died outside of Jewish territory, perhaps a violent death. After reducing his list of possible candidates for identification with the Wicked, or as he understands it, the Illegitimate, Priest to five ranging from 175 to 104 BCE, he tests each candidate against his four criteria.[54] He notes that these were all high priests, who may have been viewed as illegitimate, and that they were persons who did not assume the title 'king'. Alcimus and John Hyrcanus I are eliminated quickly in view of criterion 4, which states that he died under horrible conditions. These two high priests died of natural causes in Jerusalem. This criterion is not applicable to Jason, according to Stegemann, nor to Simon, who was murdered by a relative within the borders of Judaea. The two remaining candidates, Menelaus and Jonathan, could easily have been viewed as illegitimate, for both were non-Zadokites, representing the Jews politically, who were put to death under terrible circumstances outside of Judaea.[55] In favor of the identification with Jonathan, Stegemann emphasizes that he loved money in particular. When 1QpHab XII,7-10 says the Wicked Priest defiled the temple and robbed the poor, Stegemann understands this to mean that the Wicked Priest robbed the poor and then filled up the temple treasury with his spoils, thereby defiling it.[56]

It is not clear that one must treat הכוהן as a reference to a high priest and הרשע as a reference to his disqualification for this position due to lineage. However, in combination with the statement that he ruled in Israel, one is certainly tempted to see in this figure a priest who was also known as a ruler in Israel. If this priest had been viewed as an illegitimate high priest due to his lineage, it seems doubtful that he would have been characterized as one called by the name of Truth at first. His chief transgressions are pride, forsaking God, and rebelling against his commandments for the sake of riches. This is consistent with VIII,16-17, which says that the (Wicked) Priest rebelled against God's laws. A similar statement is made about the last priests of Jerusalem (IX,4-6; cf. 4QpNah I,11-12). Not only is the Wicked Priest noted for this pride, greed, and apostasy from God, he is accused of pursuing the Teacher of Righteousness in order to kill him (XI,4-8), of harming the poor (XII,2-3), and of desecrating Jerusalem and the temple (XII,7-9). While one cannot prove that the (Wicked) Priest was a high priest, whose legitimacy was questioned by the Qumran community, this was clearly a figure who had earned the attribute הרשע because of his apostasy from God and the Truth (האמת, VII,10-11). The הכוהן הרשע is set up in contrast to the Men of Truth, the Doers of the Law, and the Poor (XII,3). His quest for material gain distinguishes him from the Poor, whom God will save at the judgment.

Therefore, it seems that the attribution הרשע not only characterizes a particular priest, but does this by contrasting him with others who are not wicked. While his illegitimacy in regard to his function as high priest may be an aspect of that wickedness, it need not be. If הרשע had referred to the illegitimacy of a high priest, that is, his not coming from the Zadokite line, how could he have been 'called by the name of Truth at first'? The characterization of him as wicked is based on his disobedience of God's laws and his desire for material things. Thus, it would seem that Stegemann's initial criterion cannot be used independently to identify the Wicked Priest with a non-Zadokite.

Stegemann's second criterion, associating the Wicked Priest with a regnal function, is more helpful, for it suggests that the pesharist may have been concerned with a ruling high priest after all. Stegemann may be correct in claiming that, since the Wicked Priest is never called 'king', the pesharist is probably referring to a time when the high priest was the highest political leader of the Jewish people. That could suggest that the Wicked Priest was a high priest who lived at some time from the post-exilic period into the first century BCE.

His fourth criterion, that the Wicked Priest died a violent death at the hands of the Gentiles, induces Stegemann to look for a Jewish high priest who was killed by the Gentiles outside of Judaea. This criterion is based on 1QpHab IX,1-2, which speaks of the physical suffering of the Wicked Priest. This seems to have occurred at some time in the past (עשו). The beginning of this interpretive section is broken off at VIII,17 so that it is difficult to say much about this event. In fact, several other passages refer to the future judgment of the Wicked Priest. In X,3-4, it is said that this will occur among many peoples. In XI,13-15, the pesharist calls this punishment 'the cup of wrath'. 4QpPs 37 II,19 and IV,9-10 seem to allude to the future event mentioned in 1QpHab X,3-4. In the latter, the Wicked Priest will suffer among many peoples (עמים רבים). In 4QpPs 37 II,19 the wicked as a whole will be delivered up to the violent ones of the peoples (עריצי הגויים). In IV,9-10, almost an identical statement is made about the Wicked Priest: God will punish him by giving him into the hands of the violent of the peoples to execute his judgment. Thus, while 1QpHab VIII,17 could refer to the physical torture of the Wicked Priest by Gentiles in the past, the majority of statements about this event presents it as unaccomplished. The pesharist seems to be concerned more with a description of the fate of the Wicked Priest and the wicked in general than with a historical event that has already occurred. Assuming that this interpretation is correct, one cannot speak of the actual death of a high priest, the Wicked Priest, among or by the hands of Gentiles. It turns out, therefore, that Stegemann's fourth criterion can neither be used independently nor in combination with his second criterion to date and identify the

Wicked Priest. The most important criterion for identifying the Wicked Priest would seem to be the conflict between him and the Teacher of Righteousness, but since the historiographic material of the Second Temple period never refers to this conflict, one cannot date any of these figures accurately.

A better chronological benchmark for the identification of figures of Qumran history appears in 4QpNah, which Stegemann, Jeremias, and others have used to establish a *terminus ad quem* for one of the groups opposed to the Teacher and his followers—the Seekers after Smooth Things.[57] From the association of the Liar and the Seekers after Smooth Things in CD I,18-20, Stegemann infers that this is a reference to the Liar's community.[58] However, the Liar is not mentioned, and there is no recognizable reference to direct opposition to the Teacher of Righteousness.

CD I,18-20 speaks of a group of apostates, whom the Liar was responsible for misleading. This group had earned the curses of the covenant. They are accused of having sought smooth things, of having chosen illusions, of watching for breaks, of having chosen the fair of neck, of justifying the wicked, and of transgressing the covenant. Several references are made to the Seekers after Smooth Things in 4QpNah. I,2-3 refers to the collaboration between this group and Demetrius, a king of Yavan. This political perspective is absent from CD I,18-20. In I,7, reference is made to revenge on the Seekers after Smooth Things. This reminds one of CD I,17-18, which also speaks of revenge on this group. In 4QpNah II,2, this group is identified with the city Ephraim at the end of days and is characterized as pursuing lies and deceptions. In II,4-6, reference is made to the rule of the Seekers after Smooth Things and their inescapable destruction because of their guilty council. In the next passage, II,8-10, the Seekers after Smooth Things are not explicitly mentioned, but the reference to Ephraim is, in view of II,2, clearly an allusion to this group. II,8-10 speaks of a group that misled Ephraim with their deceptive doctrine, their lying tongue(s), and false lip(s). II,9-10 also says that this group misleads kings, leaders, priests, people, resident aliens, cities, families, the royal, and rulers. Thus II,4-6 bears a remarkable resemblance to the statement about the Liar in CD I,14-21. 4QpNah III,3 notes that the evil deeds of the Seekers after Smooth Things/Ephraim (l. 3) will be revealed to Israel at the end of days. III,6-8 only adds a prediction of the judgment on this group.

Stegemann's inference that the Seekers after Smooth Things were associated with the Liar is clearly substantiated by their characterization in 4QpNah. Should the statement about the collusion of Demetrius with the Liar's group be a concrete reference to historical events in Judaea c. 90 BCE, this would establish a *terminus ad quem* for the Liar, not mentioned in 4QpNah, and his followers. The Seekers after Smooth things are certainly viewed as a group. Their characterization corresponds closely to that of the Liar and the Seekers after Smooth Things in CD I,12-21. 4QpNah may have subsumed the Liar under this category of evil-doers. He is never singled out as in CD I,14; 1QpHab X,9; XI,1; 4QpPs 37 I,18-19; IV,14-15 (cf. II,17-19). In contrast to these other passages, 4QpNah I associates the Liar's group with Demetrius' attempt to gain access to and control of Jerusalem c. 90 BCE.

Stegemann has clearly presented a convincing case for identifying the Seekers after Smooth Things of 4QpNah with the Liar's community, which was in collusion with the Seleucid Demetrius. Should one identify the statement in I,2 as an allusion to the events reported in Josephus' *Ant*. 13.372-83 and *Bell*. 1.88-98, one would be able to date this group c. 90 BCE. Of course, Stegemann and Jeremias think that 4QpNah is speaking of the Liar's followers at a time posterior to the Liar's and the Wicked Priest's conflicts with the Teacher of Righteousness. Although the Liar is not mentioned in 4QpNah, one might infer that he is subsumed under the general category of Seekers after Smooth Things and that he would be contemporary with his own community. One could also infer that the Liar, not mentioned in the present context, was survived by his community. The argument from silence should not be pressed too much. Since 4QpNah neither mentions the Liar, the Wicked Priest, and the Teacher individually nor in conflict with each other as in 1QpHab II,1-3; IX,9-10; XI,4-8; 4QpPs 37 II,17-18; IV,8-9, 14-15, the most that one can infer from it is that the Seekers after Smooth Things, i.e. the Liar's community, were apparently involved in the political machinations of Judaea around the year 90 BCE.

4QpPs 37 II,17-18 seems to suggest that the Liar's group, the Seekers after Smooth Things, were also opponents of the Teacher and his adherents. In this passage, the actions of the godless against the poor as mentioned in Ps. 37.14 are interpreted as referring to the attempt of the godless of Ephraim and Manasseh to harm the Priest, the Teacher, and the men of his council. 4QpNah II,2 has already equated the city Ephraim with the Seekers after Smooth Things at the end of days. If this group was active around the year 90 BCE, then it is possible that 4QpPs 37 II,17-18 is referring to the activities of the Liar's community in the political history of Judaea. Of course, one can hardly know whether the Liar was alive at this time.

The reference to the violence of Ephraim and Manasseh against the Priest and the men of his council in 4QpPs 37 II,17-18 reminds one of other passages that speak of the intentions of the Wicked Priest to harm the Teacher of Righteousness: 1QpHab IX,9-10; XI,4-8; 4QpPs 37 IV,8-10. The first passage is just as laconic as 4QpPs 37 II, 17-18. The most that one can derive from these two passages is that an evil person or group has attempted to harm a righteous one or group of righteous ones. The former speaks merely of Ephraim and Manasseh, while the latter refers to the Godless Priest, who is guilty of something in regard to the Teacher of Righteousness and the men of his council. 1QpHab XI,4-8 and 4QpPs 37 IV,8-10 are also laconic, but do provide additional information about this conflict.

XI,2-8 presents the most event-like statement dealing with the Wicked Priest and the Teacher in all of 1QpHab. Even more than the statement about the Liar's disobedience to the Teacher in II,1-3, this passage is thought to refer to a historical episode in which the Wicked Priest attacked the Teacher and his community.

> (2) WOE TO HIM WHO GIVES HIS NEIGHBORS TO DRINK, MIXING IN (3) HIS POISON, INDEED, MAKING (THEM) DRUNK IN ORDER THAT HE MIGHT LOOK UPON THEIR FEASTS.
> (4) The interpretation concerns the Wicked Priest, who (5) pursued the Teacher of Righteousness—to swallow him up with his poisonous vexation (6)—to his place of exile. And at the end of the feast (during) the repose of (7) The Day of Atonement, he appeared to them to swallow them up (8) and to make them stumble on the Fast Day, their restful Sabbath.[59]

This passage is usually understood (1) as referring to the historical dispute between the Teacher of Righteousness and the Wicked Priest, (2) as witnessing Qumran's use of a different calendar from the one used at the Jerusalem temple,[60] and (3) as dating the conflict to a Day of Atonement.

What does this passage say concretely about the conflict? It paints the scene of the Wicked Priest's pursuit of the Teacher to his place of exile in order to kill him on the Day of Atonement. Where the Teacher's exile was located and which particular Day of Atonement is not mentioned. There is no necessity to assume that the Teacher was following a sectarian or unofficial religious calendar. The text simply says that the Wicked Priest appeared on the Day of Atonement. This important passage provides, therefore, no specific information on the nature of the conflict, where it happened, when it happened, nor its outcome.

XI,8-15 deals with the Wicked Priest as a figure of the past, but at the same time speaks of his future punishment by God. Using theological language, the pesharist accuses him of not circumcising the foreskin of his heart and of wandering on the paths of excess. XI,17–XII,6 deals with the punishment of the Wicked Priest for his mistreatment and plot to destroy the Poor. The latter can only be identified in a general way with the inhabitants of Jerusalem and its environs. This is supported by XIII,2-5, which speaks first of the Poor, then identifies Lebanon with the Council of the Community, and the Simple Ones of Judaea, who are the Doers of the Law.

While the person or persons responsible for the composition of 1QpHab may have had particular historical individuals in mind when speaking of the Teacher of Righteousness, the Liar, the Wicked Priest, the Doers of the Law (in Judaea), and the House of Absalom, they neither name them nor associate them with known and recognizable historical contexts. They do seem, however, to have been contemporaries. But nothing is reported about the specific issues disputed by the two main parties. No attempt is made to speak about the specific geographical location nor the time of the conflict(s). Therefore, while 1QpHab seems to be concerned with historical conflicts between the Wicked Priest, the Liar, and the Teacher of Righteousness, it fails to name these individuals and locate them in a known historical context.

b. *4QpPs 37*

As Stegemann has pointed out, and as analysis of 1QpHab has illustrated, both 1QpHab and 4QpPs 37 share an interest in the Teacher of Righteousness, the Wicked Priest, the Liar, and Ones Doing Violence to the Covenant.[61] The presence of this overlap in terminology allows one to affirm a clear exegetical relationship between these two documents. Does 4QpPs 37 provide more concrete information on the personalities involved in Qumran history as well as the time and place of their activity than does 1QpHab?

4QpPs 37 I,17–II,1 interprets Ps 37.7 as referring to the Liar, who led many astray with deceitful words. Those who were misled chose empty words, instead of obeying the Interpreter of Knowledge. The audience is informed that the consequence of following the Liar or of allowing oneself to be misled will be the destruction by sword, famine, and plague. The opposition of the Liar and the Interpreter depicted in this passage bears a stong resemblance to several passages in 1QpHab (II,1-3; IX,9-12; X,3-5, 9-13) and CD (I; XIX,24–XX,4, 8-12).

Continuing the future orientation related to the judgment on the Liar and the misled, II,1-4 on Ps. 37.8-9a says that those who actually return to the Law will not be cut off. Those who fail to repent will be destroyed. These statements do not provide information that is useful for historical reconstruction, but do function as admonitions directed toward those who may potentially repent and threats to those who will not.

The subsequent pericope, II,4-5, interpreting 37.10, concerns the destruction of the Wicked at the end of the forty years. This recalls the period of time that will extend from the 'gathering' of the Teacher of the *Yaḥîd* until the destruction of all the men of war, who apostasized with the Liar, that is, about forty years (CD XX,13-15). Read in light of the subsequent section, II,8-11, on Ps. 37.11, one may safely conclude that the forty years were understood as a period of affliction, perhaps a sort of abbreviated dominion of Belial. Typologically, this is a wilderness or exile period. The accent seems to be less on the entire period of forty years and specific historical conflicts in that period than on the *end* of the forty years, which lies at some unspecified time in the future, when God will destroy the Wicked and deliver the Faithful.

II,12-15 on 37.12-13 reiterates the theme of the eventual destruction of the evil ones, in this case of Those (in Judaea) Doing Violence to the Covenant and plotting against the Doers of the Law who belong to the Council of the Community. In II,15-19, the theme of the geographical expansion of the wicked from Judaea into Ephraim and Manasseh is taken up, and they are accused of wanting to stretch out their hand against the Priest and his Council at the Time of Purification or Testing. At the end of this period, the pesharist says, God will save the Doers of the Law.

The theme of salvation is echoed in III,1-2, which interprets 37.19. It is said that the Returnees from the Wilderness will live for 1000 generations and will receive, along with their offspring, the portion of Adam. The notion of divine protection during the famine associated with the period of confusion is taken up again in III,3-5.

Then a shift occurs in mood with III,7-8, which speaks of the destruction of the godless.

The pesharist returns in III,9-11, interpreting 37.21-22, to speak about the inheritance of the Community of the Poor, which will receive Israel's high mountain. The theme and mood returns once again in III,11-13 to the Ones Doing Violence to the Covenant, the Godless of Israel, who will be eternally exterminated. The shift from the theme of the Righteous to that of the Wicked is precipitated by the presence of the word [מקול]לו in 37.22.

In III,14-17 where 37.23-24 is interpreted, the Priest is identified as the Teacher of Righteousness, whom God chose to build a community.[62] The substance of this passage resembles what is recorded in 1QpHab I,16–II,10. In the latter, the Teacher/Priest is presented as a figure of the past. III,14-17 reveals nothing about the historical identity of this Teacher and his community.

IV,7-10 presents an interpretation on 37.32-33 that reminds one of the event-like statement in 1QpHab XI,2-7.

> (8) The interpretation of it concerns (the) Wicked (Pr)iest, who l(ay) in ambush for the Teache)r of Righteous(ness and sought to) murder him and the Law(9) that he sent to him: but God will not ab(andon him into his hands) nor (will he let him be condemned as guilty when) he comes to trial. But as for (him, God will) pay (him) his due, giving him (10) into the hand of the ruthless ones of the Gentiles to wreak vengeance on him.[63]

Both passages share the basic theme of an attack of the Wicked Priest on the Teacher of Righteousness at some time in the past. 4QpPs 37 IV,7-10 differs from 1QpHab XI,2-7, however, in that a promise is made of divine protection for the Teacher and destruction for the Wicked Priest. 1QpHab XI,1-7 evidences only the existence of a conflict. But 1QpHab XI,14-15 speaks of God's judgment on the Wicked Priest. Neither specific motivations for the behavior of the Wicked Priest nor concrete details of his confrontation with the Teacher are given.

Several passages in 4QpPs 37 have been investigated for their relevance to the question of the history of the Qumran community: I,17–II,1; II,1-4, 4-5, 8-11, 12-15, 15-19; III,1-2, 3-5, 7-8, 9-11, 9-13; IV,7-10. 4QpPs 37 gives the impression of being primarily concerned with the punishment of the Wicked and the salvation of the Doers of the Law. With the exception of I,17–II,1, which depicts the Liar and the Misled in contrast to the Interpreter of Knowledge, III,14-17, which speaks of the Teacher, and IV,7-10, which sets the Wicked Priest and the Teacher in opposition, the passages in 4QpPs 37 are predominantly concerned with the destruction of the Wicked. Even in passages that mention individual figures, this interest in a future judgment is not absent (e.g. II,1; IV,9-10).

As was the case in 1QpHab, the passages mentioning the Teacher, the Interpreter of Knowledge, the Liar, and the Wicked Priest fail to present information that would help the historian to make secure identifications, such as information about the locality of conflicts, affiliations of the figures with known historical persons or parties, concrete descriptions of human activities, and chronological notes. Even the statements in 1QpHab and 4QpPs 37 about the punishment of the Wicked Priest are phrased as predictions of his future fate rather than as an accomplished fact. One can only say with certainty that both 1QpHab and 4QpPs 37 presents these figures as contemporaries of the writers' past. Thus they can say nothing concrete about the specific history of the Qumran community.

c. *4QpNah*

4QpNah is related to 1QpHab and 4QpPs 37 by virtue of sharing the same exegetical approach to a biblical text, the so-called continuous pesher-interpretation. Unlike 1QpHab and 4QpPs 37, 4QpNah does not mention the Wicked Priest, the Teacher of Righteousness, the Liar, and Ones Doing Violence to the Covenant.[64] On the other hand, 4QpNah knows the Seekers after Smooth Things; these are not mentioned in 1QpHab and 4QpPs 37. But 1QpHab and 4QpNah share an interest in the Kittim, not mentioned in 4QpPs 37. 4QpPs 37 and 4QpNah both mention Ephraim and Manasseh, which are not mentioned in 1QpHab. Thus 4QpNah does share some of the same thematic interests illustrated in 1QpHab and 4QpPs 37. However, key figures associated with Qumran history, such as the Teacher, the Wicked Priest, the Liar, and the House of Absalom are absent from it. What is then the relevance of 4QpNah to the history of the Qumran community?

While it is widely thought that sections of 1QpHab, 4QpPs 37, and CD refer to the period when the Teacher of Righteousness was still active, 4QpNah presumably provides information on the period between his demise and future-looking, eschatological events mentioned in the same documents.[65] There is no compelling evidence within 4QpNah that clearly supports the assumption that it is concerned with the time after the death of the Teacher. 4QpNah reports nothing about the conflict between the Wicked Priest, the Liar, and the Teacher nor about them individually. Nevertheless, the discussion above in section 2.a demonstrated that the Seekers after Smooth Things are to be identified with the community of the Liar. It is less clear, however, whether the Liar was a figure of the past or whether he was included among the ranks of the Seekers after Smooth Things. The identification of this group with the Liar's followers is based on the appearance of both the Liar and the Seekers after Smooth Things in CD I. The pesharist of 4QpNah does not explicitly mention the Liar (nor the Teacher and the Wicked Priest), but I,2 indicates that this group was involved in this political history of Judaea—apparently in the pre-Christian period.

Unlike CD, 1QpHab, and 4QpPs 37, 4QpNah I,1-14 preserves personal names in addition to symbolic designations. In this passage, the Seekers after Smooth Things, the Liar's community, are mentioned.

> (11) WHERE THE LION WENT TO ENTER, THE LION'S CUB (12) (AND NO ONE TO DISTURB. The interpretation of it concerns Deme)trius, King of Greece, who sought to enter Jerusalem on the advice of the Seekers-after-Smooth-Things, (13) (but God did not give Jerusalem) into the power of the Kings of Greece from Antiochus until the rise of the rulers of the Kittim; but afterwards (the city) will be trampled (14) (and will be given into the hand of the rulers of the Kittim).[66]

One recognizes immediately that the method of interpretation is identical in 1QpHab, 4QpPs 37, and 4QpNah, but the specific content of the Nahum pesher is entirely different. The pesharist interprets the word ארי in the quotation of Nah. 2.12 as referring to a certain Demetrius, a Greek king, who had attempted—in collusion with the Seekers after Smooth Things—unsuccessfully to enter Jerusalem. That occurred, according to the pesharist, during the period of Greek monarchs from Antiochus until the emergence of the Kittim (=Romans?).

The direct reference to personal names distinguishes this passage from those in other pesharim. Since the pesharist seems to be listing Hellenistic monarchs from the earliest down to the latest, and one may perhaps assume that the pesharist is writing from the most recent perspective, one would naturally draw the conclusion that the pesharist lived at the time of the Kittim or Romans. While a great amount of interest has been directed toward identifying Demetrius and Antiochus,[67] the crucial issue in regard to the history of the Qumran community is the identity of Those Seeking after Smooth Things/the Liar's community. They are often identified as the Pharisees of the first century BCE.[68] Neither 4QpNah I,2 nor 4QpIsa[c] 23 ii 10, where they are mentioned in connection with the end-time, presents any specifics about their relationship to Qumran history. The concern of this passage seems to be the attempt of some Pharisees to assist Demetrius III Eukeros (95–88 BCE) to capture the city of Jerusalem. I,4-6 suggests a continuing exegetical concern with a foreign ruler.

In I,4-6, one expects a continuing exegetical concern with a foreign ruler.

> (4) THE LION TEARS ENOUGH FOR ITS CUBS AND STRANGLES PREY FOR HIS LIONESS (5) (its interpretation) concerns the Lion of Wrath, who would strike with his great ones and his partisans.[69]

If one applies the exegetical approach used in I,1-4 to the pesher on Nah. 2.5, the Lion of Wrath would also seem to be a foreign ruler. If ארי was understood as Demetrius and a long line of non-Jewish rulers, is it not logical that כפיר החרון might also refer to a foreign ruler? Perhaps, but this passage provides too little concrete information for the historian to be sure.

According to most Qumran investigators, the next section, I,6-8, gives the clue to the identity of the Lion of Wrath.

> (6) (AND IT FILLS UP) ITS CAVE(?) WITH PREY) AND ITS DEN WITH TORN FLESH. The intepretation of it concerns the Lion of Wrath, (7) (*mwt* in the Seekers-after-Smooth-Things; he would hang men up alive (8) (upon the tree,) in Israel before, for regarding one hanged alive upon the tree (it) reads. . .[70]

The large majority of scholars identifies the Lion of Wrath with Alexander Jannaeus and associates the expression 'hanging men up alive' with his crucifixion of 800 Pharisees.[71] He had reason to dislike them, for they had questioned his legitimacy and appealed to the Seleucid Demetrius III for assistance against him.[72]

If the identifications of Demetrius (l. 2) with Demetrius III and of the Lion of Wrath (l. 6) with Alexander Jannaeus are correct, then the allusion to 'hanging men up alive' (l. 8) would seem to refer logically to Jannaeus' crucifixion of a group of his Pharisaic opponents c. 90 BCE. Acordingly, these opponents would have been members of the Liar's community. Thus, although 4QpNah does not speak of the conflict between the Liar and the Teacher nor of that between the Wicked Priest and the Teacher, known from other literary contexts, it does present information that enables the historian to assign a date to the political activities of the Liar's community—the Seekers after Smooth Things.

No other personal names are mentioned in the remainder of 4QpNah. I,10-11 speaks about the presence of foreign armies in Jerusalem and of the last priests. In II,2 the devastation moves from Judaea to Ephraim, who is identified with the Seekers after Smooth Things at the end-time. This thought is continued in II,9-10. In III,4-5, Judaea and Ephraim are opposed much as the Teacher and the Wicked Priest/Liar were opposed in 1QpHab and 4QpPs 37. Manasseh is introduced as a companion figure to Ephraim in III,9 and IV,3-6.

As shown above in section 2.a, the pesharist of 4QpNah II,2 could also use the name Ephraim symbolically to refer to the Seekers after Smooth Things. He writes that this group is full of lies and deception—like the Liar. Later, in IV,3 he speaks of the dominion of Manasseh in terms similar to those used to refer to the dominion of Ephraim in II,4. The pesharist provides too little information to help the historian decide conclusively whether he understands Ephraim and Manasseh as two different groups or just one. Interestingly, Ephraim is consistently described in terms reminiscent of the Liar (see section 2.a above). In II,4, the pesharist speaks of the *memšelet* of the Seekers after Smooth Things. This reminds one of the statement about the Wicked Priest ruling in Israel in 1QpHab VIII,9-10. When 4QpNah IV,3 refers also to the end of Manasseh's dominion, this seems to echo what is said both in 1QpHab VIII,9-10 and 4QpNah II,4. Although one cannot be certain, Ephraim and Manasseh seem to be two symbolic names given to the Seekers after Smooth Things. It has already been established that this group was identical with the Liar's community. 4QpNah IV,3 suggests that Manasseh may refer to the Wicked Priest and his community. In any case, the Liar's community, if not also the Liar, can be dated to the early years of the first century BCE and also associated with the political history of the city of Jerusalem. 4QpPs 37 II,17-18 suggests that Ephraim, the Liar's community, and Manasseh were contemporary with the Teacher of Righteousness and his community and had tried to do them harm. This conflict would then date by inference to the period around 90 BCE.

Conclusion

As the pesharim have often functioned in historical studies as an important, if not the most significant, body of evidence concerning the history of the Qumran community, they required analysis in terms of their structure, language, and possible historical relevance. The actual assessment of the pesharim was preceded by a discussion of the genre 'pesher'. The 'pesher' is a form of interpreting divine oracles with roots in the dream and vision interpretation of Gen. 40–41 and Daniel. Despite the general resemblances between the biblical dream/vision interpretations and the pesher-interpretation, it was pointed out that the pesharim lack any narrative framework which might have provided valuable information for use in historical reconstruction. Modern exegetes and historians of Qumran texts provide this framework by interpreting the pesharim as primary sources for the history of the Qumran community. Thus the analysis of the language and intention of each individual pesher becomes at the same time a critical dialogue with those scholars who believe that the pesharim are primarily concerned with the sectarian history of the Qumran/Essene community.

Attention was given to three pesharim in particular—1QpHab, 4QpPs 37, and 4QpNah. The various pericopes in each document were investigated in regard to their informational value for historical study. An attempt was made to find specific and concrete statements about the Teacher of Righteousness, the Liar, the Wicked Priest, and the conflict between their respective groups. Special attention was given to the interpretation of the Seekers after Smooth Things. The texts were also interrogated for information about the locality of these figures and the period in which they lived.

Even the most event-like statements, e.g. 1QpHab II,1-3 and 4QpPs 37 IV,2-7, were found to lack specific information necessary for reconstructing history. The specific issue that created the rivalry between the Teacher of Righteousness and the Wicked Priest/the Liar, who were apparently contemporaries, is never really spelled out. The Wicked Priest and the Liar are accused generally of having rebelled against God, his Teacher, and the divine statutes. Nothing concrete is known about the members of each leader's group. They are usually characterized as Doers of the Law or the Wicked. Of Stegemann's four criteria for determining the time when the Wicked Priest was active as well as his identity, only the second seems to be helpful. The Wicked Priest may have been a high priest at some time from the early post-exilic period into the first century BCE and would therefore have exercised a regnal function. It is less clear whether הרשע refers to the illegitimacy of his high-priestly function due to family lineage. הרשע is probably used as a general term to contrast him with the righteous, specifically the Teacher of Righteousness and the Doers of the Law. Thus, while the Wicked Priest may have been a high priest, he was not necessarily a non-Zadokite. After all, he had been 'called by the name of Truth at first'. In combination with the second criterion, Stegemann used his fourth criterion—that the Wicked Priest was killed by Gentiles outside of Judaea—to determine the identity of the Wicked (high) Priest. This criterion proved also to be less than convincing. It is based on the fragmentary passage 1QpHab VIII,16–IX,2 which refers to the physical suffering of the Wicked Priest. It is unclear who caused him to suffer or when this occurred. Nowhere else in the Qumran texts is this motif presented as an event of the past. In several passages (1QpHab X,4-5; XI,12-15; XII,2-6; 4QpPs 37 II,17-19; III,7-8; IV,8-10), it seems to function as a description of God's future judgment of the Wicked Priest and the wicked. This description serves as a contrast to the salvation of the righteous. Clearly, Stegemann's second criterion does suggest that the Wicked Priest may have been a high priest, but neither it nor the other criteria actually enable one to determine when this figure and his contemporaries, the Teacher, the Liar, and the House of Absalom were active. Thus the information provided by the pesharim, concerning the Teacher, the Wicked Priest, the Liar, and the House of Absalom, is not of the kind that the historian can use independently. Assuming that the pesharim do in fact refer, by means of their cryptic language, to specific historical episodes, one would need to know more about the persons and events involved from other historical sources.

The one document that does make a connection with recorded political history and provides a chronological benchmark is 4QpNah. In I,2-8, it is said that Demetrius, widely identified as Demetrius III, attempted to enter Jerusalem at the urging of a group called the Seekers after Smooth Things. Stegemann has convincingly argued that this was the Liar's community. Thus, this community was politically active during the reign of Demetrius III. I,4-8 adds crucial information that helps the historian to understand this political involvement better. It mentions the Lion of Wrath, who took revenge on the Seekers after Smooth Things. Although the text is damaged at this point, it does say that he 'hung men up alive'. Most Qumran scholars understand I,2-8 as referring to Alexander Jannaeus' crucifixion of a group of Pharisees, who had requested that Demetrius III take Jerusalem. Accordingly, Demetrius is Demetrius III, the Lion of Wrath is Alexander Jannaeus, and the Seekers after Smooth Things are a group of Pharisees. All three were important actors in the political history of Jerusalem c. 90 BCE.

Even if the Seekers after Smooth Things should be Pharisees in the early years of the first century BCE, several other issues are not clarified in 4QpNah. If the Liar's community consisted of Pharisees, who were then the Teacher of Righteousness and his community? While one might think of them as Sadducees or even Essenes, this is not clear from the context of 4QpNah (nor from the other pesharim). Certainly, the current consensus views the Teacher of Righteousness and his community as Essenes, but Josephus depicts the Essenes as Jews who were politically passive, leaving the course of history in God's hands. Of course, even this characterization is not applied consistently. This may also be an oversimplification. But Josephus' narrative of Jewish politics in the Second Temple period from the Hasmonean period concerns almost exclusively the Pharisees and Sadducees. One might entertain the possibility that the Seekers after Smooth Things (and the Liar) and the Teacher's community were originally members of the same sectarian group—the Pharisees. None of the sectarian documents from Qumran provides the necessary information to substantiate this identification.

The other problem suggested by the juxtaposition of CD, 1QpHab, 4QpPs 37, and 4QpNah is the chronological relationship of the Seekers after Smooth Things of the latter to the conflict between the Teacher of Righteousness and the Liar as well as between the Teacher and the Priest. 4QpNah reports nothing about these conflicts, so that one cannot factually determine whether the Teacher, the Liar, and the Wicked Priest were figures of the past or contemporaries of the Seekers after Smooth Things mentioned in 4QpNah I (and other columns) or even later figures. One can at least date the Seekers after Smooth Things to c. 90 BCE and know that they probably consisted of Pharisees who were involved in the political history of that time.

Chapter 7

4QTESTIMONIA AND THE HISTORY OF THE QUMRAN COMMUNITY

A. *Structural Considerations*

Several analysts think that 4QTest preserves information that is relevant to the history of the Qumran community. Cross and others have drawn attention to the expressions 'accursed man, one of Belial' and 'instruments of violence' (l. 25), which they believe allude to and can be identified with known historical figures.[1] Stegemann admits that the various pericopes (*Worte*) of 4QTest may have had concrete historical referents at some time, but points out that the present form of the document, an authoritative collection of citations or testimonia, deals with figures of the end-time and should, for that reason, be disqualified from consideration as possible evidence for Qumran history.[2] In order to reassess the value of 4QTest for reconstructing the history of the Qumran community, attention should first be given to its structure, genre, and language.

Only one page consisting of a series of biblical citations plus one non-biblical citation along with its interpretation is extant: Deut. 5.28-29; 18.18-19; Num. 24.15-17; Deut. 33.8-11, and a citation from an apocryphal psalm of Joshua that is similar to Josh. 6.26.[3]

George Brooke has outlined 4QTest, thereby helping to highlight its chief interests.[4]

I. Those favoured by God — 4QTest 1-20
 A. Exod. 20.21 (Sam) — 1-8
  1. Introductory formula
  2. Yahweh speech proper
   a. Concerning Yahweh's attitude to the people (MT: Deut. 5.28-29)
    (1) Concerning the correctness (הטיב) of their words

(2) Wish for their continual well-being (הטיב)
b. Concerning future action with the prophet (MT: Deut. 18.18-19)
(1) Raise him up
(2) Put words into his mouth
(3) Require account of those who do not heed him

B. Num. 24.15-17 9-13
1. Introductory formula
2. Oracle
a. Announcement
b. Oracle proper
(1) Concerning הגבר
(2) Concerning כוכב and שבט

C. Deut. 33.8-11 14-20
1. Introductory formula
2. Content of blessing
a. Command
b. Statement of future work of priesthood
(1) To cause precepts to shine to Jacob,
Law to Israel
(2) To offer incense and burnt offerings
c. Blessing proper
(1) Blessing
(2) Request for smiting of haters

II. Those cursed by God 21-30
A. Introduction
B. Quotation and Commentary (4QPssJosh)
1. Josh. 6.26b (less יריחו = LXX)
2. Commentary
a. Concerning the accursed man
(1) Announcement of existence of man of Belial
(2) Description of purpose of existence
(a) To be a fowler's net to his people
(b) to be a cause of destruction of his neighbors
b. Concerning two sons (or) Concerning the brother

b. Concerning two sons (or)
Concerning one brother
(1) Identification as vessels of violence
(2) Their actions

According to this outline, ll. 1-20 concern those whom God favors and ll. 21-30 concern those who are cursed by God. Closer examination of the citations forming ll. 1-20 reveals that they also deal with the theme of 'the curse' that dominates ll. 21-30. In order to grasp the meaning of the terms used in these lines, the structure of ll. 1-20 must also be analyzed.

The dichotomy between the obedient and the disobedient is accentuated by the juxtaposition of Deut. 5.28-29 and Deut. 18.18-19.

(ll. 3-4) לשמור את כול מצותי כול היומים
(ll. 6-7) האיש אשר לוא ישמע אל דברי

This juxtaposition contrasts the themes of the obedience of the people (העם) with the disobedience of anyone (האיש) who might not obey God's future prophet. The consequences of these two opposite kinds of behavior, obedience and disobedience, are also paralleled in the citations.

The obedient	למעאן יטב להם ולבניהם לעולם	(l. 4)
The disobedient	אדרוש מעמו	(ll. 7-8)

In the following section, Num. 24.15-17 seems to suggest that Bileam is the future prophet promised in Deut. 18.18-19, whose oracle should be believed. Bileam's oracle functions as a concrete example of God's word נאום (l. 9). The prophet is praised as one who hears, knows, and see God's plan.

(ll. 10-11) נואם שומע אמרי אל וידע דעת עליון
אשר מחזה שדי יחזה נופל וגלו עין

The specific 'word' or 'oracle' under consideration concerns 'the star out of Jacob and the scepter out of Israel' that will shatter the forehead of Moab and annihilate all the sons of Seth.[5]

The dichotomy in ll. 1-8 between the obedient and the disobedient is not explicitly pursued in ll. 9-13. Rather, a future, divine destruction by means of the 'Star' and the 'Scepter' is emphasized.

The verbs מחץ and קרקר in ll. 12-13 echo the intent of the divine threat found in the first pericope: אדרוש מעמו (l. 8). The בני שית and the פאתי מואב stand in relation to האיש אשר לוא ישמע as כוכב and שבט do to God.

In ll. 14-20 a structure similar to that of ll. 1-8 is present. The obedient is identified with Levi, who observes God's word and keeps his covenant.

כי שמר אמרתכה ובריתך ינצר (l. 17)

The MT of Deut. 33:9c preserves the plural forms שמרו and ינצרו, which refer to the Levites rather than to Levi alone. The other verbs in ll. 17-18 and in Deut. 33.10 (MT) are also plural, indicating conclusively that the Levites are the subject. In ll. 19-20 a blessing on the Levites and a curse on their enemies are uttered. The blessing corresponds to the promise of welfare for the obedient in l. 4.

למאען יטב להם ולבניהם לעולם (l. 4)
ברך (l. 19)

The command to smite the enemies of the Levites (l. 19) echoes earlier threats in 4QTest.

אדרוש (l. 8)
מחץ פאתי מואב וקרקר את כול בני שית (ll. 12-13)
מחץ מתנים קמו ומשנאו בל יקומו (l. 19)

The last two words of Deut. 33.11, בל יקומו ('so that they not rise again') emphasize the utter extermination of the enemies of the Levites in the future.[6]

In order to understand the character of ll. 1-20, it is necessary to note how the compiler's selection and arrangement of biblical quotations would have suggested a forward-looking, prophetic perspective to his ancient readers. The initial quotation of Deut. 5.28-29 sets the scene for the train of thought that will follow: God tells Moses that he hopes the people will be obedient so that it will be good for them and their children all the days (לעולם, כול היומים). The quotation of Deut. 18.18-19, concerning the future prophet that God will cause to arise, is used to adumbrate the people's potential for disobedience. Then Bileam's oracle concerning the Star and the Scepter (Num. 24.15-17) is introduced, presenting Bileam as the promised prophet who speaks concerning one who will arise to destroy Israel's enemies at some future time. Concluding Part I of 4QTest (according to Brooke's outline), Deut. 33.8-11 is quoted in order to emphasize the obedience of Levi as well as his functions as teacher of law and as one who sacrifices to God. This quotation concludes with the command to annihilate Levi's (the Levites') enemies. Had 4QTest ended at this point, one would have the impression that the compiler is concerned primarily with the eventual destruction of the disobedient among the Israelites and Israel's enemies.

According to Brooke's outline, Part II of 4QTest, ll. 21-30, pursues the companion themes of disobedience and its consequences, which are already foreshadowed in ll. 6-7: 'and whoever should not obey my words which the prophet says in my name, I will require of him'. This section opens with an introduction to a citation. The introduction is mostly non-biblical, but the words בעת make the verbal connection with Josh. 6.26:

(l. 21) בעת אשר כלה ישוע להלל ולהודות בתהלותיהו

Joshua's subsequent speech is introduced by ויאמר rather than the biblical לאמר. Then follows the quotation of Josh. 6.26.

(ll. 22-23) ארור היש אשר יבנה את העיר הזות בבכורו
ייסדנה ובצעירו יצב דלתיה

Besides a few orthographic variations, the citation of Josh. 6.26 in 4QTest 22-23 preserves several textual deviations from the MT. (1) The phrase לפני יהוה is absent. LXX[B] and LXX[L] transpose it before λέγων. This omission from 4QTest does not seem to be significant. (2) MT יקום does not appear in 4QTest 22. Perhaps this is simply an attempt to avoid repeating a word used already in line 20. It is also lacking in the LXX. (3) Whereas the MT uses the consecutive form of ובנה after the imperfect יקום, 4QTest 22 uses the imperfect form יבנה. (4) Finally, the identifying phrase את יריחו that stands in apposition to העיר הזאת in the MT is absent from 4QTest 22(=LXX). This omission may be significant, but, as with all of the deviations, this depends upon how they are or are not treated in the explanatory material that follows the citation.

4QTest 23-30

(23) ואנה איש ארור אחד בליעל
(24) עומד להיות פ[ח י]קוש לעמו ומחתה לכול שכניו ועמד
(25) [ ]מ[לה]יות שניהמה כלי חמס ושבו ובנו את
(26) [העיר הזות ויצ]יבו לה חומה ומגדלים לעשות לעוז רשע
(27) [ורעה גדולה] בישראל ושערוריה באפרים וביהודה
(28) וע]שו חנופה בארץ ונצה גדולה בבני
(29) [יעקוב ושפכו ד]ם כמים על חל בת ציון ובחוק
(30) ירושלים[7]

In contrast to the use of biblical quotations in ll. 1-20, elements in the quotation of Josh. 6.26 are taken up one by one and explained in ll. 21-30. Although an introductory formula separating the text and its interpretation is lacking, this kind of interpretation is essentially identical with the pesher. In the explanation, the curse formula ארור is treated as an attribute of the noun. Furthermore, 'an accursed man' is designated as 'one of Belial' (l. 24). In the quote, this figure is accused of rebuilding a city, but in the explanation he is accused of becoming a trap to his people and a terror to all his neighbors (ll. 24-25). In l. 25, which is damaged at an important place in the explanation, a transition seems to have been made from 'the accursed one of Belial' to an elucidation of the words כלי חמס and שניהמה. These expressions are interpreted as 'two instruments of violence'. The connection with the citation is made again in the description of the activities of these 'instruments'. They are accused of שבו ובנו 'repeatedly rebuilding' [this city and esta]blishing for it a wall and towers. The 'building' theme (יבננה, l. 22) is echoed in l. 25 (בנו). The theme of 'erecting' (יצב, l. 23) is taken up in l. 26 (יצ[י]בו). The words מגדלים and חומה (l. 25) recall the word דלתיה (l. 23). Only one element is not reiterated in the order of its appearance in the citation, the expression את יריחו. Several elements in ll. 26-30 compensate for this omission: mention is made of Israel, Ephraim, Judaea, the land, the sons of Jacob, the daughter of Zion, and Jerusalem. The use of these terms tends to apply the prophecy to the geographical territory of Israel and Judaea.

The rationale for the juxtaposition of ll. 21-30, the quotation of Josh. 6.26 and its interpretation, with the first part of 4QTest (ll. 1-20=Deut. 5.28-29; 18.18-19; Num. 24.15-17; Deut. 33.8-11) is difficult to discover. The compiler may have intended to contrast the 'accursed man, one of Belial' with the positive figures in ll. 1-20—the future prophet, Bileam, the Star and the Scepter, and Levi. In any case, ll. 21-30 pursue the negative aspect of the dichotomy established in the foregoing lines between the obedient and the disobedient, the Star-Scepter and Moabites-Sethites, and Levi (the Levites) and his enemies.

Forming a contrast to the juxtaposition of biblical passages in ll. 1-20, the essentially pesher type of interpretation of Josh. 6.26 induces readers, probably the ancient as well as the modern ones, to attempt to identify the man of Belial. The man of Belial and his sons (or brother) are made responsible for doing evil in Israel, Ephraim,

Judah, the land, among the sons of Jacob, against the daughter of Zion, and in Jerusalem. There are no obvious exegetical grounds for associating the activities of the man of Belial and his sons with the conflict involving the characters delineated in 1QpHab, 4QpPs 37, and CD—the Teacher of Righteousness, the Wicked Priest, the Liar, and the House of Absalom.

It was noted above that the selection and arrangement of the biblical quotations in ll. 1-20 form a prophetic and future-oriented section. Both individually and collectively, these quotations suggest that those who do not obey God's prophet as well as Israel's and Levi's enemies will eventually be destroyed. The quotation of Josh. 6.26 in ll. 22-23 is also temporally open-ended. Taken together with the phrase ארור האיש ('cursed is the one who'), the imperfect verb forms יבנה, ייסדנה, and יצב imply that this prophecy might refer to the activities of a man of Belial at some undetermined time—either in the present or in the future. Lines 23-24 do explain the elements in the quotation, but do not determine the time of the accursed man's activity more specifically. The verbal forms in the interpretative section itself do not really clarify the temporal perspective: עומד and עמד in l. 24, שבו ובנו in l. 25, [יצ]יבו in l. 26, and [ע]שו or [יע]שו in l. 28, and ושפכו in l. 29. Lohse translates the verbs in l. 24 as a present tense.[8] Except for the last verb עמד, which he also treats as a present tense, he renders the remainder of the verbs in the future tense. Cross translates every verb as a future tense.[9] Clearly, nothing in the quotation of Josh. 6.26 and its interpretation urges one to understand the activity of the man of Belial and his sons (or brother) as already accomplished.

B. *Relevance for the History of the Qumran Community*

Several analysts assume that the expressions 'an accursed man, one of Belial' and 'the two instruments of violence' allude to enemies of the Qumran community and have identified them with figures of Judaean history in the second and first centuries BCE.[10] One group thinks that these terms refer to a father and his two sons. Another interprets them as two brothers. Owing to the fragmented condition of l. 25, where the transition is made from a description of the activity 'an accursed man, one of Belial' to 'the two instruments of violence', one cannot determine which view is empirically correct.[11] Nevertheless, the citation of Josh. 6.26 does refer to a man and his two sons, and one may assume that 4QTest 23-30 would as well.

Frank M. Cross, Jr thinks there can be no mistake about the historical persons intended by the allusions.

> The passage assuredly applies to an archenemy of the sect. The application of the passage to Simon and his older and younger sons, Judas and Mattathias, and their deaths in Jericho seems to the writer almost inevitable. The slaughter in Jerusalem and its environs described in the last lines reflects the attack of Antiochus Sidetes upon Judaea in 134–132 BC. immediately following Simon's death.[12]

In this statement, Cross makes three claims that deserve further consideration. (1) 'An accursed man, one of Belial' alludes to Simon Maccabeus; 'the two instruments of violence', to his sons Judas and Mattathias (ll. 23-25). (2) 4QTest alludes to their death in Jericho. (3) Lines 26-30 allude to the attack of Antiochus VII Sidetes upon Judaea in 134–132 BCE. Taking the last point first, ll. 26-30 make no clear allusion to any particular person. Where one places the responsibility for the slaughter in Jerusalem depends upon one's restoration of the verb in l. 29. Cross now seems to restore a pual sg. ושפך, translated '[shall be poured out]'.[13] This restoration would leave the text entirely unclear about the relationship between the activities of the 'accursed man' in ll. 21-25 and the evil done in the Holy Land and Jerusalem in ll. 26-30. If the 'accursed man' should be Simon Maccabeus and the two vessels of violence his sons, as Cross maintains, one might expect ll. 26-30 to continue the theme of their evil activities and not to switch to the attack of the Seleucid monarch, Antiochus Sidetes, on Judaea in 134–132 BCE. In any case, Cross's restoration is too equivocal to permit any precise historical identifications. Lohse restores ושפכו, implying that the two vessels of violence, and perhaps the man of Belial, is or will be responsible for the sacrilege and bloodshed in Jerusalem and the Holy Land. The restoration of a plural form would also be consistent with the verb forms used in ll. 25-28. But, as with Cross's restoration, this one is also speculative. As for the second claim, that 4QTest alludes to the deaths of Simon and his sons in Jericho, it need only be pointed out that neither the citation nor the interpretation mentions the city Jericho nor the deaths of 'an accursed man, one of Belial' and 'the two instruments of violence'. The text speaks simply of the evil done in Israel, Ephraim, Judah, Zion, and Jerusalem. The crucial issue is the first point raised by Cross, whether the 'accursed man' and the 'two instruments of violence' are to be identified with a father and his two sons—in particular Simon, Judas, and Mattathias.

A comparative look at how Josh. 6.26 was interpreted both in 1 Kgs 16.33-34 and in 4QTest should clarify the exegete's/historian's difficulty in using the statements of the latter in a historical reconstruction. Whereas the word האיש is rendered by the vague expression אחד בליעל in 4QTest, 1 Kgs 16.34 identifies this 'man' with a historical person bearing a name, Hiel of Bethel. The name of 'the city' is absent from the citation in 4QTest, but is associated with Israel, Ephraim, Judaea, and Jerusalem in the explanation. In 1 Kings 'the city' is Jericho. In 4QTest 'the firstborn' and 'the youngest' are rendered with the expression 'two instruments of violence'; in 1 Kgs 16.34, with the names of Hiel's sons, Abiram and Segub. 1 Kgs 16.34 dates the fulfillment of the prophecy in Josh. 6.26 to the reign of Ahab (874–853 BCE): 'It was in his time. . ., just as Yahweh had foretold through Joshua son of Nun'. 4QTest 23-30 is also concerned with the meaning and fulfillment of the same prophecy, but the chronological information that would clearly associate it with a specific historical period is lacking. While the author of ll. 23-30 may have undertood the 'accursed man' and the 'two instruments of violence' as real historical persons, he does not reveal enough information to allow the Qumran historian to know which persons are meant. The narrative of the fulfilment of Josh. 6.26 in 1 Kings does this explicitly by reference both to named persons and by mention of the reign of an Israelite king. The interpretative approaches in 4QTest 21-30 and 1 Kgs 16.33-34 represent two modes of speaking of the fulfillment of prophecy. 4QTest seems to expect a second fulfillment of Josh. 6.26, or it ignores 1 Kgs 16.33-34, which is revealed only in highly ambiguous language.

The association of the 'accursed one' with Belial might be expected to preserve clues to this person's identity. An interest in 'Belial' is a feature of several other Qumran texts: 1QS II,5-7; 1QM XIII,14; CD IV,13-20; V,17-19; 4QpPs 37 II,9-10; 4QFlor I,8-9; II,2.

Except for CD V,17-19, no passages clearly refer to historical figures. In this passage, Belial is mentioned in the context of the history of Israel. At the time of Moses and Aaron, whom the Prince of Lights raised up, Belial also arose with Jannes and his brother to mislead Israel. This appeal to ancient history is used to underscore the similarity and continuity of the present activity of Belial with his past activity. Some passages speaking of the sons or the traps of Belial seem to refer to the eschatological future. 4QpPs 37 II,8-11 explains Ps. 37.11 as an allusion to the future preservation of the community of the poor from the traps of Belial. 4QFlor I,7-11(12) interprets 2 Sam. 7.11-14 as referring to the future rest that the Doers of the Law will enjoy, when God destroys the sons of Belial. Thus, although 4QTest's reference could be to known historical figures, it need not.

Conclusion

4QTest 1-20 preserves a collection of biblical quotations dealing with the obedient and disobedient in the last days. Lines 21-30 preserve a quotation from an unpublished apocryphal psalm of Joshua. The theme of the curse in Josh. 6.26 makes the connection with the foregoing, which speaks of the total annihilation of Levi's enemies. The prophecy of Josh. 6.26 is interpreted in ll. 23-25 as referring to the deeds of the 'accursed man, one of Belial' and 'two instruments of violence'. Some Qumran scholars identify these figures with known historical figures. Most of them interpret these references as allusions to a father and his two sons. A minority opinion thinks in terms of a man and his brother. Since the beginning of l. 25 is damaged, one cannot determine the relationship of the 'accursed man' to the 'instruments' with confidence. Owing to the damaged state of the text also at l. 29, it is impossible to know who would be responsible for pouring blood out on the ramparts of Jerusalem. Moreover, these figures are not named, and that is the key obstacle to their historical identification.

It is also difficult to establish a time-frame against which to understand their wicked deeds in the Holy Land. The quotation of Josh. 6.26 in ll. 21-22 is itself a prophecy open to a future fulfillment, which is explained in ll. 23-30. The verbs in ll. 22-23a, the quotation, are imperfect in form. The verb forms from l. 25 on are converted perfects and seem to require a future translation (as Cross, Lohse, and others have done). Analysis of other texts dealing with Belial did not provide information on the historical identities of the 'accursed one' and the 'instruments'. Except for CD V,17-19, the concern is with cursing Belial and God's judgment on him and his lot at some undetermined time. 4QFlor I,8-11(12) and 4QpPs 37 II,8-11 seem to understand this judgment on the sons of Belial as well as the salvation of the faithful as an event of the eschatological future.

Clearly, the difficulty in determining the precise chronological framework for understanding the statements in 4QTest 23-30 and in interpreting the references to an 'accursed man' and the 'instruments' prevent one from identifying them with known historical persons.

The structure of 4QTest as a whole suggests that its author was concerned to speak, albeit cryptically, about positive and negative figures of the eschatological future. Cross's view that the first three sections of 4QTest 1-20 deal with future figures—a prophet like Moses, priestly and royal messiahs, and a righteous teacher (or priestly messiah) seems to be correct. One need not assume, however, that this last figure already exists. The quotation does indeed speak of Levi or the Levites in the past, but its point is to underscore his/their continuing validity as teachers of the law for the present and future. These positive figures are matched in the second half of 4QTest 21-30 by reference to the accursed man of Belial and two instruments of violence. In CD V,17-19, the opposition of the Prince of Lights, Moses, and Aaron to Belial, Jannes, and his brother is used as a historical example representative of the kind of conflict between the forces of good and evil and its resolution in the age of the writer. 4QTest does the same with regard to the future, but does not mention the protagonists and antagonists by name.

Chapter 8

THE HODAYOT AND THE HISTORY OF THE QUMRAN COMMUNITY

A. *The Personal Experiences of the Teacher: The* Lehrerlieder

In his publication of 1QH, E.L. Sukenik presented the view that this document was composed by the Teacher of Righteousness who is mentioned in CD, 1QpHab, and 4QpPs 37.[1] Palaeographical analysis reveals that 1QH was perhaps authored, and certainly copied, in the Herodian period. Hand B, a later Herodian hand, replaces Hand A in col. X1,22 (see above Chapter 3 on Palaeography of the Dead Sea Scrolls). Thus 1QH was composed at an earlier time. In the 1960s Gert Jeremias offered a modification of this thesis on form-critical grounds, attributing only part of 1QH to the Teacher.[2] This view was shared by several of his colleagues at the Qumranforschungsstelle, and became widely accepted outside of West Germany.[3] The consequence of the modification of Sukenik's view for the historian is that only a certain group of the *hodayot* in 1QH is thought to be directly relevant to the history of the Qumran community. These are the *Lehrerlieder*, which report information on the life of the Teacher, his intimate relationship to God, his fear of adversaries, his concern for his community, and his claim to authority. Unlike the material in CD and the pesharim, these individual thanksgiving hymns are thought to come from the pen of the Teacher of Righteousness. If Jeremias's thesis is correct, the hymns would provide the only first-hand, eyewitness information about persons and events mentioned in the other Qumran documentation.

Geza Vermes has criticized this approach to the *Lehrerlieder*.

> Subjecting some of the Hymns to a form-critical analysis, and assuming furthermore that the Teacher of Righteousness was their author, they have deduced from vague poetic hints a whole detailed

> story of an internal struggle among the sectaries. But I am afraid that the matter is far too conjectural for any serious consideration.[4]

Vermes has questioned both the thesis of the Teacher's composition of the *Lehrerlieder* and their use in discussions about the internal history of the Qumran community. In order to reassess the correctness of using this material in a historical reconstruction, attention must first be given to Jeremias's modification of Sukenik's position and then to the nature of the language of the *Lehrerlieder*.

Jeremias's initial observation on 1QH is that it is not a unified work, but rather a collection consisting of hymns, psalms, and thanksgiving songs.[5] In col. I, a hymn, the Creator is praised. In X,1-12, a psalm, God is also praised as Creator. The psalms in XI,3-14, XII, and XIV have a didactic character. Sometimes an 'I' speaks. Jeremias distinguishes this 'I' from the one speaking about his personal relationship to God and his environment in the thanksgiving songs.[6] Jeremias points out that the one praying in the Old Testament psalms usually remains in the background. In contrast to this, he says, the one speaking in the first person singular in the thanksgiving songs from Qumran is an imposing personality who distinguishes himself from all other people.[7] This 'I' does not reflect the feelings of an ordinary person who has recently recovered from some sickness or mistreatment by his fellow human beings. Rather, it reflects the feelings of one who has had to suffer specifically because of his proclamation of God's marvelous secrets. Sometimes one finds a speaking 'we' instead of an 'I'.[8] However, only the psalms in which the very personal 'I' is speaking are thought to bear on the question of the identity and experiences of their author. Thus 1QH II,1-19; II,31-39; III,1-18; IV,5-V,4; V,5-19, 20–VII,5; VII,6-25; VIII,4-40 constitute Jeremias's collection of *Lehrerlieder*.[9]

In support of his view that 1QH is not a literary unity, Jeremias presents an analysis and comparison of the vocabulary of the *Lehrerlieder* and the other psalmic material in 1QH.[10] He comes to the conclusion that one can clearly distinguish the specific *Lehrerlieder* from the rest of 1QH on the basis of their distinctive vocabulary and use of figurative language. In contrast to the *Lehrerlieder*, the rest of 1QH is characterized by the use of wooden expressions and monotonous repetitions.[11]

After having separated the individual thanksgiving songs from the remainder of 1QH, Jeremias then poses the question whether the Teacher of Righteousness wrote them.[12] His affirmative answer to this question is tied closely to his interpretation of the 'I' that speaks in these psalms. He denies that the one speaking is a typical 'I' or an 'Ur-I' and maintains that it is the 'I' of a real, historical teacher who is keenly aware of his responsibility to a community. Not only does he view himself as a community's leader and teacher, the one represented by the speaking 'I' also claims to be the one who brings it salvation. From this, Jeremias infers that only an authoritative figure could have made the claim that God distinguishes through him the righteous from the wicked (VII,12).[13]

In addition to these general considerations in favor of the view that the Teacher composed the *Lehrerlieder*, Jeremias points out parallels with statements about the Teacher in other Qumran documents.[14] 1QpHab II,7-8 speaks of the Teacher (actually the Priest) as one taught by God and, according to Jeremias, as one who brings the only valid interpretation of the Law to the community. Similar statements are made in some of the *Lehrerlieder* (II,18; IV,27-29; VIII,16-17, 35-36). Jeremias maintains that it is impossible that two such imposing teachers could have existed in one and the same community during the same period of time and could have claimed to be the community's authoritative teacher and the messenger of God. Just as God taught the Teacher divine secrets in 1QpHab VII,5, so the one praying in the *Lehrerlieder* says that God had instructed him in the secrets of truth (II,17-19). Furthermore, both the *Lehrerlieder* and the pesharim seem to know of the Teacher's conflict within his own community (see especially the discussion of IV,5-V,4 below). 4QpPs 37 III,15-16 speaks of the Teacher as the founder, the builder, of a community. In the *Lehrerlieder*, he is said to have made the community possible (Jeremias does not cite any particular passage). Jeremias maintains that these correspondences with statements in the pesharim are not coincidental and says that they would circumstantially support the identification of the 'I' speaking in the *Lehrerlieder* with the Teacher mentioned in other Qumran texts.[15]

Jeremias emphasizes, however, that the *Lehrerlieder* are dealing with the desires and feelings of the Teacher, essentially private matters, and reveal almost nothing about the Teacher as a public figure in relationship to his followers and his adversaries.[16] For him, the distinctive value of the *Lehrerlieder* lies in their presentation of autobiographical concerns, such as the Teacher's relationship to God, his piety, and other experiences, which are neglected in the pesharim and CD.[17]

Stegemann, who agrees with Jeremias's form-critical separation of the *Lehrerlieder* from the remainder of 1QH and who also believes that the Teacher composed them, maintains, however, that they are valuable historical sources for information about the Teacher in relation to his adversaries.[18] In that respect, he parts ways with his colleague Jeremias.

Stegemann points out that the terminology denoting enemies in the *Lehrerlieder* is not historically intelligible, however, until one knows something about the enemies from other credible sources, such as CD and the pesharim.[19] While he is not at all skeptical about the historical or biographical value of statements about the Teacher's enemies in the *Lehrerlieder*, he does realize there are potential difficulties involved in using this information independent of that found in other sources in historical reconstruction. These difficulties are, however, not insurmountable.

> Diese Schwierigkeiten dürften sich aber einigermassen reduzieren lassen, falls es gelingt, zu den erforderlichen Vorkenntnissen zu gelangen. Denn die Bezugnahmen auf historische Personengruppen und Ereignisse sind der Sache nach und in ihrem Bezug zur Person des 'Lehrers' durchaus deutlich und nur deshalb praktisch unverständlich, weil keine Namen oder konkrete Sachbezeichnungen, sondern traditionelle biblische Wendungen und Termini dafür benutzt werden und der Autor seine Schilderungen nicht in der Form von 'Erlebnisberichten', sondern unter Verwendung von Stilelementen ähnlich denen der biblischen Psalmen vorträgt.[20]

In this statement, Stegemann underscores the major problems confronting anyone who tries to interpret the *Lehrerlieder* as historical sources about the Teacher and his enemies. (1) Persons are not named and events are not described concretely enough. (2) The *Lehrerlieder* are not historical reports in narrative form; rather, they are poetic descriptions built up out of traditional, biblical language known especially from the Psalms.

In the context of discussing difficulties in using the Qumran documentation to talk about enemies of the Teacher and his community, Stegemann makes the further point that the presentations of enemies in 1QH are by nature polemical, not intended to be historically objective, and suggests that they could reflect distorted descriptions of such enemies.[21] The possibility could also arise that these descriptions tend to level out different enemies, thus confusing their separate identities and the relative chronological order of their historical appearances.[22] Since Stegemann presumes that it is the Teacher who is reporting first-hand information about his enemies, he thinks that the chance of misrepresentation of them due to the chronological distance from the persons involved would be practically nil.

Still, Stegemann identifies the enemies of the *Lehrerlieder* with the community of the Liar ('die Lügenmann-Gemeinde')[23]: גבול רשעה (II,8), אנשי רמיה (II,16), פושעים (II,8, 11), רשעים (II,10, 24), בוגדים (II,10), לצים (II,11), עריצים (II,11, 21), מליצי תעות (II,14), דורשי חלקות (II,15), קהלת רשעים (II,12), מליצי כזב (II,31; IV,9f.), דורשי חלקות (II,32), דורשי רמיה (II,34), מליצי כזב (IV,7, 9f.), נביאי כזב, מפותי תעות (IV,16), אנשי מרמה and חוזי תעות (IV,20). Similar terminology is used in CD and the pesharim.

Thus two elements in the *Lehrerlieder* cause Qumran scholars to attribute them to the Teacher of Righteousness and to identify the one speaking with him. The first is the intensely personal and authoritative address of the 'I'. The second are the speaker's statements about his own personal and historical situation—chiefly his own situation *vis-à-vis* his enemies.

The problem of identifying the 'I' of the *Lehrerlieder* is not unlike the one of identifying the 'I' of the Old Testament psalms. Some scholars have favored a collective interpretation of the 'I'. R. Smend held the view that the Old Testament psalms were used as a 'Gesangbuch des zweiten Tempels' and drew the conclusion that the 'I' referred in most cases to the Jewish community of the Second Temple period.[24] E. Balla believed that the 'I' referred to an individual in the overwhelming majority of cases.[25] Both Smend and Balla did concede, however, that there were exceptions to their exclusively collective and individual interpretations. Based on statements made by de Wette, H. Birkeland offered an interpretation of the 'I', which affirmed the correctness both of the collective and the individual positions. He perceived that the 'I' could be understood both as an individual and as a representative of the community. For him this person was the king.[26] E. Gerstenberger thinks that one should not identify all instances of a speaking 'I' either with an individual or a nation: between these two extremes there are other possibilities, e.g. family situations, social associations, depending upon the actual use of the psalms.[27]

In Qumran studies, a collective and individual interpretation of the 'I' speaking in 1QH is associated with the name S. Holm-Nielsen, whose commentary on the *Hodayot* was published before Jeremias's dissertation. He recognizes that these poems are individual to the person reading them. At the same time, they can be used collectively for liturgical or instructional purposes.[28] He opts for liturgical usage within the community.[29]

On the form-critical level, which was also Jeremias's starting-point, Holm-Nielsen divides cols. II–IX into exegetical units almost exactly as Jeremias, Stegemann, and others had done. Instead of speaking of *Lehrerlieder*, which assumes the function and identity of the one speaking, he prefers to speak of this body of literary material as individual psalms of thanksgiving.[30] The dominating mood in these psalms is one of confidence, even in cases where some lamentation is found.[31]

Holm-Nielsen is skeptical about the historical import of these individual psalms of thanksgiving for the reconstruction of the history of the Qumran history. He recognizes that the portrayals of misery do give one the impression that an individual is speaking about his own personal dilemma, but points out that similar expressions are used in the Old Testament psalms to depict distressing situations of the individual (e.g. Pss. 22; 31; 42; 107).[32] In view of this literary observation, he suggests that one should not attempt to associate the scenes of misery in 1QH with a particular historical circumstance, unless the context actually urges such an interpretation.[33] Rather, he says, one should treat expressions and phrases that contribute to the creation of scenes of distress both in the Old Testament psalmic literature and 1QH 'as abstract rather than concrete, as illustrations and symbols rather than as portrayals of historical occurrences'.[34]

In a later publication, roughly contemporary with the appearance of Jeremias's work *Der Lehrer*, he does admit that these poetic works may have originally alluded to actual historical events and personal feelings. But since they were probably used in the worship of the Qumran community, any individual who read the 'I' could have identified himself with this figure and his dilemma, thereby seeing himself in the words and situations of the psalmist.[35] This claim may be also made for the 'I' of the Old Testament psalms.

B. *The Hodayot as Historical Sources*

It is undeniable that different readers may have perceived themselves in the situation of the 'I' in 1QH II–VIII. Nevertheless, Jeremias, Stegemann, and others were not speaking of the later use and understanding of the 'I' and the enemies in the *Lehrerlieder* but clearly of the original historical referents at the time of composition. Jeremias used the *Lehrerlieder* to talk about the spiritual life of the Teacher; Stegemann, about his historical adversaries. Thus Holm-Nielsen is not at all in disagreement with Jeremias, who admitted that the *Lehrerlieder* could not be used to reconstruct public history. His disagreement is with Stegemann and other scholars, who, he thinks, are unwarrantedly optimistic about the identification of the enemies mentioned in 1QH with those known from 1QpHab, 4QpPs 37, and CD. It would be profitable, therefore, to address the issue of the nature of the language about the 'I' and the enemies in 1QH before drawing any conclusions about the usefulness of this information for historical reconstruction.

The individual thanksgiving psalms, often called songs of the Teacher, are essentially praises to God who has already saved the speaker from some crisis. Within these praises the speaker often makes reference to himself and his adversaries. He never identifies himself or his enemies by name, but simply speaks of himself as an important person by virtue of his relationship to God and contrasts himself with his adversaries who are also God's opponents.

In II,(?)-19 the 'I' speaks of himself as a 'foundation of truth and insight for the righteous of way' (l. 10). This is hardly a historical description. The image of a foundation is used to underscore the speaker's stability before God. There is no adequate way to translate that depiction into historical terms. As for the 'righteous way', this is clearly a theological category, not necessarily a historical or sociological one. The speaker calls himself an interpreter of (God's) knowledge (l. 13, מליץ דעת) and a spirit of jealousy against the seekers of smooth things (l. 15). Furthermore, he refers to himself as one taught by God (l. 17). The language of this psalm does induce one to think of the one praying as the leader or role model for a group of righteous ones who are opposed by a group of wicked persons.

On the face of it, these statements could be viewed as allusions to the Teacher of Righteousness mentioned in 1QpHab and 4QpPs 37. But the crucial questions are whether the one speaking in these individual thanksgiving psalms about his personal situation is the Teacher of Righteousness and whether historians can identify this speaker on the basis of the information presented in his depiction of his personal situation. He views himself as living in a realm of ungodliness (ll. 8, 11-12). He describes the ungodly as storm waves on the sea (ll. 12-13), as interpreters of error (l. 14), seekers of smooth things, and deceitful people (ll. 14-16). He always uses biblical imagery to present them as a dominion of evil. Since specific examples of this general description of evil adversaries are never given, one should probably avoid historicizing this language.

Stegemann points out that several of the terms for the adversaries are quite general—לצים, בוגדים, רשעים, פושעים, אנשי רמיה, גבול רשעה, עריצים.[36] Other terms present the enemies under the aspect of a false doctrine: דורשי חלקות, מליצי תעות.[37] The expression קהלת רשעים gives this undefined group a communal character.[38] CD, 1QpHab, and 4QpPs 37 also use this sort of nebulous, non-specifying language, but do occasionally refer to particular evil individuals by means of code names such as the Wicked Priest, the Liar, and the House of Absalom. Besides sharing a similar vocabulary with other Qumran documents, II,(?)-19 adds no concrete information, neither on the historical identity of the speaker and his enemies nor concerning their specific conflict with the speaker.

In II,31-(39), the speaker thanks God for having delivered him from the enemy. He designates himself as (the ?) poor (l. 32, אביון) and his foes as interpreters of lies (l. 31, מליצי כזב) and seekers of deceit (l. 34, דורשי רמיה). This stereotyped language about the enemies reminds one of similar language in the pesharim and CD about the Liar and those whom he influenced. Unlike those documents, which emphasize the Liar's misleading persons, this psalm concentrates on the attempted violent acts against the one thanking God for deliverance. Its conventionalized phraseology about enemies and the absence of names prevent one from saying anything about the actual identities of the protagonist and the antagonists nor concerning the historical nature of the conflict between them.

III,(1)-18 begins with the motif of deliverance from an enemy. The places of affliction are the depths of the sea (l. 6) and a besieged city (l. 7). In addition to these images, the speaker even likens himself to a woman giving birth for the first time (ll. 7-12). Then he abruptly returns to the image of shaky foundations that are like a ship on a storm-tossed sea (ll. 13-18). This poetic language can be used to describe either real or imagined distress. Nevertheless, the more the speaker uses figurative language and comparisons to express his feelings and personal situation, the less concrete and historically useful become the statements about both the speaker himself and his adversaries.

The psalm IV,5–V,4 has been thought to provide a valuable statement corroborating the Teacher's personal situation as known from 1QpHab and 4QPs 37. The speaker says 'they have expelled me from my country like a bird from its nest, and all my friends and relatives have been driven from me; and they esteem me as a broken vessel'. Holm-Nielsen points out that the ideas of expulsion from one's own land and abandonment by one's kith and kin need not signify concrete, historical circumstances, although they could, since they are found in the suffering motives of the Old Testament's psalms of lament (e.g. Pss. 31.12-18; 17.10; 42.7; 88.19; cf. 1QH IX,34).[39] In favor of a historical interpretation, Jeremias thinks 1QH IV,8-9 refers to an event alluded to in 1QpHab XI,4-8 and 4QpPs 37 IV,8-9.[40] The former speaks of the Wicked Priest's attempt to swallow up the Teacher of Righteousness at his place of exile.

> Its interpretation concerns the Wicked Priest who pursued the Teacher of Righteousness to the house of his exile that he might confuse him with his venomous fury.

Paralleling this statement, 4QpPs 37 IV,8-9 adds only that the Wicked Priest wanted to kill the Righteous One.

> Its interpretation concerns the Wicked [Priest] who w(atch)es the Right(eous One and seeks) to kill him. . . .

There does seem to be some sort of interdependence between these two passages. What is their relationship to the statement in 1QH IV,8-9 concerning the speaker's expulsion and abandonment?

The bird motive in IV,8-9, וידיחני מארצי כצפור מקנה, does not appear in 1QpHab XI,4-8, but the notion of expulsion is thought to be reflected in the expression 'his house of exile' ([א]בית גלותו). Even if the Teacher's place of exile should have a concrete reference point in history and geography, the poetic description of the expelled bird in 1QH need not. In any case the themes of expulsion and exile are absent from 4QpPs 37 IV,8-9. In conjunction with the theme of expulsion, a second point of contact between 1QH IV,8-12 and 1QpHab XI,2-8 is observable. The picture of one giving the righteous vinegar to drink in order to watch their error, to cause them to behave madly at their festivals, and to catch themselves in their nets, found in 1QH IV,11-12, is echoed in 1QpHab XI,2-3 (quotation of Hab. 2.15) and 6.

1QH IV		1QpHab XI	
l. 11	משקה	l. 2	משקה
l. 11	חומץ	ll. 5-6	כעס חמתו
ll. 11-12	למע הבט אל תעותם	l. 3	למען הבט אל מועדיהם
l. 12	להתהולל במועדיהם		
l. 12	להתפש במצודותם	l. 6	ובקץ מועד מנוחת

A superficial comparison of the common phraseology of the two passages might induce one to read the information given in 1QpHab into the context of 1QH. On closer examination, the inadequacy of such an approach becomes obvious. In 1QH the enemy appears as a group of lying interpreters who mislead God's people. Not once does the speaker refer to an individual. This applies throughout the so-called songs of the Teacher. In contrast to this, 1QpHab interprets the participles משקה and מספח as well as the perfect form הבט as references to the activities of one person, the Wicked Priest. רעיהו is understood as referring to the Teacher of Righteousness. Furthermore, the activities of the enemies in 1QH are not identical with those of the Wicked Priest in 1QpHab. In the former, they are accused of attempting to seduce the one speaking to God to exchange God's law for smooth things. The speaker seems to be less concerned with the details of the conflict than with the overall structure of the situation—a righteous one confronted by the wicked.[41] In 1QpHab, the Wicked Priest is attempting to kill the Teacher during a festival held at his house of exile. Several scholars think this is an allusion to an actual historical conflict with the Wicked Priest, who came to Qumran to murder the Teacher on the Qumran community's Day of Atonement (according to its own calendar reckoning).[42] Clearly, the information presented in 1QpHab is more specific than that in 1QH, but the presence of similar phraseology does not legitimize reading the Teacher and the Wicked Priest in the context of 1QH IV,8-12.

It was pointed out above that the more the speaker uses non-human imagery to depict his enemies, the less he seems to be interested in particular human enemies and their crimes against him. This seems also to be the situation in V,5-19. In ll. 6-14 he speaks of his enemies as lions (ll. 6-7, 10, 13-14) whose fangs are like the poison of dragons (l. 10). As for the reference to the lions, one is reminded of Dan. 6.1-28, Ps. 22.14, and other biblical passages. This imagery frames another kind of imagery. The speaker views himself as a fisherman and a hunter who spreads a net in order to catch the unrighteous.[43] This imagery reminds one of Jer. 16.16 and Hab. 1.14-

17. The 'sons of unrighteousness' (l. 8) are equated by virtue of the poetic context with the bloodthirsty lions. No suggestion is made as to the possible historical identity of these creatures. This imagery of dangerous animals is mentioned primarily to draw attention to God's act of salvation. In l. 16 the speaker points out that his situation of distress is actually a process of purification, not a recognizable, historical conflict: 'and you (God) lay him in (the crucible as gold) in the power of the fire, and as silver, which is purified in the oven of the silversmiths to a sevenfold purity'. This imagery can be found in Zech. 13.9 and Mal. 3.3. The point of the psalm is not to bring specific charges against adversaries for which there is any actual redress, but to underscore the belief that both distress and enemies function as part of God's plan of purification and redemption. Thus V,5-19 adds nothing concrete to the historical discussion about particular characters of Qumran history.

To Jeremias's list of *Lehrerlieder* Stegemann adds II,20-30 and VI,34–VIII,3. In II,20-30, the speaker refers to himself as one who is under attack, because he clings to God's covenant.[44] Besides general designations such as violent ones (עריצים, l. 21) and evil ones (רשעים, l. 24), the adversaries are said to be a company of falseness and a congregation of Belial/worthlessness (סוד שוא ועדת בליעל, l. 22). In ll. 25-26, the speaker describes the attack on his soul in military terms. Bearing their weapons, the enemy troops are depicted as having surrounded the speaker. Arrows are landing all about him and lances appear to him as trees on fire. Once this picture is established, the speaker shifts abruptly to a violent water image. The noise of the enemy is likened to the pounding of powerful waters and hard pouring rains. The imagery shifts again, when the speaker describes the enemy as ones who spread out nets and set traps in which they catch themselves. The consistent use of comparison suggests that the speaker is not trying to communicate specific historical information about his adversaries. Stegemann points out that this hymn's language about collective enemies does not refer to any organized group.[45] The speaker even points out in II,23-24, as in V,5-19, that the adversaries are part of God's plan for the righteous. The activities of the evil ones against the righteous are merely a prelude to God's eventual judgment on them. In VII,34–VIII,3, which is only partially preserved, the speaker does not refer to an enemy attack, but simply thanks God for not allowing him to fall into the community of falseness.[46] The major emphasis in both II,20-30 and

VII,34–VIII,3 is on the speaker's perception of having been preserved from the violent attacks of his and God's enemies rather than on his or their identities.

Conclusion

Several psalms in 1QH, which are usually attributed to the Teacher of Righteousness and presumably deal with events in his life, have been investigated in regard to their potential information value for the reconstruction of the history of the Qumran community: II,(?)-19; II,31-39; III,1-18; IV,5–V,4; V,5-19; II,20-30; VII,34–VIII,3. Analysis of these passages indicated that their author/the speaker had little, if any, concern with reporting specific and recognizable information about particular historical enemies and conflicts. In quite general terms, he depicts all of reality as a conflict between the righteous and the wicked. Although the wicked are always mentioned as a collective entity, they remain unnamed, unidentified, and without historical context. They are depicted theologically as a realm of wickedness, sometimes by means of expressions that one might tend to interpret historically, e.g. 'interpreters of errors', sometimes by means of imagery from the world of nature, e.g. 'storm-tossed sea', 'lions', and 'vipers', and sometimes by means of battle imagery. In agreement with Jeremias, it was determined that IV,8-9 and IV,11-12 preserve statements about the situation of the psalmist that one could interpret as event-like. In the former passage, the speaker refers to his exile; in the latter, to the evil activity of the enemy, who gives the righteous vinegar to drink in order to confuse and mislead them. Both of these statements bear a resemblance to what is said in 1QpHab XI,4-8 and 4QpPs 37 IV,8-9, suggesting a possible ideological, if not documentary, interdependence. Nevertheless, neither of these two passages nor both of them in combination preserve concrete information about the identity of the speaker, his enemies, the substance of their disputes, the geographical location, and the time of these conflicts. This applies as well to II,20-30, in which the speaker's adversaries are characterized as enemy troops, violent waters, and sons of unrighteousness. Poorly preserved, VII,34–VIII,3 lacks even poetic references to enemies. Its emphasis falls on the speaker's gratitude to God for deliverance.

Thus the individual thanksgiving psalms in 1QH prove not to be useful, independent of other Qumran documents, in reconstructing the history of the Qumran community. In his discussion of the Dead

Sea Scrolls that are relevant to the reconstruction of the history of the Qumran community, Stegemann emphasized correctly that the language of the *Lehrerlieder* concerning enemies of the speaker is certainly unintelligible without the information about protagonists and antagonists in 1QpHab, 4QpPs 37, and CD. That is, those documents occasionally speak about conflicts between individuals such as the Teacher of Righteousness, the Wicked Priest, and the Liar. The so-called songs of the Teacher assume an autobiographical stance, which has induced several scholars to view their statements as historically credible. These scholars tend to read the songs of the Teacher in light of the conflict passages in these other documents. Examination of IV,5–V,4, which speaks of the expulsion and abandonment of the speaker, demonstrated that one may not simply interpret it in light of 1QpHab XI,2-8, which does bear some similarities in phraseology. The pesher takes an exegetical step not present in 1QH by identifying particular elements in the biblical text with particular individuals who are in conflict with each other. The so-called depictions of suffering in 1QH also emphasize the conflict situation, but no attempt is made to identify the 'I' and the collective group of wicked ones. One has the impression that the speaker is not referring to specific, historical enemies, since there is no concern with detailing their activities. They are simply presented as a group opposed to the one speaking, who has been preserved by God. The enemies function in these psalms of thanksgiving to God as a temporary foil to the righteous one in God's eventual plan to judge the wicked and to vindicate the righteous one (e.g. this is clearest in II,20-30 and V,5-19).

Thus these psalms are not useful as independent pieces of evidence concerning persons involved in the history of the Qumran community. Even if the more concrete statements in the pesharim and CD should have actual historical referents, it is not clear that the individual psalms of thanksgiving necessarily allude to historical situations. Their language is more generalizing, tending to place the righteous one and the wicked in a conflict situation which is resolved both in the prayer of the 'I' and at the time of God's judgment of the wicked.

GENERAL SUMMARY AND CONCLUSION

The primary goal of this work was to investigate all the currently available evidence for the history of the Qumran community. At the same time it was a dialogue with several representatives of the current consensus on Qumran history, i.e. those who interpret the earliest evidence against a Maccabean context—Gert Jeremias, Hartmut Stegemann, Jerome Murphy-O'Connor, Philip R. Davies, and Frank M. Cross, Jr.

The non-literary evidence was investigated first, since it is thought to provide the broad chronological background against which to reconstruct the history alluded to in the literary documentation. The archaeological evidence from the site Qumran was investigated (Chapter 2); then the palaeographical data was reassessed (Chapter 3). Then the literary evidence for the history of the Qumran community—both non-Qumranic and Qumranic evidence—was re-examined. The non-Qumran evidence for the existence of the Qumran/Essene community, the ancient reports of Philo, Josephus, and Pliny as well as 1 and 2 Maccabees, were discussed (Chapter 4). Then the Qumran literary documentation itself was investigated in terms of its value for reconstructing a history of the community. CD (Chapter 5), 1QpHab, 4QpPs 37, and 4QpNah (Chapter 6), 4QTest (Chapter 7), and 1QH (Chapter 8) were examined independently of each other in order to determine the specific contributions of each document to the historical reconstruction.

After discussing the current consensus on the history of the Qumran community and the various pieces of evidence for that history, the archaeological evidence from Qumran and its environs was examined in Chapter 2. The evidence from the caves where the scrolls were found and the Qumran complex itself witness to the same material culture, which dates roughly to the late Hellenistic and Roman periods in Judaea. Although this shared material culture does not prove conclusively that the group that stored the scrolls in the caves also inhabited Qumran, it does—along with the argument from the proximity of the two—provide circumstantial evidence for that possibility. The general period reflected by the material remains from the caves and the building complex runs approximately from the late second century BCE to 68/69 CE.

While the broad chronological horizon is fairly clear, difficulties do arise in attempting to date specific phases of Qumran's settlement history precisely. One cannot assign a precise date to the earliest Hellenistic settlement at Qumran (Ia), because the ceramic data from this stratum cannot be distinguished from that of Ib. Nor can one determine with certainty when Ia ended and Ib, Qumran's 'definitive form', was erected. On the basis of the numismatic and ceramic data, it can at least be stated that the Ib installation dates approximately to the late second and early first century BCE.

Just as the inception of Qumran Ia and Ib cannot be determined precisely, the termination of Ib is also open to various interpretations. The most popular view associates signs of burning and structural damage at the site with the earthquake of 31 BCE as reported by Josephus. Karcz and Kafri have argued cogently against this view, explaining the structural damage as a result of the complex having been erected on unstable Lisan Marl. In addition to casting doubt on the seismic explanation, they doubt whether one can actually date this damage. Owing to the ambiguity of this evidence, one should probably not speak of a period of total abandonment at Qumran from 31 to 4 BCE. Debris did in fact accumulate at various locations on the site, which might indicate that certain parts of the Qumran complex fell into disuse for an undetermined period of time, but even the subsequent settlers of Period II seem to have managed for almost a century without repairing the damage to the water system (see loc. 48-49).

The evidence for Period II, both numismatic and ceramic, is less disputed and indicates that Qumran was resettled or refurbished during the reign of Herod Archelaus (4 BCE–6 CE). It continued to be inhabited by Jews until 68/69 CE, when the site was abandoned and reoccupied by the Romans. Thus the overall periodization is relatively secure: Qumran was first settled in the second century BCE, in the penultimate or final quarter of that century, and continued to be occupied by Jews until 68/69 CE.

In Chapter 3, the palaeographical data was examined with regard to its value for reconstructing the history of the Qumran community.

Like the archaeological study of Qumran, the palaeographical analysis of the Dead Sea Scrolls also provides indicators for the chronological framework against which to understand the literary sources. The hands of the Dead Sea Scrolls date roughly from 250 BCE to c. 70 CE. His study of the characteristic traits of these scripts leads Cross to designate the Qumran documents as Archaic dating c. 250–150 BCE, Hasmonean dating c. 150–30 BCE, and Herodian dating c. 30 BCE–70 CE.

The oldest documents, consisting primarily of biblical materials, derive from the Archaic period. The so-called sectarian writings are absent from this period, but are found in the late Hasmonean and Herodian periods. The oldest extant sectarian document is 1QS that dates c. 100–75 BCE. 4QTest, which may refer to historical figures under the guise of the code names 'man of Belial' and 'instruments of violence', dates also roughly to this time. Except for 4QTest, 4QD is the oldest of the historically valuable documents. Although fragmentary, it represents the oldest witness to the later manuscripts known now as CD, which contain information on the Teacher of Righteousness, the Liar, chronology, and geography. Other sectarian documents that deal with these figures as well as the Wicked Priest date to the Herodian period—c. 30–1 BCE (or later). These are 1QpHab, 4QpPs 37 and 4QpNah. Sometimes thought to preserve the thoughts and feelings of the Teacher, 1QH also dates to this period.

The sectarian documents preserving potentially valuable historical information were copied, therefore, in hands that date roughly from 75 to 1 BCE or later. That would indicate that CD's (actually 4QD's) compiler was concerned in part with figures that were active and events that occurred in the period before 75 BCE. Not concerned with the conflict between the Teacher, the Liar, and the Wicked Priest, 1QS would be about twenty-five years older, presumably originating from the same group. Hence, the dating of the sectarian documents on palaeographical grounds is consistent with the general periodization established independently on archaeological grounds. These documents date roughly from the end of the second century BCE into the first century CE.

In Chapter 4, the ancient reports of Philo, Josephus, and Pliny were examined for potential evidence about the identity and history of the Qumran community. Clearly, Philo knew about the Essenes of his time in Palestine even if he probably was not an eyewitness to their way of life. For the most part, his general information about the common life of the Essenes is consistent with that of Josephus. He was of no direct assistance, however, in answering specific questions about Qumran or Essene history. His interest in presenting the Essenes to his audience was in large part philosophical, with the goal of describing the wisest and the most free among his own people the Jews. It was determined that Josephus was quantitatively and qualitatively a different kind of historical source. Although philosophical concerns are by no means absent from his digressions on the Essenes, he does claim to have studied with them and does provide valuable information on their daily routine, their initiation procedures, and other information that might distinguish them from other Jewish groups. The initiation procedures of the Essenes did prove to be very similar, although not identical, to those in 1QS. Unlike Philo, Josephus is able to speak of three Essenes by name—Judah, Simon, and John. The first two were significant for Josephus who admired their prophetic, predictive powers. The last one, John, served as a Jewish commander in the war against the Romans. We have no way of knowing whether these Essenes were involved in the history of the Qumran community. Josephus locates them chiefly in Jerusalem. For the reconstruction of the specific history of the Qumran community, his reports are therefore unhelpful. Taken together, the ancient reports of Philo and Josephus do confirm the fact that the Essenes were a Jewish group that lived from the second century BCE to the first century CE. This is consistent with the results of archaeological investigation at Qumran and of palaeographical analysis of the Dead Sea Scrolls. When this group originated cannot be determined precisely, although Josephus does introduce the Essenes into his narrative about the history of the mid-second century BCE, he does not clarify their relationship to that history. The identification of the early Essenes with the Hasidim of the early second century BCE goes beyond the evidence. We know nothing about the identity of their members, with the exception of Judas Maccabeus, nor of their historical development from the second century BCE into later times.

Neither Philo nor Josephus and 1 and 2 Maccabees report anything about a specific Essene community that inhabited the area around Qumran during that period. In contrast to these Jewish writers, the Roman naturalist Pliny does preserve the valuable information that Essenes inhabited a site above Engedi and near the

Dead Sea in the last half of the first century BCE. Although he knows practically nothing about the internal makeup and ideology of this group, and certainly nothing about the Teacher of Righteousness, the Wicked Priest, and the Liar, his geographical location of the Essenes in the vicinity of Qumran suggests that its inhabitants during the Hellenistic and Roman periods were possibly Essenes. To say more than this would go beyond the available evidence.

These three bodies of evidence—the archaeological, the palaeographical, and the literary—all point to the existence of a Jewish group, similar to the Essenes, at Qumran from the late second century BCE to the last half of the first century BCE. The ancient reports of Philo and Josephus about the Essenes present them as a phenomenon that existed throughout Palestinian Syria. Pliny knows of an Essene association located in the vicinity of Qumran. This piece of information might suggest that an Essene-like group may have inhabited the Qumran complex and placed the Dead Sea Scrolls in the nearby caves.

In Chapter 5, CD was examined in terms of the value of its information for the discussion about the history of the Qumran community. Several potentially valuable historical elements were analyzed in their respective literary contexts—references to a Teacher of Righteousness, a Liar, a Damascan covenant, and chronological notes. These elements help to concretize and historicize the theological message of CD. This message concerns God's disdain for the disobedient and love for the repentant. Within this overall scheme, the Teacher functions as God's messenger to a particular remnant community. The compiler of CD seems to understand his community as historically related to an earlier group that had escaped to the land of the north at the time of the exile and formed a new covenant in the land of Damascus. The Teacher and his group are contrasted in col. I with the Liar and the traitors/the Seekers after Smooth Things.

Without the chronological notes in I,5-11, one could only say that these figures lived before the time of the writer or compiler of CD. The insertion of the first chronological note has the effect of dating the emergence of the remnant community 390 years after the Babylonian exile—around the beginning of the second century BCE. According to the second note, God gave this remnant a teacher twenty years later in order to guide them in the way of his heart. This would have occurred two decades later, if one takes the information literally. The context of col. I suggests also that the Liar and the traitors/the Seekers after Smooth Things were roughly contemporareous with the Teacher. Nevertheless, there is no explicit reference to a conflict between the Teacher and the Liar as can be found in 1QpHab and 4QpPs 37 concerning the Teacher's conflicts with the Liar and the Wicked Priest.

This evidence indicates that the compiler of CD lived after the time when the Teacher and the Liar were active, since he apparently refers to the Teacher's death in XIX,35–XX,1 and 13-14. It is impossible to determine whether the compiler actually knew the Teacher and the Liar personally, for he does not present any information on their identities. Nor is it clear how many years had passed from the time of the Teacher's activity to the compilation of CD. The compiler himself seems to belong to a later group which he called the Men of Perfect Holiness (XX,2). Living after the Teacher's death, this group continued to revere his instructions. The most important piece of information that CD presents concerning the Teacher and the remnant community dates them to the early years of the second century BCE. Nevertheless, CD's compiler does not associate these figures with the history of that period as known from other sources such as 1 and 2 Maccabees and Josephus. Without clear reference to this important historical framework, all attempts to identify the Teacher, the remnant group, the Liar, and the traitors/the Seekers after Smooth Things must be characterized as highly speculative.

In Chapter 6, statements in three pesharim about the chief actors of Qumran history were examined. 1QpHab, 4QpPs 37, and 4QpNah were found to be replete with references to the Teacher of Righteousness, the Wicked Priest, the Liar, and traitors. In regard to the Teacher and the Liar, known already from CD, it was hoped that the pesharim would contain additional information about their possible relationship.

1QpHab does in fact provide some information in that regard. In V,9-12, the pesharist refers also to the House of Absalom that did not help the Teacher of Righteousness against the Liar. This passage makes it clear that a conflict had taken place between these two figures. This account stands in contrast to CD I, where they are simply juxtaposed and no information is given about a particular conflict. The pesharist, however, does not deem it necessary to clarify what was actually at issue in the conflict between the Teacher and the Liar. The Liar is simply accused of having rejected the Law in the midst of their community. The House of Absalom is accused of indifference, which could be construed as a form of treachery. Since the figures are never named or brought into association with known Jewish history, one cannot presume to identify them.

In VIII,3-13, the pesharist introduces the Wicked Priest about whom he reveals more than any other figure mentioned in the pesharim. The Wicked Priest is said to have been called by the name of Truth when he arose, but he became puffed up with pride and a desire for wealth as he began to reign over Israel. Stegemann provides a substantial discussion in favor of identifying this individual as a non-Zadokite high priest. It was determined that the Wicked Priest may have in fact been a high priest, but since he was at one time called by the name of Truth, it is doubtful whether the pesharist, who presumably viewed all non-Zadokites as ineligible to execute any high priestly functions, would speak of him in such terms.

Stegemann then attempts to determine the general period when a high priest would have also enjoyed regnal powers. This period could have extended maximally from the post-exilic period into the first century BCE. Based on the chronological information derived from archaeological and palaeographical study, Stegemann is able to restrict the period of the Wicked Priest's activity from the year 200 to c. 100 BCE. He offers another criterion that is supposed to aid the historian in identifying this figure within this century: he must have been killed by Gentiles outside of Judaea. This criterion proved upon inspection, however, to be ambiguous as Stegemann wanted to apply it, because, with the exception of the fragmentary passage in 1QpHab VIII,16–IX,2 all statements about the ultimate fate of the Wicked Priest in 1QpHab and 4QpPs 37 are characteristically descriptive and concerned with God's future judgment of the Wicked Priest as well as the rest of the wicked.

Thus it would seem that only Stegemann's second criterion permits one to speak of the Wicked Priest as a figure of the period 200–100 BCE. Nevertheless, the lower limit is not entirely clear. He appeals, however, to 4QpNah I,2-3, which seems to associate the Seekers after Smooth Things with the political history of Judaea around the year 90 BCE, for a more solid chronological benchmark. Since the Seekers after Smooth Things have been identified with the Liar's community based on the information preserved in CD I,12-21, one can infer that 4QpNah provides the chronological index required for determining the general period in which the Seekers after Smooth Things, the Liar, the Teacher, and the Wicked Priest were active. Admittedly, 4QpNah does not mention the Teacher, the Wicked Priest, and the Liar, but these figures were contemporaries of the last-named figure whose community was active c. 90 BCE. Furthermore, it is impossible to know with certainty whether 4QpNah is concerned with a community that had outlived the Liar and the other figures or whether these figures were still alive. Only the chronological information in CD I,5-11 suggests that the Teacher, the Liar, traitors/Seekers after Smooth Things, and the Wicked Priest by association were figures of the second century BCE.

Several passages in 1QpHab indicate that a conflict had existed between the Teacher of Righteousness and the Poor and the Wicked Priest: 1QpHab IX,9-10; XI,4-5; XII,2-6. IX,9-10 merely provides evidence for such a conflict. XI,4-5 suggests that the Wicked Priest had attempted to kill the Teacher of Righteousness on a Day of Atonement. XII,2-6 refers to the Wicked Priest's mistreatment of the Poor—presumably an allusion to the Teacher's adherents. 4QpPs 37 also makes a few statements about such conflicts. II,13-14 refers to the attempt of the Violent Ones of the Covenant to destroy the Doers of the Law. This reminds one of 1QpHab XII,2-6. Using the names Ephraim and Manasseh symbolically to refer to these Violent Ones, the pesharist speaks in II,17-18 of their desire to kill the Priest, i.e. the Teacher, and his community. In IV,8-9, the pesharist again mentions the Wicked Priest's attempt to kill the Righteous One, i.e. the Teacher or the Priest. The pesharists clearly know of such conflicts, but never associate the chief actors with recognizable history, nor do they clarify the issues at the center of the conflicts.

As mentioned above, 4QpNah's chief historical significance lies in its apparent association of the Liar's community, the Seekers after Smooth Things, with the political history of Judaea c. 90 BCE. Specifically, 4QpNah I,2-3 presents the Liar's community in collaboration with the Seleucid Demetrius III Eukerus, by appealing to him to capture Jerusalem and remove Alexander Jannaeus from power. Assuming that I,2-3 is alluding to the event reported by Josephus about some Pharisees of the early first century BCE, then the Seekers after Smooth Things must have been Pharisees. These Pharisees were opposed to the Lion of Wrath, who would then be identified with Alexander Jannaeus. Hence, while 4QpNah does not mention the conflicts involving the Liar, the Wicked Priest, and the Teacher, which form the key issues in 1QpHab and 4QpPs 37, it does associate the Liar's community with the political history of Judaea c. 90 BCE. The chronological information in CD I indicates that the Liar, the Teacher, and the Wicked Priest by association with the Teacher, were active at some time before 90 BCE, but after the early years of the second century BCE.

Thus 1QpHab and 4QpPs 37 do contain important information about one or more conflicts involving characters that the pesharists perceived as righteous or wicked. In particular, reference is made to a conflict involving the Liar and the Teacher and a conflict involving the Wicked Priest and the Teacher. Other statements concern conflicts between these wicked figures and the Poor or the Doers of the Law. The information presented in 4QpNah I,2-8 dating the Seekers after Smooth Things (=the Liar's community) c. 90 BCE seems to provide an important chronological benchmark for the general period of the Liar's and the Teacher's communities.

In Chapter 7, 4QTest was investigated for its relevance to the history of the Qumran community. Cross thinks that the terms 'accursed man, one of Belial' and 'intruments of violence' refer to the character known from 1QpHab and 4QpPs 37 as the Wicked Priest and his sons. As the fulfillment of the prophecy Josh. 6.26 which is reported in 1 Kgs 16.33-34 concerns a father and his two sons, this sort of interpretation is most natural. Cross identifies these figures with Simon Maccabeus and his two sons Judas and Simon. It is not clear, however, whether the 'accursed one of Belial' was a high priest, nor whether one should identify him with the Wicked Priest. He is neither characterized as having once been called by the name of Truth nor accused of having attempted to kill the Teacher of Righteousness.

Not only does the information presented in ll. 21-30 not permit the historian to speak with any certainty about the true identities of these figures, the temporal aspect of their activities also remains an unresolved issue. The quotation of Josh. 6.26 in ll. 21-22 is itself a prophecy open to a future fulfillment. The verb forms in ll. 22-23a and from l. 25 on seem to require a future translation, suggesting that the interpretation given in ll. 23-30 most probably refers to a future, eschatological event. In any case, no demonstrable connection is made with the conflicts involving the Teacher, the Liar, and the Wicked Priest as reported in 1QpHab and 4QpPs 37 and the political activities of the Liar's community as reported in 4QpNah. Therefore, one may conclude that 4QTest preserves no clear-cut information on the history of the Qumran community.

In Chapter 8, several of the *hodayot* in 1QH were examined in respect of their potential information value concerning the one speaking and his experiences—II,(?)-19; II,31-39; III,1-18; IV,5-V,4; V,5-19; II,20-30; VII,34-VIII,3. Some scholars, particularly Jeremias and Stegemann, believe that these *hodayot*, which they designate as *Lehrerlieder*, are autobiographical and reflect the actual words and experiences of the Teacher of Righteousness. Close inspection of these individual thanksgiving hymns indicated that the speaker, who may or may not have been the author, was not concerned with reporting specific and recognizable information about himself and his enemies. More clearly than in any of the other Qumran documents, the speaker is concerned to depict reality as divided into the righteous and the wicked. His prayers to God are primarily concerned with thanking God for having saved him from the wicked, whom he consistently presents as a collective entity without name and historical context. Neither the identity of the one speaking nor that of his enemies can be determined from the contexts of the *hodayot*. Hence, these *hodayot*, better not referred to as *Lehrerlieder*, cannot be used independently as evidence for the history of the Qumran community or even for the life of its Teacher.

This examination of the non-literary and the literary evidence for the history of the Qumran community began with no commitment to a particular thesis on the history of that history. It was acknowledged, however, that a consensus has emerged understanding the origin and earliest history of the Qumran community against a Maccabean context. According to this thesis, the Wicked Priest was either Jonathan or Simon Maccabeus and the Teacher of Righteousness was a contemporary Zadokite high priest.

Analysis of the archaeological data from Qumran and the caves does allow one to postulate a Jewish community at Qumran at least from the end of the second century BCE on; how much earlier cannot be determined. Moreover, the proximity of the caves to the site and the fact that both share an identical material culture dating from the late second/early first century BCE into the first century CE allow one to infer that one and the same group inhabited the site and the caves during this period. Since the sectarian scrolls were found in these caves, it is thought that the community living at Qumran had written and stored them there roughly at the time of the Roman attack on the site in 68/69 CE. Palaeographical analysis of the scripts of the sectarian Dead Sea Scrolls agrees with the general periodization provided by archaeology. More specifically, however, palaeographical analysis is able to date the copying of the historically relevant Qumran documents between the years 75 and 1 BCE. Accordingly, events and persons alluded to in these documents would belong to the time before 75 BCE. The ancient reports of Philo, Josephus, and Pliny about the Essenes also had them on the scene in Judaea in this period. Pliny alone located them in the vicinity of Qumran, which suggests that the inhabitants of Qumran and its caves may have also been Essenes. More than this cannot be inferred from the archaeological, the palaeographical, and the ancient, non-Qumranic literary evidence.

The external evidence, which indirectly dates the events and persons alluded to in the sectarian Dead Sea Scrolls before the year 75 BCE, is consistent with the literary evidence from Qumran. The compiler of CD presents the Teacher of Righteousness, the remnant, the Liar, and the traitors/the Seekers after Smooth Things as figures of the early second century BCE. Understood literally, the two chronological notes in I,5-11 date these figures before the middle of the second century—410 years after the Babylonian exile. Nothing is said concretely about their historical relationship nor about the enmity between them. In 1QpHab and 4QpPs 37, statements are made depicting the Liar and the Wicked Priest in conflict with the Teacher of Righteousness and his adherents. Analysis of 1QpHab VIII,3-13 indicated, in agreement with Stegemann, that the Wicked Priest may have been a high priest of the second century BCE, but not necessarily a non-Zadokite high priest. Unfortunately, the pesharist does not reveal what is at issue in the conflict between the Teacher and the Wicked Priest nor does he associate these figures with the political history of that century. This applies as well to the conflict between the Liar and the Teacher. Hence, it is impossible to determine the identities of the key actors and events related to the history of the Qumran community.

Only 4QpNah, which says nothing about these figures and their web of conflicts, provides a chronological benchmark for speaking about the historical existence of one of the Teacher's enemies—the community of the Liar. In I,2-3, the Seekers after Smooth Things are reported to have attempted to entice Demetrius (III Eukerus) to capture Jerusalem. This event is reported by Josephus in *Ant*. 13.372-83. This valuable piece of information dates the Liar's community to the year 90 BCE, identifies them as Pharisees, and has them involved in the political history of the early first century BCE. Therefore, CD I and 4QpNah I provide the general chronological framework against which to understand the history alluded to in the other documents—roughly from the first quarter of the second century to 90 BCE.

Since CD, 1QpHab, and 4QpPs 37 do not contain more specific and concrete information about the identities of the chief actors of the scrolls, it is difficult to determine where they fit into the recorded history of the second century and early first century BCE. The literary evidence does witness to conflicts between the Liar, the Wicked Priest, and the Teacher, but nothing more than that. The possibility has been established, however, that the Wicked Priest was a high priest. Furthermore, the Liar's group has been identified as Pharisees. One might speculate that the conflicts alluded to in the pesharim and CD involved disputes between different sectarian groups or perhaps with more justification as disagreements within one particular group, but even this sort of speculation would go beyond the evidence. Therefore, one must conclude that it is impossible to say more than has been said above about the history of the Qumran community on the basis of the evidence that is presently available.

NOTES

Notes to Chapter 1

1. Solomon Zeitlin (*JQR* [1948/49-1965/66]) objected not only to the interpretation of the archaeological finds, but also to the secrecy surrounding the discovery, purchase, and publication of the scrolls. While certain aspects of his own views are unacceptable, his observation that details in the various reports of the finds are not always in agreement and his critique of Qumran sensationalism are accurate (*idem*, *The Dead Sea Scrolls and Modern Scholarship*, esp. pp. 81-93).

2. G.R. Driver, *The Judean Scrolls. The Problem and a Solution.*

3. Geza Vermes, 'Dead Sea Scrolls', *IDBSup*, pp. 210-19; *idem*, 'The Essenes and History', *JJS* 32 (1981), pp. 18-31; Michael A. Knibb, 'The Dead Sea Scrolls: Reflections on Some Recent Publications', *ET* 90 (1979), pp. 294-300; Hans Bardtke, 'Literaturbericht über Qumran. X. Teil. Der Lehrer der Gerechtigkeit und die Geschichte der Qumrangemeinde', *TRu* 41 (1976), pp. 97-140; E.-M. Laperrousaz, 'Qumran et découvertes au désert de Juda', *DBSup* 9, pp. 790-98; Deborah Dimant, 'Qumran Sectarian Literature', in *Jewish Writings of the Second Temple Period*, ed. Michael E. Stone, pp. 483-550.

4. Ben Zion Wacholder (*The Dawn of Qumran*) dates the Teacher to c. 195 BCE and identifies his adversaries with Simon the Just II and Onias III. H.H. Rowley is concerned to identify characters and issues in the scrolls with the Maccabean era and, therefore, belongs to this early period. He does not bring the Essenes into connection with the archaeology of Qumran and the palaeography of the scrolls; see his *The Internal Dating of the Dead Sea Scrolls; idem, The Relevance of Apocalyptic; idem*, 'The History of the Qumran Sect', *BJRL* 49 (1966), pp. 203-32; *idem*, 'The Kittim and the Dead Sea Scrolls', *PEQ* 88 (1956), pp. 92-109; cf. Matthew Black, *The Scrolls and Christian Origins*, pp. 3-24; J.C. Greig, 'The Teacher of Righteousness and the Qumran Community', *NTS* 2 (1955/56), pp. 119-26; I. Rabinowitz ('The Guides of Righteousness', *VT* 8 [1958], pp. 391-404) interprets the expression teacher of righteousness as a reference to past, present, and future figures—Nehemiah (a second Moses), Mattathias/Judas Maccabeus, and the Messiah. Similarly, A.S. van der Woude thinks that the title Wicked Priest could have been applied to most of the high priests from Judas Maccabeus on. Archaeological and palaeographical data have little significance for him ('Wicked Priest or Wicked Priests? Reflections on the Identification of the Wicked Priest in the Habakkuk Commentary', *JJS* 33 [1982], pp. 349-59);

cf. Morton Smith ('The Dead Sea Sect in Relation to Ancient Judaism', *NTS* 7 [1961], pp. 347-60), who speaks of a plurality of wicked priests and righteous teachers.

5. This widely advocated theory is discussed below in section C. The scholars falling into this category are many, but four are selected for their lasting contribution to the consensus: Gert Jeremias, *Der Lehrer der Gerechtigkeit*; Hartmut Stegemann, *Die Entstehung der Qumrangemeinde*; Jerome Murphy-O'Connor, 'The Essenes and their History', *RB* 81 (1974), pp. 215-44; *idem*, 'Demetrius I and the Teacher of Righteousness', *RB* 83 (1976), pp. 400-420; *idem*, 'The Essenes in Palestine', *BA* 40 (1977), pp. 100-24, and several other articles discussed below; and Frank M. Cross, Jr, *The Ancient Library of Qumran and Modern Biblical Studies*. Jeremias, Stegemann, and Murphy-O'Connor identify the Wicked Priest with Jonathan Maccabeus; Cross, with Simon Macabeus. Geza Vermes seems to have been one of the first to advocate the Maccabean thesis. Unfortunately, his *Les manuscrits du désert de Juda* was not available for examination; see however his works mentioned in note 3 above. F.J. Weinert associates 4Q159 with Murphy-O'Connor's thesis of Babylonian origins ('4Q 159: Legislation for an Essene Community Outside of Qumran?', *JSJ* 5 [1974], pp. 179-207; *idem*, 'A Note on 4Q159 and a New Theory of Essene Origins', *RQ* 34 [1977], pp. 223-30). Philip R. Davies (*The Damascus Covenant. An Interpretation of the 'Damascus Document'*) tends toward the thesis of Babylonian origins. Cf. M.A. Knibb ('Exile in the Damascus Document', *JSOT* 25 [1983], pp. 108-14), who objects to the Babylonian thesis and instead maintains that the Essenes emerged in a Palestinian context in the third and second centuries BCE.

6. J. van der Ploeg (*The Excavations at Qumran*) identifies the Wicked Priest with Alexander Jannaeus and the Kittim with Pompey and the Romans. A. Dupont-Sommer (*The Jewish Sect of Qumran and the Essenes*) identifies Aristobulus II as the Wicked Priest.

7. J.L. Teicher dates the main characters and events of the scrolls to the first century CE; the Teacher of Righteousness and the Wicked Priest are identified respectively with Jesus and Paul. See especially his articles in *JJS* 1-6 (1951-55) with the title 'The Teaching of the Pre-Pauline Church in the Dead Sea Scrolls'. Similarly, Barbara Thiering associates Qumran history with the group that returned to Qumran after the earthquake of 31 BCE and with the early Christians. While she does not question the accepted view of archaeology at Qumran and the relative chronology inferred from it, her identification of the Teacher of Righteousness and the Wicked Priest with John the Baptist and Jesus puts her somewhere between Teicher, Driver, and Roth. She also offers new datings of some of the Qumran hands. See her 'Once More the Wicked Priest', *JBL* 97 (1978), pp. 191-205; *idem*, *Redating the Teacher of Righteousness*; *idem*, *The Gospels and Qumran. The Qumran Origins of the Christian Church*. Robert Eisenman (*Maccabees, Zadokites,*

Christians and Qumran) belongs, by virtue of his association of the Qumran texts and archaeology with first-century Christianity in Palestine (Jesus and James), to the Christian theory. He offers, however, a substantive critique and reinterpretation of the archaeological (pp. 24, 32-34) and of the palaeographical (pp. 28-31) data. See also his *James the Just in the Habakkuk Pesher*.

8. G.R. Driver, *Judean Scrolls*; C. Roth, *The Historical Background of the Dead Sea Scrolls*.

9. Y. Baer, 'Serek ha Yahad—The Manual of Discipline: A Jewish Christian Document from the Beginning of the Second Century C.E.', *Zion* 29 (1964), pp. 1-60. I Sonne, 'A Hymn against Heretics in the Newly Discovered Scrolls', *HUCA* 23 (1950/51), pp. 275-313. The latter attributes some of 1QH to Jewish gnostics of the second century CE. Cf. M. Wallenstein ('A Hymn from the Scrolls', *VT* 5 [1955], pp. 277-83).

10. See note 1 above on Zeitlin. S.B. Hoenig considered 1QSa to be an early Karaite composition. See his 'The Age of Twenty in Rabbinic Tradition and 1QSa', *JQR* 49 (1959), pp. 209-14; *idem*, 'The Dead Sea Psalm Scroll', *JQR* 58 (1967), pp. 162-63; *idem*, 'The Sectarian Scrolls and Rabbinic Research', *JQR* 59 (1968), pp. 24-70. A.N. Polak identifies the Kittim with the Seljuk Turks of the eleventh and twelfth centuries CE. See also his 'The Dead Sea Scrolls: A New Approach', *JQR* 49 (1959), pp. 89-107.

11. Frank M. Cross, Jr, *The Ancient Library*, pp. 81, 87-89; H. Stegemann, *Die Entstehung*, p. 4; J. Murphy-O'Connor, 'The Essenes and their History', *RB* 81 (1974), p. 215.

12. Robert Eisenman, see note 8 above; Zeitlin, dispersed throughout his writings (see note 1 above); G.R. Driver, *Judean Scrolls*, pp. 393-420.

13. Geza Vermes, *Les manuscrits du désert de Juda* (not available for examination).

14. *Ibid*., 'The Essenes and History', *JJS* 32 (1981), pp. 20-21.

15. Gert Jeremias, *Der Lehrer der Gerechtigkeit*.

16. *Ibid*., pp. 10-166.

17. *Ibid*., pp. 10-139.

18. *Ibid*., pp. 140-66.

19. *Ibid*., pp. 168-267.

20. *Ibid*., esp. pp. 168-80.

21. *Ibid*., pp. 319-53.

22. Hartmut Stegemann, *Die Entstehung*.

23. *Ibid*., pp. 9-16.

24. *Ibid*., p. 10.

25. *Ibid*., pp. 10-11.

26. *Ibid*., pp. 12-15.

27. *Ibid*., pp. 14-15.

28. *Ibid*.

29. *Ibid*., p. 5.

30. *Ibid*., p. 20.

31. *Ibid.*, pp. 20-21.
32. *Ibid.*, pp. 21-24.
33. *Ibid.*, pp. 24-25.
34. *Ibid.*, pp. 25-27.
35. *Ibid.*
36. *Ibid.*, pp. 41-53, 82-87.
37. *Ibid.*, pp. 53-69.
38. *Ibid.*, pp. 69-82.
39. *Ibid.*
40. *Ibid.*
41. *Ibid.*, pp. 87-95.
42. *Ibid.*, pp. 95-115.
43. *Ibid.*, pp. 115-20.
44. *Ibid.*, pp. 120-27.
45. *Ibid.*, pp. 128-84. See also pp. 39 and 198.
46. *Ibid.*, pp. 186-97.
47. *Ibid.*, pp. 198-246a.
48. *Ibid.*, pp. 207-24. According to Stegemann (p. 224), the Teacher was a Sadducee before joining the Essene-Qumran community.
49. *Ibid.*, p. 242.
50. *Ibid.*, pp. 242-43.
51. *Ibid.*, pp. 253-54.
52. Jerome Murphy-O'Connor, 'An Essene Missionary Document? CD II,14–VI,1', *RB* 77 (1970), p. 215.
53. Since 1QS plays no part in understanding historical episodes involving members of the Qumran community, i.e. the Teacher, the Wicked Priest, the Liar, Murphy-O'Connor's contribution to understanding this document will not be discussed here.
54. Murphy-O'Connor, 'An Essene Missionary Document?', pp. 201-29; *idem*, 'A Literary Analysis of Damascus Document VI,2–VIII,3', *RB* 78 (1971), pp. 210-32. Murphy-O'Connor's concern with the pre-Teacher phase of the community's history is based on his particular interpretation of CD I,9-12.
55. Stegemann, *Die Entstehung*, pp. 23, 128.
56. See note 54 above. Murphy-O'Connor thinks of the Qumran community archaeologically as that community which settled at Qumran along with its Teacher of Righteousness in the middle of the second century BCE and remained there until c. 70 CE, with only a thirty-year occupational hiatus. From a literary standpoint (CD I,5-10), this is the Teacher's community. Murphy-O'Connor believes that an earlier community, originating in and emigrating from Babylon, authored two documents (CD II,14–VI,1 and VII,4–VIII,3), which the later Qumran community took up and adapted to form the Damascus Document as we know it. The earlier community is often called the pre-Qumran/pre-Teacher (Essene) community.
57. *Ibid.*

58. *Ibid.* See also F.J. Weinert (note 5 above).
59. *Ibid.*, 'The Essenes and their History', pp. 226-29.
60. *Ibid.*, 'Damascus Document VI,2–VIII,3', pp. 228-31.
61. *Ibid.*, 'The Critique of the Princes of Judah (CD VIII,3-19)', *RB* 79 (1972), pp. 200-16.
62. *Ibid.*, 'The Essenes and their History', p. 224; *idem*, 'The Essenes in Palestine', p. 106.
63. *Ibid.*, 'The Essenes and their History', pp. 219-20.
64. See note 62 above.
65. *Ibid.*, 'The Essenes and their History', p. 225.
66. *Ibid.*
67. *Ibid.*, pp. 236-37.
68. See note 5 above.
69. Stegemann, *Die Entstehung*, p. 21.
70. Cross, *The Ancient Library*, pp. 112-18.
71. *Ibid.*, p. 113.
72. For the distinction between non-Qumranic and Qumranic literature, see *ibid.*, p. 9; *idem*, 'Die Bedeutung der Qumranfunde für die Erforschung der Apokalyptik', in *Apocalypticism in the Mediterranean World and the Near East*, ed. David Hellholm, pp. 503-18. Cf. also Baruch Levine, 'The Temple Scroll: Aspects of its Historical Provenance and Literary Character', *BASOR* 232 (1978), p. 7; George Nickelsburg, 'The Epistle of Enoch and the Qumran Literature', *Essays in honour of Yigael Yadin*, JJS 39 (1982), pp. 333, 347; W.H. Lipscomb and J.A. Sanders, 'Wisdom at Qumran', in *Israelite Wisdom. Theological and Literary Essays in Honor of Samuel Terrien*, ed. John G. Gammie, Walter A. Brueggemann, W. Lee Humphreys, pp. 280-21, 283 n. 3. See also Lawrence Schiffman ('The Temple Scroll in Literary and Philological Perspective', in *Approaches to Ancient Judaism*, ed. W.S. Green, pp. 147-51) who makes a distinction based on orthography and language.
73. Stegemann, 'Die Bedeutung der Qumranfunde', p. 511. 'Als "spezifische Qumrantexte" können zunächst nur solche Werke aus den Qumranfunden gelten, die der Gestalt des "Lehrers der Gerechtigkeit" eine autoritative Funktion beimessen, die die spezifische Ordnung der Qumrangemeinde kennen, auf andere Weise deren Sonderstellung im Rahmen des Judentums reflektieren oder wegen ihres formalen oder terminologischen Konnexes mit solchen Schriften diesen *notwendigerweise* zuzuordnen sind'. See also his discussion in 'Some Aspects of Eschatology in Texts from the Qumran Community and in the Teachings of Jesus', *Biblical Archaeology Today. Proceedings of the International Congress on Biblical Archaeology, Jerusalem, April 1984* (IEJ, 1985), pp. 408-26, specifically 409-10.
74. Stegemann, 'Die Bedeutung der Qumranfunde', p. 511.
75. The provenance of several non-biblical documents among the Qumran finds is still debated: these are CD, 1QM, the Songs of the Sabbath Sacrifice, and the Temple Scroll.

76. Stegemann, *Die Entstehung*, pp. 19-28.
77. *Ibid.* See also pp. 39-41.
78. *Ibid.*, p. 39.
79. *Ibid.*
80. *Ibid.*, p. 20.
81. *Ibid.*, Joseph Amoussine ('The Reflection of Historical Events of the First Century BC in Qumran Commentaries (4Q 161; 4Q 169; 4Q 166)', *HUCA* 48 [1977], pp. 123-24) takes issue with Stegemann's claim that these fragmentary pesharim 'ganz geringfügig sind und nur wenige geschichtliche Angaben bieten'.
82. Stegemann, *Die Entstehung*, p. 39.
83. *Ibid.*, pp. 39-40. 'Als die entscheidenden, weil umfänglichsten bzw. am vollständigsten erhaltenen Vertreter der mit den Qumrantexten erstmalig bekanntgewordenen Gattung der pešarim wurden in Kapitel II bereits 1QpHabakuk, 4QpNahum und 4QpPs 37 gekennzeichnet, die auch inhaltlich manches miteinander gemeinsam haben, andererseits Unterschiede im Sachbezug ihrer Aussagen und in der verwendeten Terminologie zeigen, die vielleicht von den jeweiligen Bibeltexten, vielleicht aber auch von verschiedenem Interesse der einzelnen pešarim oder von Unterschieden im historischen Ort (etwa verschiedenes Abfassungsdatum) herrühren könnten und nicht nur Angaben über die Gemeinde selbst, sondern auch solche über Aussenstehende betreffen'.
84. *Ibid.*, p. 40.
85. *Ibid.*
86. *Ibid.*
87. *Ibid.*
88. *Ibid.*
89. *Ibid.*
90. *Ibid.*
91. *Ibid.*, pp. 21-27.
92. *Ibid.*
93. *Ibid.*, pp. 23-24.
94. *Ibid.*, pp. 26-27.
95. *Ibid.*, p. 23. Concerning CD, he says: 'Zweitens verfolgt die Geschichtsdarstellung in CD nach Ausweis ihres formalen Rahmens den besonderen Zweck der religiösen Belehrung von Mitgliedern der Qumrangemeinde, hat also eine ganz besondere *Tendenz*, die Auswahl und Darbietung historischer Daten bestimmt haben wird und leichter zu erkennen ist, wenn man über die geschichtliche Wirklichkeit schon von anderer Seite her, wenn auch vielleicht in bescheidenem Ausmass informiert ist, als wenn man ohne solche Hilfe versuchen müsste, sie allein aus der Stoffdarbietung selbst zu erheben'. Compare this with his very explicit later remark: 'Eine Untersuchung über die Entstehung der Qumrangemeinde setzt am besten bei den Gegneraussagen in den Qumrantexten ein und orientiert sich zweckmässigerweise zunächst

ausschliesslich an der Textgruppe der pešarim. Die sachlichen und formalen Gründe für dieses Vorgehen wurden bereits in den beiden ersten Kapiteln dieser Untersuchung dargestellt und ebenfalls die Gesichtspunkte angeführt für die Reihenfolge, in der die weiteren Texte (Damaskusschrift, 'Lehrerlieder' in 1QHodajot und sonstige Qumranschriften) nacheinander herangezogen werden sollen. Die Behandlung formal verschiedener Texte grundsätzlich je für sich und nacheinander soll freilich nicht ausschliessen, dass auch schon etwa bei der Analyse der pešarim Angaben z.B. der Damaskusschrift oder der Hodajot herangezogen werden; doch darf deren Heranziehung nicht dazu dienen, die Argumente zu liefern, sondern lediglich der Kontrolle *unabhängig* von den anderen Schriften gewonnener Ergebnisse. Nach dieser Absicherung gegen voreilige Kombinationen gilt es nun, die Gegneraussagen der pešarim auf ihre Sachbezüge und mögliche Auskunft über historische Daten hin zu befragen'.

96. Martin Noth, *The History of Israel* (2nd edn), p. 44: 'The study of historical sources cannot and must not be confined to the collecting and the arranging of the relevant information'.

97. *Ibid.*: 'In certain circumstances the task of interpreting the relative usefulness and significance of the sources is even more important'.

98. *Ibid.*: 'it is absolutely necessary to investigate the sources of these records, to ask what occasioned them, why they were made and made in this form, what they are intended to connote and what they are capable of signifying historically. And this question must be applied to each single tradition'.

99. *Ibid.*: 'Only when we have grasped the circumstances under which they arose and what they are driving at, can we answer the vital question as to how they arrived at their particular selection from the wealth of events and why they presented it in the particular way they did'.

100. *Ibid.*: 'Only when we have answered that can we discern the subjects on which they can be expected to supply information and the weight which may be attached to what they say and to what they suppress'.

101. *Ibid.*, p. 45 n. 1: 'Anyone who does not ask these questions misjudges the situation and inevitably gives tacit answers, only these answers will not be considered and well founded, and will therefore not withstand closer examination'.

Notes to Chapter 2

1. See Chapter 1 n. 13. Most recently Robert Eisenman has addressed the use of the archaeological data in reconstructing the history of the Qumran community (*Maccabees, Zadokites, Christians and Qumran*, pp. 24, 32-34). Although Norman Golb ('Who Hid the Dead Sea Scrolls?', *BA* 48 [1985], pp. 68-82) has not directly criticized the use of the archaeological data from

Qumran to reconstruct the history of the community of the Dead Sea Scrolls, in a preliminary fashion he has raised the issue of the identity of the group that hid the scrolls.

2. Frank M. Cross, Jr, *The Ancient Library*, p. 87.

3. Martin Noth, *The History of Israel*, 2nd edn, pp. 45-51.

4. Roger Moorey, *Excavation in Palestine*, p. 111: 'History is much concerned with events, archaeology almost exclusively with the background against which events take place. The short term interplay of cause and effect in human affairs constitutes a significant part of history's subject matter. This is not so in archaeology, whose raw material is most readily interpreted in terms of the broad, economic, social and technological factors affecting human life'. Cf. the remarks in Anthony Snodgrass, 'Archaeology', in *Sources for Ancient History*, ed. Michael Crawford, pp. 139, 145, and 166.

5. Noth, *The History*, p. 47: 'In general, it must not be expected to yield positive evidence concerning particular historical events and processes, except when it leads to the happy discovery of written documents'.

6. *Ibid.*: 'But it can certainly shed a far-reaching light on the presuppositions and conditions of life and the changes they underwent in the course of time, and it can thereby reveal the background against which the historical personalities acted and the historical events took place; and insofar as these phenomena and movements are always closely related to that background, it makes a substantial contribution to our insight into the historical process'.

7. *Ibid.*, p. 47: 'Even archaeological discoveries can only be understood and appreciated in relation to information from literary sources'. Cf. Moorey, *Excavation*, p. 111: 'Archaeologists in Palestine, as elsewhere, certainly uncover direct evidence of events, usually of the catastrophic kind, such as earthquakes and burnings of cities by enemies. But the extent to which they may be reconstructed from archaeological evidence alone is highly circumscribed. The details upon which the precision of historical reconstruction rests are supplied only by written sources. The most decisive events in world history have left no immediate trace whatsoever in the archaeological record'.

8. Roland de Vaux, 'On the Right and Wrong Uses of Archaeology', in *Essays in Honor of Nelson Glueck. Near Eastern Archaeology in the Twentieth Century*, ed. James A. Sanders, p. 70.

9. *Ibid.*

10. *Ibid.*; *idem*, 'Method in the Study of Early Hebrew History', in *The Bible in Modern Scholarship*, ed. John Philip Hyatt, pp. 27-28.

11. *Ibid.*, p. 70.

12. *Ibid.*; *idem*, *The Archaeology of Qumran*, p. viii.

13. F. de Saulcy, *Narrative of a Journey Round the Dead Sea and in the Bible Lands, in 1850 and 1851. Including an Account of the Discovery of the Sites of Sodom and Gomorrah*, I, pp. 49-50; C. Clermont-Ganneau,

'Kumran', in *Archaeological Researches in Palestine during the Years* 1873-1874 II, pp. 14-16; G. Dalman, 'Jahresbericht', *PJ* 10 (1914), pp. 9-12; *idem*, *PJ* 16 (1920), pp. 40-41; E.W.G. Masterman, 'Observations on the Dead Sea Levels', *PEFQS* (1902), p. 161; *idem*, 'Notes on some ruins and a rock-cut aqueduct in the wady Kumran', *PEFQS* (1903), p. 267. See also Masterman's several reports in *PEFQS* (1902-1913, 1917).

14. Roland de Vaux, *The Archaeology of Qumran*. See also E.-M. Laperrousaz, *Qumran: L'Établissement essénien des bords de la Mer Morte. Histoire et archéologie*; J.A. Sanders, 'History and Archaeology of the Qumran Community', *BASOR* 231 (1978), p. 79; Philip R. Davies, *Qumran*. For bibliographical information on the archaeological work at Qumran, see Elaine Vogel, 'Bibliography of Holy Land Sites', *HUCA* 42 (1971), pp. 54-55; Elaine K. Vogel and Brooks Holtzclaw, 'Bibliography of Holy Land Sites, Part II', *HUCA* 52 (1981), p. 71; Hans Bardtke, 'Qumran und seine Funde', *TRu* 29 (1963), pp. 261-62, 268-69.

15. De Vaux, *The Archaeology*, pp. 1-3.

16. *Ibid*., pp. 3-40.

17. On stratum Ia, see *ibid*., pp. 3-5.

18. On Ib, see *ibid*., pp. 5-24.

19. *Ibid*., pp. 8-10.

20. *Ibid*., pp. 11-12.

21. *Ibid*., p. 12.

22. *Ibid*., pp. 12-15.

23. *Ibid*., pp. 17-18.

24. *Ibid*., p. 17.

25. *Ibid*., p. 18.

26. *Ibid*.

27. On the numismatic evidence, see *ibid*., pp. 18-19.

28. *Ibid*., pp. 20-22. See also Plate XXXIX.

29. *Ibid*., pp. 20-21.

30. *Bell*. 1.270-72; *Ant*. 15.121-122.

31. De Vaux, *The Archaeology*, pp. 23-24.

32. On stratum II, see *ibid*., pp. 24-41.

33. *Ibid*., pp. 28-29.

34. *Ibid*.

35. *Ibid*.

36. *Ibid*., p. 29.

37. *Ibid*.

38. *Ibid*., p. 30.

39. *Ibid*., pp. 22-23, 33-34.

40. *Ibid*.

41. *Ibid*., pp. 35-36.

42. *Ibid*., p. 36.

43. *Ibid*., p. 34.

44. *Ibid.*, pp. 36-37.

45. *Ibid.*, pp. 34-35. M. Sharabani ('Monnaies de Qumran au Musée Rockefeller de Jerusalem', *RB* 87 [1980], pp. 274ff.) has published all the material from Hoard A that was found in the Rockefeller Museum in Jerusalem.

46. *Ibid.*, p. 35.

47. *Ibid.*

48. *Ibid.*, pp. 35-36.

49. On stratum III, see *ibid.*, pp. 41-44.

50. *Ibid.*

51. *Ibid.*, p. 44.

52. *Ibid.*

53. *Ibid.*

54. *Ibid.*, pp. 42-43.

55. *Ibid.*, p. 43.

56. *Ibid.*

57. *Ibid.*, p. 45.

58. *Ibid.*

59. *Ibid.*, n. 3, citing an article by A. Kindler.

60. *Ibid.*, p. 45.

61. On the remains recovered from the caves, see *ibid.*, pp. 49-53. Joseph A. Fitzmyer (*The Dead Sea Scrolls Major Publications and Tools*, pp. 11-39) has a useful listing of textual discoveries according to the particular caves where they were found.

62. *Ibid.*, p. 54 n. 1.

63. De Vaux originally characterized the pottery as late Hellenistic. He discerned no ceramic wares dating to the Roman period ('À propos des manuscrits hébreux', *RB* 57 [1950], p. 429): 'La céramique est très abondante et relève toute—sauf un petit groupe sur lequel on va revenir—d'une même époque. Elle se classe indiscutablement à la fin de l'âge héllénistique, au IIe siècle av. J.-C. Elle peut aller jusqu'au début du Ier s. av. J.-C., mais elle est certainement antérieure à l'époque romaine'. Concerning de Vaux's reinterpretation of the age of the ceramic wares, G. Vermes (*The Dead Sea Scrolls*, p. 12) says: 'In the spring of 1952, de Vaux, who was in the process of completing his first campaign at Qumran, prepared a report for the French Académie des Inscriptions in which he advanced his new interpretation of the archaeological facts and confessed his previous mistakes: "*Je me suis trompé. . . Je me suis trompé. . . Je me suis trompé. . .* "'.

64. De Vaux, *The Archaeology*, pp. 95-111.

65. *Ibid.*, pp. 45-48.

66. *Ibid.*, pp. 57-58.

67. *Ibid.*, pp. 58-86.

68. Pesah Bar-Adon, 'Another Settlement of the Judean Desert Sect at 'En el-Ghuweir on the Shores of the Dead Sea', *BASOR* 227 (1977), pp. 1-25;

idem, 'The Expedition to the Judean Desert, 1960. Expedition C', *IEJ* 11 (1961), pp. 25-30.

69. *Ibid.*, pp. 8, 12, 16 fig. 17.

70. De Vaux, *The Archaeology*, p. 88.

71. Bar-Adon, 'Another Settlement', pp. 5-7, fig. 10:1,12. (storage jars); fig. 12:1-6, 9-11 (jugs, juglets); fig. 14:1-9, 11-12 (cooking pots); fig. 15:1-6 (flasks); fig. 15:7-12 (bowls); fig, 15:13-15, 17 (bowls); fig. 15:20 (lamps). Bar-Adon speaks of the ceramic ware as extending from 200 or 150 BCE to 70 CE. Occasionally, he extends this upper range to the Bar-Kokhba period, as in the case of some craters (fig. 14:14) and lamps (fig. 15:20, c. 75 BCE–135 CE).

72. *Ibid.*

73. Davies, *Qumran*, p. 53. See also Paul W. Lapp, *Palestinian Ceramic Chronology*, p. 11 n. 20.

74. See nn. 28-29 above. Still, there are other explanations. (A) The early de Vaux, Dupont-Sommer, and Laperrousaz advocate the view that the fire and the earthquake were two causally/chronologically distinct events. (R. de Vaux, *RB* 61 [1954], p. 235; A. Dupont-Sommer, *Les Écrits esséniens*, pp. 349-50; E.-M. Laperrousaz, *Qumran*, p. 44). According to this proposal, the fire would be evidence of an attack on the Qumran complex—related to the struggles of Hyrcanus II and Aristobulus II (67–63 BCE). The coins of Ib, which extend at least into the reign of Antigonus Mattathias and perhaps into the reign of Herod the Great, do not lend credence to this possibility. (B) Another thesis associates the fire with military confrontation at Qumran, specifically a Parthian onslaught in the year 40 BCE, but dismisses the apparent evidence of seismic activity (J.T. Milik, *Ten Years*, p. 52; B. Mazar, T. Dothan, and I. Dunayevsky, *En-Gedi*, p. 5 n. 16; B. Kanael, 'Two Observations on the Chronology of Khirbet Qumran', *EI* 5 [1958], p. 93; P. Bar-Adon, 'The Expedition to the Judean Desert', *IEJ* 11 [1961], pp. 25-30; *idem*, 'Another Settlement', *BASOR* 227 [1977], pp. 18-20; R.H. Smith, 'The "Herodian" Lamp of Palestine. Types and Dates', *Berytus* 14 [1961], p. 58 n. 15; Davies, *Qumran* p. 56; Eisenman, *Maccabees*, p. 24). The seismic evidence cannot be simply ignored, and the numismatic data dating at least to 37 BCE militate against Ib ending in 40 BCE.

75. D.H. Kallner-Amiran, 'Revised Earthquake-Catalogue of Palestine—I', *IEJ* 1 (1950/51), pp. 223-46; *idem*, 'A Revised Earthquake-Catalogue of Palestine—II', *IEJ* 2 (1952), pp. 48-57. There were also other known earthquakes in the years 19, 30, and 33 CE.

76. A. Schalit, *Koenig Herodes*, pp. 122-23 n. 98, 5 n. 19.

77. S.H. Steckoll, 'The Qumran Sect in Relation to the Temple of Leontopolis', *RQ* 6 (1967), p. 69; *idem*, 'Marginal Notes on the Qumran Excavations', *RQ* 7 (1969), pp. 33-34 n. 8.

78. I. Karcz and U. Kafri, 'Evaluation of Supposed Archeoseismic Damage in Israel', *Journal of Archaeological Science* 5 (1978), pp. 237-45.

79. *Ibid.*, p. 251.

80. *Ibid*., pp. 241-42: 'Though this interpretation [that of de Vaux] enjoys official status (as witnessed by the text on tourist post-cards), the actual field evidence *per se* is inconclusive. The settlement is located in Lisan Marl, a late Pleistocene formation which consists of alternating calcareous and clayey layers. This sub-stratum is unstable and is prone to differential swelling desiccation, and compaction which result in cracks, rills and landslides. Furthermore, a small sediment-settling basin is located just behind the damaged staircase, so that its collapse may have been caused by seepage, percolation or piping (Figure 3). The nontectonic explanation of the Qumran displacement was originally offered by Zavistock, who supervised the excavations, but was subsequently rejected (de Vaux, 1961). Joints and fissures, subject to similar reservations occur also in several other buildings and structures at Khirbet Qumran'.

81. *Ibid*., p. 242.

82. Both the Herodian coins and many others from Qumran have not yet been published. Originally, Father Spijkerman was entrusted with their publication. Ms Marcia Sharabani says she has published all of the Qumran coins that were housed at the Rockefeller Museum in Jerusalem only (Hoard A, see n. 44 above). The lists of Qumran coins that were drawn up by Spijkerman and Seyrig are, according to Ms Sharabani, safely locked away at the Rockefeller Museum. The remainder of the Qumran coins are presumably in the Amman Museum. According to Père Benoit, O.P., 408 coins from Qumran were originally brought to Amman. King Hussein gave President Nixon three of them. They are housed in the presidential repository in Washington, D.C., where gifts to the Presidents of the USA are kept. Fifty other coins were displayed, along with Qumran documents and artifacts, in the USA and England. These items were returned to Amman on June 16, 1966 and were checked by the American Embassy on June 18, 1966, reporting that 'all items were accounted for and in good condition'. Nevertheless, no one seems to know the whereabouts of these coins. Presumably, 353 coins are still housed in the Amman Museum. Under the auspices of the École biblique et Archéologique Française, Mr Christian Augé of the Institut d'Art et d'Archéologie in Paris is charged with the publication of these coins still in the Amman Museum. Père Benoit assured the writer that no Qumran coins are presently housed in the École Biblique. Special appreciation goes to Ms Marcia Sharabani and Père P. Benoit, O.P. who kindly discussed these matters with the writer in Jerusalem in April, 1984.

83. See n. 23 above.

84. Lapp, *Palestinian Ceramic Chronology*, p. 15.

85. *Ibid*., p. 16.

86. *Ibid*., p. 18.

87. *Ibid*., p. 20.

88. *Ibid*., p. 12.

89. *Ibid*., pp. 11-12.

90. De Vaux, *The Archaeology*, p. 33 n. 2, where he says: 'The pottery of Qumran now appears less "autonomous" or "original" than I stated it to be at an earlier stage'.

91. *Ibid.*, pp. 147, 161-62, 185, 187.

92. Bar-Adon, 'Another Settlement', pp. 5-7.

93. *Ibid.*, p. 7.

94. Smith, 'The "Herodian" Lamp', p. 65.

95. Recognizing the difficulties involved in distinguishing Ib and II pottery chronologically, wares which are indeed similar, Laperrousaz suggests a way of taking into account both the similarities between the wares of Ib and II and their differences (*Qumran*, pp. 45-47). He does this by postulating the end of Ib between the years 67–63 BCE and the beginning of IIa during the reign of Herod the Great. Like de Vaux, he thinks there was probably an abandonment of the site during Herod's reign. IIb would have begun in the reign of Herod Archelaus. Understanding the signs of conflagration at Qumran Ib as results of military activity in the 60s BCE enables Laperrousaz to account for the similarity of Ib and IIa pottery. IIa functions as a transition into the actual typological watershed, IIb. He claims that de Vaux has occasionally mistaken stratum Ib for IIa and vice versa. Laperrousaz's assessment of the ceramic and the stratigraphic situation could conceivably account for the presence of the Herodian coins—deriving from the settlement of Qumran in the reign of Herod the Great. While Laperrousaz has offered an alternative explanation to that of de Vaux, he too is probably attempting to be overly precise in dating the evidence of burning above de Vaux's Ib/his Ia remains. His attempt to account for the similarities of the ceramic forms of Ib and II (de Vaux) by shifting the beginning of Ib back to 67–63 BCE and the beginning of IIa to the reign of Herod the Great still assumes a period of abandonment of approximately thirty years. This assumption is indefensible. Still, more attention needs to be given to his period of transition—IIa (from the reign of Herod the Great to Herod Archelaus). In the present context, the correctness or incorrectness is not relevant to the main conclusions of this chapter.

Notes to Chapter 3

1. Hartmut Stegemann, *Die Entstehung*, pp. 9-16; J. Murphy-O'Connor, 'The Essenes and their History', *RB* 81 (1974), pp. 215-16; Frank M. Cross, Jr, *The Ancient Library*, 87. In contrast to these scholars, several others have questioned the assumption that datings based on palaeographical analysis are superior to clues provided in the Qumran literature in determining the chronological background for reconstructing the history of the Qumran community (see Chapter 1 nn. 1, 5, 8, 9). Others have doubted the accuracy of the palaeographical datings themselves: S. Zeitlin, 'The Hebrew Scrolls:

Once More and Finally', *JQR* 41 (1950-51), pp. 17-19; *idem*, 'The Hebrew Scrolls and the Status of Biblical Scholarship', *JQR* 42 (1951-52), p. 153; *idem*, 'The Fiction of the Recent Discoveries near the Dead Sea', *JQR* 44 (1953-54), p. 102; Ernest Lacheman, 'Reply to the Editor', *BASOR* 116 (1949), pp. 16-17; *idem*, 'A Matter of Method in Hebrew Palaeography', *JQR* 40 (1949-50), pp. 15-39; *idem*, 'Can Hebrew Palaeography be called "Scientific"?', *JQR* 42 (1951-52), pp. 377-85; *idem*, 'Hebrew Palaeography Again', *JQR* 44 (1953), pp. 116-22; J.L. Teicher, 'Method in Hebrew Palaeography', *JJS* 2 (1950-51), p. 201; G.R. Driver, *The Judean Scrolls*, pp. 16-35. Robert Eisenman, *Maccabees*, pp. 28-31, 78-79; Isaiah Sonne, 'A Hymn Against Heretics in the Newly Discovered Scrolls', *HUCA* 23 (1950-51), pp. 275-313.

2. Cross, *The Ancient Library*, p. 87.

3. *Ibid*., 'The Development of the Jewish Scripts', *The Bible and the Ancient Near East*, pp. 140-45, 181-88.

4. *Ibid*.

5. N. Avigad, 'The Palaeography of the Dead Sea Scrolls', in *Scripta Hierosolymitana*, IV (1975), pp. 56-87; S. Birnbaum, *The Hebrew Scripts* II, *passim*.

6. Robert Eisenman (*Maccabees*, p. 81 n. 152) has pointed out the problems inherent in Birnbaum's attempt to quantify a series of Hebrew scripts.

7. Cross, 'The Development', Figure 1, line 3.

8. *Ibid*., line 4.

9. *Ibid*., line 5.

10. *Ibid*., line 6.

11. According to a letter from John Strugnell to Ben Zion Wacholder in the latter's *The Dawn of Qumran*, pp. 205-206. This may not be an early copy of the Temple Scroll. Perhaps it derives from an expanded *torah* MS.

12. Cross, 'The Development', Figure 1, line 7.

13. *Ibid*., Figure 2, line 1.

14. *Ibid*., pp. 158, 198 n. 116; Eugene C. Ulrich, '4QSam[c]: A Fragmentary Manuscript of 2 Sam. 14–15 from the Scribe of the *Serek Hay-yahad* (1QS)', *BASOR* 235 (1979), pp. 1-2.

15. Cross, 'The Development', p. 158.

16. Avigad, 'The Palaeography', p. 71.

17. Barbara Thiering, *Redating the Teacher of Righteousness*, pp. 39-45. Her valuable reassessment of the dating of Hasmonean semiformal scripts—1QS, 4QTest, 4QpIsa[c]—has yet to receive a fair hearing.

18. Cross, *The Ancient Library*, p. 89 n. 17.

19. Thiering, p. 47.

20. See n. 31.

21. Thiering, p. 45.

22. See nn. 30-31.

23. See n. 34; J.T. Milik, 'Milki-sedeq et Milki-reša', *JJS* 23 (1972), p. 135.

24. Thiering, pp. 46-47.

25. Cross, 'The Development', p. 119; Birnbaum, *The Hebrew Script*, pp. 138-43.

26. Avigad, 'The Palaeography', p. 70.

27. See above n. 24.

28. Strugnell, 'Notes en marge du volume V des "Discoveries in the Judaean Desert of Jordan"', *RQ* 7 (1970), p. 211.

29. Cross, 'The Development', p. 138.

30. *Idem*, *DJD*, p. 217.

31. Many of the texts that Cross used in his typology of Jewish scripts are still unpublished—above all 4Q texts.

32. J.T. Milik, *Ten Years*, p. 41; Cross, *The Ancient Library*, pp. 114-15. Maurya P. Horgan (*Pesharim*, pp. 3-4) questions their claim.

Notes to Chapter 4

1. E.L. Sukenik, *Megillot Genizoth*, p. 26, cf. p. 34. See recently Geza Vermes, 'The Essenes and History', *JJS* 32 (1981), pp. 19-31.

2. See Philo, Josephus, and Pliny in the Loeb Classical Series. The ancient reports are collected in A. Adam and Christoph Burchard, *Antike Berichte über die Essener*, 2nd edn, pp. 1-38. A. Dupont-Sommer (*The Essene Writings*, pp. 21-38) has an English translation of the relevant texts.

3. David Graf, 'The Pagan Witness to the Essenes', *BA* 40 (1977), pp. 125-29.

4. Adam and Burchard, *Antike Berichte*, pp. 38-61.

5. *Ibid.*, pp. 41-51. On the controversial report of Hippolytus and the Church Fathers as witnesses, see M. Black, 'The Account of the Essenes in Hippolytus and Josephus', in *The Background of the New Testament and Its Eschatology*, ed. W.D. Davies and D. Daube, pp. 172-75; *idem*, 'The Patristic Accounts of Jewish Sectarianism', *BJRL* 41 (1959), pp. 285-303; Christoph Burchard, 'Die Essener bei Hippolyt. (Hippolyt, Ref., IX 18,2-28,2 und Josephus, Bell. 2,119-161)', *JSJ* 8 (1977), pp. 1-41; A. Dupont-Sommer, 'On a Passage of Josephus Relating to the Essenes (Antiquities 18.22)', *JSS* 1 (1956), pp. 361-66; M. Smith, 'The Description of the Essenes in Josephus and the Philosophumena', *HUCA* 29 (1958), pp. 273-313; S. Zeitlin, 'The Account of the Essenes in Josephus and the Philosophumena', *JQR* 49 (1958-59), pp. 292-99.

6. S. Wagner, *Die Essener in der wissenschaftlichen Diskussion*, pp. 1-192.

7. The English translations used here are taken from Dupont-Sommer.

8. Josephus says that the Pharisees numbered more than 6000 (*Ant.* 17.2.3,42).

9. Strabo of Amaseia also speaks of the Jews as farmers and merchants. See M. Stern, *Greek and Latin Authors on Jews and Judaism*, I, pp. 287, 312.

10. F.H. Colson, 'Introduction to *Quod omnis probus liber sit*', *Philo* IX, p. 4.

11. Cf. Megasthenes in Stern, *Greek and Latin Authors*, I, p. 46.

12. Colson, 'Introduction to *De vita contemplativa*', *Philo* IX, p. 104.

13. Josephus hellenizes the Jewish sects (αἵρεσις) by depicting them as three Greek schools of philosophy, which differ from one another chiefly in respect to their views of fate, free will, and the immortality of the soul. The Pharisees are likened to the Stoics (*Ant*. 5.12), the Essenes to the Pythagoreans (15.371), and the Sadducees to the Epicureans (implied). Furthermore, just as a well-bred aristocrat attended the three academies and then chose his path, so Josephus experimented with each of the Jewish philosophies, eventually gravitating to the Pharisees. See Shaye J.D. Cohen, *Josephus in Galilee and Rome. His Vita and Development as Historian*, pp. 106-107. He maintains that Josephus' membership with the Pharisees is probably much more complex than he himself has reported (pp. 107, 144-51).

14. David L. Mealand ('Philo of Alexandria's Attitude to Riches', *ZNW* 69 [1978], pp. 258-64) says that Philo's descriptions of the Essenes and Therapeutae tell us perhaps more about Philo's views than those of these groups. See also his 'Community of Goods at Qumran', *TZ* 31 (1973), pp. 129-39.

15. Although several non-Jewish writers have knowledge of less than flattering versions of Jewish history, of its geography, and of other pieces of information concerning the Jews and Judaism, many of them associate the Jews with the seventh/Sabbath day—sometimes calling it the Day of Saturn. See the following writers in Stern, *Greek and Latin Authors*, I: 1. Agatharcides of Cnidus (pp. 106-107), 2. Meleager (p. 140), 3. Tibullus (p. 319), 4. Horace (p. 325), 5. Pompeius Trogen (pp. 335, 337), 6. Ovid (pp. 348-49), 7. Apion (p. 396), 8. Seneca (p. 431), 9. Persius (p. 436), 10. Petronius (p. 444), 11. Pliny the Elder (p. 499), 12. Fronius (p. 511), 13. Plutarch (pp. 549, 553, 558); II: 1. Tacitus (pp. 18, 25), 2. Juvenal (pp. 102-103), and 3. Suetonius (pp. 110-11). On the confrontation of Jewish and non-Jewish worlds in the Hellenistic-Roman periods, see A. Momigliano, *Alien Wisdom. The Limits of Hellenism*, pp. 74-122.

16. Cf. Luke 4.16-20.

17. Doron Mendels ('Hellenistic Utopia and the Essenes', *HTR* 72 [1979], pp. 207-22) discusses an interesting Greek parallel to the Essenes. On the common meals see Iamblicus in *Diodorus Siculus Bibliotheke* 2.59.1-3, 5; on the baths, 2.57.3.

18. See n. 14. Mendels, *ibid*. Hans-Josef Klauck, 'Gütergemeinschaft in der klassischen Antike, in Qumran und im Neuen Testament', *RQ* 11 (1982), pp. 47-79.

19. Joseph M. Baumgarten, 'The Essene Avoidance in Oil and the Laws of Purity', *RQ* 6 (1967), pp. 183-92.

20. A. Dupont-Sommer, 'On a Passage of Josephus', pp. 361-66; J. Carmignac, 'Conjecture sur un passage de Flavius Josephe relatif aux esséniens', *VT* 7 (1957), pp. 318-19; Stanley Isser, 'The Conservative Essenes: A New Emendation of Antiquities XVIII.22', *JSJ* VII (1976), pp. 177-80; H. Kruse, 'Noch einmal zur Josephus-Stelle Antiquities 18,1,5', *VT* 9 (1959), pp. 31-39; G.R. Driver, *The Judean Scrolls*, pp. 31-39.

21. See n. 17.

22. This applies primarily to *Bell.* 2: Essenes (113-61), Pharisees (162-63), and Sadducees (164-65).

23. Cohen (*Josephus*, p. 197) hints strongly that Josephus has to some extent created his list of Jewish generals involved in the First Jewish War.

24. *Ibid.*, p. 232.

25. Helgo Lindner, *Die Geschichtsauffässung des Flavius Josephus in Bellum Judaicum*, pp. 45-47.

26. Wagner, *Die Essener*, pp. 210-20.

27. See n. 1.

28. Dupont-Sommer, *The Essene Writings*, pp. 21-67, esp. 42-61 (French, pp. 55-74). See also Todd S. Beall, 'Josephus' Description of the Essenes Illustrated by the Dead Sea Scrolls' (unpublished Ph.D dissertation, The Catholic University of America, 1984). Accepting the Essene-Qumran community thesis, Beall offers a translation of the relevant passages in Josephus as well as a discussion of key terms and phrases.

29. Driver, *The Judean Scrolls*, pp. 100-121.

30. Dupont-Sommer, *The Essene Writings*, p. 61.

31. Driver, *The Judean Scrolls*, p. 121.

32. See n. 27.

33. See n. 28.

34. On the Sabbath Code in CD, see Lawrence H. Schiffman, *The Halakhah at Qumran*; on the problem of identifying the community behind the Sabbath Code with the Essenes, see especially pp. 134-46; cf. Schiffman's *Sectarian Law in the Dead Sea Scrolls*, p. 1, where he does not exclude the possibility of the Essene identification, but asserts rather that the evidence is at present insufficient to substantiate such a claim.

35. John Strugnell, 'The Angelic Liturgy at Qumran—4Q Serek Širot 'Olat Haššabbat', *VTSup* 7 (1959), pp. 318-45; Carol A. Newson, *The Songs of the Sabbath Sacrifice: Edition, Translation and Commentary*. On Old Testament and intertestamental angelology, and especially on angelology in the Dead Sea Scrolls, see Stephan F. Noll, 'Angelology in the Qumran Texts' (unpublished Ph.D. dissertation Victoria University of Manchester, 1979).

36. Driver, *The Judean Scrolls*, p. 109.

37. *Ibid.*, pp. 110-12.

38. *Ibid.*, p. 112.

39. Two different perspectives are presented in James VanderKam', The Origin, Character, and Early History of the 364-Day Calendar: A Reassessment of Jaubert's Hypothesis', *CBQ* 41 (1979), pp. 390-411; *idem*, '2 Maccabees 6, 7a and Calendrical Change in Jerusalem', *JSJ* 12 (1981), pp. 52-74; and in Philip R. Davies, 'Calendrical Change and Qumran Origins: An Assessment of VanderKam's Theory', *CBQ* 45 (1983), pp. 80-89.

40. De Vaux, *The Archaeology*, p. 47.

41. A.R.C. Leaney, *The Role of Qumran and its Meaning*, p. 32.

42. Philip R. Davies ('Hasidim in the Maccabean Period', *JSS* 28 [1977], pp. 127-40) has rightly questioned the widespread view that the Hasidim were a *well-defined sectarian* group out of whose midst the Pharisees and the Essenes emerged.

Notes to Chapter 5

1. Paul Kahle, *The Cairo Geniza*, pp. 1-11.

2. S. Schechter, *Documents of Jewish Sectarians*, 1910=reprinted with a prolegomenon by Joseph A. Fitzmyer.

3. H.H. Rowley, *The Zadokite Fragments*, pp. 1-3. Cf. the sketch of the history of interpretation of CD in Davies, *The Damascus Covenant*, pp. 3-47.

4. Paul Riessler, *Altjüdisches Schrifttum*, p. 1324.

5. S. Wagner, *Die Essener*, pp. 210-20.

6. J.T. Milik, *Ten Years*, pp. 38, 124.

7. This information derives from J.A. Fitzmyer, *Tools*, pp. 20-21, 31.

8. Milik, *Ten Years*, pp. 151-52.

9. *Ibid*., p. 152.

10. I. Rabinowitz, 'A Reconsideration of "Damascus" and "390 Years" in the "Damascus" ("Zadokite") Fragments', *JBL* 73 (1954), pp. 12-33 (see the notes to his translation).

11. S. Iwry, 'Was there a Migration to Damascus? The Problem of שבי ישראל?', *EI* 9 (1969), p. 83.

12. A.-M. Denis, *Les thèmes de connaissance dans le Document de Damas*, pp. 8-10, *passim*.

13. H. Stegemann, *Die Entstehung der Qumrangemeinde*, pp. 131-46.

14. *Ibid*., p. 146.

15. *Ibid*., pp. 146-83.

16. J. Murphy-O'Connor was the first scholar to attempt to distinguish pre-Qumranic and Qumranic documents in CD.

17. J. Murphy-O'Connor, 'An Essene Missionary Document? CD II, 14-VI, 1', *RB* 77 (1970), pp. 201-29.

18. *Idem*, 'A Literary Analysis of Damascus Document VI,2-VIII,3', *RB* 78 (1971), pp. 212-20.

19. *Ibid.*, pp. 212-17.
20. *Ibid.*, pp. 220-28.
21. *Ibid.*, p. 228.
22. *Ibid.*, pp. 228-32.
23. *Ibid.*
24. *Ibid.*
25. *Ibid.*, pp. 227-29.
26. *Idem*, 'The Critique of the Princes of Judah (CD VIII,3-19)', *RB* 79 (1972), p. 212.
27. Philip R. Davies, *The Damascus Covenant. An Interpretation of the 'Damascus Document'*, pp. 2, 22-23, 199-200.
28. *Ibid.*, pp. 48-55.
29. *Ibid.*, p. 50
30. *Ibid.*, pp. 50-53.
31. *Ibid.*, pp. 53-54.
32. *Ibid.*, pp. 56-104.
33. *Ibid.*, pp. 72-73.
34. *Ibid.*, p. 76.
35. *Ibid.*, pp. 83-104.
36. See n. 32.
37. *Ibid.*, pp. 105-41.
38. *Ibid.*, pp. 50, 119.
39. *Ibid.*, p. 133.
40. See n. 37.
41. *Ibid.*, pp. 142-72.
42. *Ibid.*, p. 169.
43. *Ibid.*
44. *Ibid.*, pp. 170-71.
45. *Ibid.*, pp. 142-72.
46. *Ibid.*, pp. 172-95.
47. *Ibid.*, pp. 172-75.
48. *Ibid.*
49. *Ibid.*, pp. 175-79.
50. *Ibid.*, pp. 174, 181-82.
51. *Ibid.*, pp. 182-86.
52. *Ibid.*, pp. 186-90.
53. *Ibid.*, pp. 190-94.
54. *Ibid.*, p. 194.
55. *Ibid.*, pp. 194-97.
56. *Ibid.*, p. 197.
57. *Ibid.*, p. 198.
58. *Ibid.*, pp. 198-201.
59. *Ibid.*, p. 199.
60. *Ibid.*, pp. 199-200.
61. *Ibid.*, p. 202.

62. K. Baltzer, *Das Bundesformular*.
63. Davies, *The Damascus Covenant*, p. 54.
64. *Ibid*., pp. 105-37.
65. See (1) CD X, 4; (2) XII,19; (3) XII,21; XIII,22; (4) XII,22; XIV,3; (5) XIII,7; (6) XIII,20; XIV,18.
66. See n. 37 above. Davies is referring to expressions like 'Teacher of Righteousness', 'Wicked Priest', 'Liar', and 'House of Absalom', which are found in 1QpHab and 4QpPs 37 as well as in the so-called Qumranic interpolations into the pre-Qumran *admonition*.
67. The situation with regard to CD, the *Admonition* and the Laws, resembles that of the Pentateuch. A key difference is that the major figures of CD's *Heilsgeschichte* remain unnamed. Instead, they usually receive sobriquets. These figures are assigned to the realms of good and evil, of obedience and disobedience, of God and Belial. Appropriately, several superscriptions in the legal material present CD's laws as valid for the Time of Godlessness (XIII,20; XIV,18).
68. Davies, *The Damascus Covenant*, pp. 53-54.
69. Since Qumran scholars tend either to discuss either the *Admonition* or the Laws to the exclusion of the other, the actual literary relationship of the two in CD has been neglected. Davies has initiated this discussion, concluding that the Laws belonged originally with the pre-Qumranic *Admonition* (see n. 37 above). Due to several lexical connections between the Laws and 1QS, 1QSa, 1QSb, and 1QM, which are not found both in the Laws and the *Admonition*, one might need to reevaluate Davies's claim.
70. See Chapter 1 nn. 5, 7-9.
71. *Ibid*., n. 5.
72. Davies, *The Damascus Covenant*, pp. 2, 22-23, 199-200.
73. The reference to the *bōgᵉdîm* provides a lexical cross-reference to the pesharim, or, according to Davies's theory of the Qumranic redaction of CD, from the latter to the former.
74. Although God is the subject in ll. 10-11, the introduction of the teacher in l. 12 complicates the matter. In any case, God is the one who instructs, even if through his agent 'a teacher'.
75. Stegemann, *Die Entstehung*, p. 132.
76. Davies, *The Damascus Covenant*, p. 64.
77. *Ibid*., pp. 64-75.
78. Jeremias, *Der Lehrer der Gerechtigkeit*, p. 152 n. 1; Stegemann, *Die Entstehung*, p. 132. In a study on the tenses of CD, Talia Thorion-Vardi ('The Use of the Tenses in the Zadokite Documents', *RQ* 12 [1985], pp. 70-71) understands *'asāh* as a relative future to *wayyōdāʿ*, which is relative past to the speaker. Like Jeremias and Stegemann, she makes the claim, but offers no arguments from context or other examples of this usage. Even if she should be correct, the temporal relationship of *'aśāh* to the speaker's contemporary situation remains unclear.

79. A. Jaubert, 'Le pays de Damas', *RB* 65 (1958), p. 236; Davies, *The Damascus Covenant*, pp. 67-68.

80. Davies, *The Damascus Covenant*, pp. 67-68.

81. *Ibid*., p. 78.

82. Both the heavenly and the terrestrial worlds share in the history of obedience and disobedience recorded in CD. The Watchers are accused of having had evil thoughts and lustful eyes. This *may* be a circumlocution for not keeping God's commandments, which is said explicitly of their offspring, the Giants (II,18-20). If that should be the case, then one would have to ask which commandments should have been followed by the heavenly world. Is this perhaps a reference to specific pre-Mosaic commandments?

83. Davies, *The Damascus Covenant*, pp. 78-91.

84. *Ibid*., pp. 80-81.

85. *Ibid*., p. 80.

86. *Ibid*., pp. 83-104.

87. Stegemann, *Die Entstehung*, p. 148.

88. Davies, *The Damascus Covenant*, p. 83.

89. *Ibid*.

90. *Ibid*., pp. 105-19.

91. *Ibid*., pp. 105-19.

92. *Ibid*., pp. 110-19.

93. *Ibid*., pp. 119. A similar tradition is also found in 2 Tim 3.1-9.

94. See n. 83.

95. Most Qumran scholars identify the *dōreš* with the Teacher of the Qumran community. For one example, see Murphy-O'Connor, 'Damascus Document VI,2-VIII,3', p. 230. S. Also John J. Collins's, review of Philip R. Davies, *The Damascus Covenant*, in *JBL* 104 (1985), p. 533.

96. *Ibid*., pp. 228-29.

97. *Ibid*., p. 229.

98. *Ibid*.

99. Stegemann, *Die Entstehung*, p. 148; Davies, *The Damascus Covenant*, p. 124.

100. Davies, *The Damascus Covenant*, pp. 119-20.

101. See Murphy-O'Connor in n. 95 above.

102. The Law of Moses seems to be the primary authority for the compilers of the Laws of cols. IX–XVI. There is a reference, however, to another document, widely thought to be a direct reference to the book of *Jubilees* (XVI,3-4). Confusion arises in the broader context in which this reference is embedded: 'therefore a man shall bind himself by oath to return to the Law of Moses, for in it all things are strictly defined. As for the exact determination of their times to which Israel turns a blind eye, behold it is strictly defined in the Book of the Divisions of the Times into their Jubilees and Weeks. And on the day that a man swears to return to the Law of Moses, the Angel of Persecution shall cease to follow him provided that he fulfils his

word: for this reason Abraham circumcised himself on the day that he knew' (XVI,1-5). The reference to the book of Jubilees is framed by appeal to the authority of the Law of Moses, thus suggesting that the interpolation of ll. 3-4 is not presenting a competing authority for the Law of Moses but rather a sort of proof-text for it.

103. Neither a date for the 'death' of the Teacher of the *Yahîd* nor for the arrival of a messiah is given. The parallel formulation in XX,13-14 answers the question 'how long?' suggested by XIX,35–XX,1. This is a period of forty years. XX,13-14 also replaces the messiah with the destruction of the men of war.

104. The reference to the 'men of war' is an allusion to Deut. 2.14: 'and the time of our leaving Kadesh-barnea until we crossed the brook Zered was thirty-eight years, until the entire generation, that is the men of war, had perished from the camp, as the Lord had sworn to them' (RSV). This is a rough estimation of the length of the Age of Wrath when God hides his face from the land, because he is angry with the wicked. Cf. Num. 1.33-35; 26.65; Deut. 1.34-35, 42-43; 2.16; CD III,7-9.

105. Most Qumran scholars make little out of the forty years, but presume that the Age of Wrath was ushered in by the death of the Teacher of Righteousness. There is no information in CD, the pesharim, or 1QH to support any speculation concerning the precise date of the Teacher's death.

106. Davies, *The Damascus Covenant*, p. 188.

107. This particular tradition is witnessed at Qumran in 4QpIsa[c] fragment 23, col. II, ll. 15-20. It is clear that the book of Isaiah was important for the people who composed and preserved the sectarian Dead Sea Scrolls. This is proven by the presence of an incomplete scroll of the book (1QIsa[b]), a complete scroll of it (1QIsa[a]), fragments of pesharim on it (4QpIsa[a-e]), and scattered allusions to and quotations of it in other Qumran documents, e.g. CD.

108. Davies, *The Damascus Covenant*, pp. 177-79.

109. Cited in *ibid*., p. 195.

110. *Ibid*., p. 64.

111. I,20; II,3; XX,26f.; IV,13; V,18; XX,8-9.

112. II,17–III,10; V,2, 17-19.

113. VI,10-11; XX,1.

114. XX,20, 25-26, 33-34.

115. See Chapter 6 below.

116. See n. 13 above.

117. *Ibid*.

118. The message of CD concerns a progression from disobedience and destruction to restoration/preservation. The anticipated contrition of humans is balanced by God's mercy. The confession of col. XX epitomizes obedience and contrition. The one confessing perceives genealogical guilt for

which he is responsible. Hence the need for confession.

119. Agreeing with Davies's view that one should translate the verb עשה as a past tense. See nn. 79-80 above.

120. Davies, *The Damascus Covenant*, pp. 72-73.

121. *Ibid.*, pp. 108-13.

122. See n. 57.

123. Stegemann, *Die Entstehung*, p. 39.

124. Davies, *The Damascus Covenant*, pp. 16-17.

125. Stegemann, *Die Entstehung*, pp. 240-41. Stegemann actually views the community at Qumran as a local manifestation of the more widespread Essene movement. The name 'Damascus' is a symbolic expression meaning outside of Judaea.

126. Cross, *The Ancient Library*, pp. 81-82.

127. Throughout the writings of Murphy-O'Connor; Davies, *The Damascus Covenant*, p. 203 (implied, not explicitly argued).

128. Davies, *The Damascus Covenant*, p. 17.

129. George J. Brooke, *Exegesis At Qumran. 4QFlorilegium in its Jewish Context*, p. 308. Cf. Davies, *The Damascus Covenant*, pp. 145-48.

130. *Ibid.*

131. On the question of the original text and the relationship of MSS A and B, see J. Murphy-O'Connor, 'The Original Text of CD 7.9-8.2=19.5-14', *HTR* 64 (1971), pp. 379-86; George J. Brooke, *Exegesis at Qumran*, pp. 302-309; Philip R. Davies, *The Damascus Covenant*, pp. 145-48.

132. Davies, *The Damascus Covenant*, pp. 184-85.

133. *Ibid.*, p. 177.

134. *Ibid.*, pp. 171-72.

135. *Ibid.*, p. 16.

136. *Ibid.*, p. 5.

137. Representatives of the prevailing consensus on the history of the Qumran community do not take this twenty years literally. It is thought to be an estimate. Murphy-O'Connor says it refers to a half-generation or ten years.

138. *Ibid.*, pp. 12-13.

139. *Ibid.*, pp. 26-27.

140. R.H. Charles, 'The Zadokite Fragments', in *Apocrypha and Pseudepigrapha of the Old Testament*, II, p. 800.

141. Stegemann, *Die Entstehung*, pp. 132-33.

142. Murphy-O'Connor, 'An Essene Missionary Document?', pp. 226-27.

143. Davies, *The Damascus Covenant*, pp. 67, 199.

144. *Ibid.*

145. I,3; IV,5; V,20; VI,10,14; VII,21; XII,23–XIII,1; XIX,10.

146. IV,4; VI,10-11.

147. I,12, 16; II,8, 10; IV,9; V,19; XX,8-9.

148. II,17; III,9; V,3-5; XIX,35–XX,1; XX,13-15.

149. (II,9-10); II,21; IV,9-10, 13; V,15, 17; VI,10-11; VII,3, 6, 12; VIII,2; IX,6; X,10.

150. See n. 136.

151. *Ibid.*; M.A. Knibb, 'Exile in the Damascus Document', *JSOT* 25 (1983), pp. 294–300.

Notes to Chapter 6

1. M. Burrows, *et al.* (eds.), *The Dead Sea Scrolls of St. Mark's Monastery*, I (New Haven, 1950).

2. W.H. Brownlee, *The Midrash Pesher of Habakkuk*. Cf. also his 'Wicked Priest, the Man of Lie, and the Righteous Teacher—The Problem of Identity', *JQR* 73 (1982), pp. 1-37, which is primarily interested in historical identifications.

3. Maurya Horgan (*Pesharim: Qumran Interpretations of Biblical Books*, p. 6) warns: (1) that the pesharim are interpreted history (2) that the language about specific figures is ambiguous and figurative, and (3) that the individual pesharim may be complex products of different stages of tradition.

4. George Brooke, 'Qumran Pesher: Towards the Redefinition of A Genre', *RQ* 10 (1981), pp. 483-503. See especially the literature presented there on the 'Pesher in the History of Scholarship'.

5. Philip R. Davies, *The Damascus Covenant*, pp. 2, 21-26, 200.

6. J. Carmignac, 'Le document de Qumran sur Melkisedeq', *RQ* 7 (1969-71), pp. 360-61.

7. Horgan, *Pesharim*, p. 94.

8. *Ibid., passim*.

9. Asher Finkel, 'The Pesher of Dreams and Scripture', *RQ* 4 (1963-64), pp. 357-70.

10. See Chapter 1 Section C above.

11. Horgan, *Pesharim*, p. 248 n. 76.

12. Stegemann, *Die Entstehung*, p. 10.

13. *Ibid.*, pp. 10-11.

14. *Ibid.*, pp. 14-15.

15. *Ibid.*, p. 11.

16. *Ibid.*, pp. 11-12.

17. *Ibid.*, pp. 12-15.

18. *Ibid.*, pp. 12-13.

19. *Ibid.*, p. 13.

20. *Ibid.*

21. *Ibid.*

22. *Ibid.*, pp. 20-21.

23. *Ibid.*, p. 39.
24. *Ibid.*, p. 40.
25. *Ibid.*
26. *Ibid.*, p. 19: 'Die der Zahl nach meisten, am weitesten ins Detail gehenden und ihren historischen Bezugspunkten nach differenziertesten Aussagen über die Qumrangemeinde und ihre geschichtliche Umwelt bietet die Textgruppe der *pešarim*. Diese stehen deshalb mit Recht allgemein im Mittelpunkt der Diskussion über die Geschichte der Qumrangemeinde'.
27. The text and restorations derive from E. Lohse, *Die Texte aus Qumran*, pp. 229-30. See M. Horgan (*The Pesharim*, pp. 24-26) for other restorations.
28. *Ibid.*, p. 57.
29. *Ibid.*
30. *Ibid.*, p. 59.
31. Karl Elliger, *Studien zum Habakuk-Kommentar*, p. 171.
32. Brownlee, *The Midrash Pesher*, pp. 55-56.
33. See above Chapter 5 nn. 78-79.
34. See the discussion of this issue in Chapter 5 Section C.
35. Paul Winter, 'Two Non-allegorical Expressions in the Dead Sea Scrolls', *PEQ* 91 (1959), pp. 38-39, 42; David Noel Freedman, 'The "House of Absalom" in the Habakkuk Scroll', *BASOR* 114 (1949), pp. 11-12.
36. Brownlee, *The Midrash-Pesher*, p. 92: Jeremias, *Der Lehrer*, p. 86.
37. Brownlee, *ibid.*
38. J. Teicher, 'The Habakkuk Scroll', *JJS* 5 (1954), p. 57.
39. Stegemann, *Die Entstehung*, p. 95.
40. *Ibid.*, p. 98.
41. *Ibid.*
42. *Ibid.*, pp. 99-100.
43. *Ibid.*, ch. 4, n. 328.
44. *Ibid.*, ch. 4, n. 329.
45. See above n. 41.
46. *Ibid.*
47. *Ibid.*, pp. 101-102.
48. *Ibid.*, p. 106.
49. *Ibid.*, pp. 109-11.
50. *Ibid.*, p. 110.
51. *Ibid.*, pp. 115-16.
52. *Ibid.*, pp. 202-204.
53. *Ibid.*, p. 204.
54. *Ibid.*, pp. 204-207.
55. *Ibid.*, pp. 205-206.
56. *Ibid.*, p. 206.
57. *Ibid.*, pp. 76-79, 120-27; Jeremias, *Der Lehrer*, pp. 127-39.
58. Stegemann, *ibid.*, p. 72.
59. Horgan, *Pesharim*, p. 19.

60. S. Talmon, 'Yom-Ha-Kipporim in the Habakkuk Scroll', *Bib* 32 (1951), pp. 542-63; *idem*, 'The Calendar Reckoning of the Sect from the Judean Desert', *Scripta Hierosolymitana* 4, ed. C. Rabin and Y. Yadin, pp. 162-99; Brownlee, *The Midrash Pesher*, p. 179-89; Horgan, *Pesharim*, pp. 30, 246-47.

61. Stegemann, *Die Entstehung*, p. 40.

62. Not only is the restoration of this text difficult, the syntax is also peculiar. At the beginning of line 16, Allegro restores [*d*]*br*; Horgan, following Skehan and Strugnell, retores [*b*]*hr*, which fits nicely with *bō'* (see *Pesharim*, p. 219).

63. Horgan, *Pesharim*, p. 198.

64. See above n. 59.

65. Horgan, *Pesharim*, pp. 7-8.

66. *Ibid*., p. 163.

67. Horgan (*Pesharim*, pp. 161, 174) points out the majority view that identifies Demetrius with Demetrius III Eukeros (95–88 BCE), Antiochus with Antiochus IV Epiphanes (169 BCE), and the Kittim with the Romans. I. Rabinowitz ('The Meaning of the Key ('Demetrius')—Passage of the Qumran Nahum Pesher', *JAOS* 98 [1978], pp. 394-99) offers the minority view that identifies Demetrius with Demetrius I Soter (162–150 BCE).

68. Horgan, *Pesharim*, p. 161.

69. *Ibid*., p. 163. Our translation deviates significantly from that of Horgan. Her restoration of line 5 with 'concerns Demetrius, who made war' would juxtapose Demetrius and the Lion of Wrath so that they would appear to be opponents. She is certainly correct that the text is broken off at the beginning of ll. 4-5, but neither the extent nor the nature of the material that is now lost can be determined. On the basis of the exegetical method of the pesharist, one would expect 'a lion'—figure to be a foreign ruler. B. Thiering ('Once More the Wicked Priest', *JBL* 97 [1978], pp. 194-202) made this point about expecting a modicum of consistency in the pesharist's application of exegetical method.

70. *Ibid*.

71. Josephus, *Ant*. 13.372-383.

72. *Ibid*.

Notes to Chapter 7

1. There are two approaches to the interpretation of the 'accursed one of Belial' and 'the two instruments of violence'. One group of scholars treats the former as a father and the latter as two sons: Frank M. Cross, Jr, *The Ancient Library*, pp. 147-55; *idem*, *Canaanite Myth and Hebrew Epic*, pp. 337-40; H. Burgmann, 'Der Josuafluch zur Zeit des Makkabäers Simon (143-134 v. Chr.)', *BZ* NF 1 (1975), pp. 26-40, esp. 38-40: *idem*, 'Gerichtsherr und

General-ankläger: Jonathan und Simon', *RQ* 9 (1977), pp. 3-72, esp. 12; *idem*, 'Der Gründer der Pharisäergenossenschaft des Makkabäer Simon', *JSJ* 9 (1977), pp. 153-91, esp. pp. 157 n. 5, 167 n. 33, 172 n. 40-173, 183-91; J.H. Charlesworth, 'The Origin and Subsequent History of the Authors of the Dead Sea Scrolls: Four Transitional Phases among the Qumran Essenes', *RQ* 10 (1980), p. 226. These scholars identify the father with Simon Maccabeus and his two sons with Judas and Mattathias. Others identify the father with John Hyrcanus I and the sons with Aristobulus I and Alexander Jannaeus: O. Betz, 'Donnersöhne, Menschenfischer und der Davidische Messias', *RQ* 3 (1961-62), p. 42 n. 4; M. Treves, 'On the Meaning of the Qumran Testimonia', *RQ* 2 (1960), pp. 569-71. John M. Allegro ('Further Messianic References in Qumran Literature', *JBL* 75 [1956], pp. 182-87) identifies the father with Alexander Jannaeus and the sons with Hyrcanus II and Aristobulus II. J.T. Milik (*Ten Years*, pp. 61-64) identifies them with Mattathias and his sons Judas and Simon. A few scholars interpret the references to 'the accursed man' and the 'two instruments of violence' as two brothers: Geza Vermes, *The Dead Sea Scrolls in English*, p. 247; Raymond E. Brown, 'The Teacher of Righteousness and the Messiah(s)', in *The Scrolls and Christianity*, ed. M. Black, p. 39; P. Skehan, 'Two Books on Qumran Studies', *CBQ* 21 (1959), p. 75; P. Winter, 'Two Non-Allegorical Expressions in the Dead Sea Scrolls', *PEQ* 91 (1959), pp. 40-42. These scholars identify the brothers with Jonathan and Simon Maccabeus.

2. Hartmut Stegemann, *Die Entstehung*, pp. 8-9.

3. This apocryphal psalm of Joshua comes from Cave 4 and belongs to the lot assigned to John Strugnell. It is not yet published.

4. George J. Brooke, *Exegesis at Qumran. 4QFlorilegium in its Jewish Context*, pp. 311-13; see also John Luebbe, 'A Reinterpretation of 4Q Testimonia', *RQ* 12 (1986), pp. 187-98.

5. *Ibid*., p. 350. Brooke thinks that the author of 4QTest was aware of the interpretation of Num. 24.15-17 in CD A VII,18-20, which understands the 'star' as the eschatological Interpreter of the Law and the 'scepter' as the kingly Messiah of David.

6. The Hebrew expression כל יקומו appears only four times in the OT in the exact form cited in 4QTest 20: Deut. 33.11; Isa. 14.21; 26.14, 43.17; and Ps. 140.11. In all these contexts, destruction is wished upon Israel's and the righteous ones' enemies. Elements in the language of Psalm 140 bear a striking resemblance to the language of 4QTest 23-30: 'evil men', 'violent men', 'the wicked', 'trap', 'net', 'snares', 'the slanderer', 'the violent man'.

7. This reconstructed text comes from J. Allegro, *DJD*, V, p. 58.

8. E. Lohse, *Die Texte aus Qumran*, pp. 251, 253.

9. Cross, *Canaanite Myth*, p. 338.

10. In support of his view that two brothers are intended, Vermes (*The Dead Sea Scrolls*, p. 144) points out that Gen. 49.5 refers to Simeon and

Levi, who destroyed Shechem, as 'instruments of violence'. One hopes that the future publication of 4QPssJosh could clarify this issue. Allegro and Cross seem to restore 4QTest 24-29 according to this text. But their notes suggest that this is not entirely the case, for the crucial beginning of l. 25, which they claim speaks of a father and two sons, is apparently missing. That leads one to suspect that 4QPssJosh may also be damaged at the place corresponding to 4QTest 25.

11. See note 1.
12. Cross, *The Ancient Library*, pp. 149, 152.
13. *Ibid.*, *Canaanite Myth*. In *The Ancient Library*, p. 149, he restored a qal sg. ('shall flow?').

Notes to Chapter 8

1. E.L. Sukenik, *Ozar hammegilloth haggenuzoth*, p. 34: J. Licht, *The Thanksgiving Scroll*, pp. 22, 24; S. Mowinckel, 'Some Remarks on Hodayoth 39.5-20', *JBL* 74 (1956), p. 276. For other advocates of this view, see, D. Dombrowski Hopkins, 'The Qumran Community and 1 Q Hodayot: A Reassessment', *RQ* 10 (1981), p. 331.
2. Gert Jeremias, *Der Lehrer der Gerechtigkeit*, pp. 168-239. He points out others who had already doubted the literary unity of 1QH (see p. 169 n. 3).
3. For example, see Jerome Murphy-O'Connor, 'The Essenes and Their History', *RB* 81 (1974), p. 217.
4. Geza Vermes, 'The Essenes and History', *JJS* 32 (1981), p. 27.
5. Jeremias, *Der Lehrer der Gerechtigkeit*, p. 170.
6. *Ibid.*
7. *Ibid.*
8. *Ibid.*, p. 171. See Fragments 10, 18, and perhaps 55.
9. *Ibid.*
10. *Ibid.*, pp. 171-73.
11. *Ibid.*, pp. 171-72.
12. *Ibid.*, p. 174.
13. *Ibid.*, pp. 174-75.
14. *Ibid.*, pp. 176-77.
15. *Ibid.*, p. 177.
16. *Ibid.*, p. 166: 'Um so stärker empfindet man, wie bedauerlich es ist, dass die Gestalt des Lehrers keine schärferen Konturen gewinnt. Das liegt nicht nur daran, dass biographische Angaben fast völlig fehlen, sondern hat vor allem seinen Grund darin, dass die bisher besprochenen Texte in einem gewissen Abstand nur von der überragenden Bedeutung des Lehrers berichten, aber fast gänzlich über seine persönliche Stellung zu Gott, seine Frömmigkeit, sein eigenes Erleben schweigen. Diese Lücke wird durch die

Selbstzeugnisse des Lehrers in den Hodayot ausgefüllt...'.

17. *Ibid.*, p. 264: 'Wichtiger für unsere Fragestellung aber war, dass sie zugleich einen Einblick in das Fühlen und Wollen ihres Verfassers erlaubten. Von seinem äusseren Schicksal erfuhren wir freilich nichts Neues über das hinaus, was uns aus der Damaskusschrift und den Pescharim bereits bekannt war, weil der Lehrer bei der Schilderung seines äusseren Ergehens weitgehend auf traditionelle Wendungen und Motive zurückgriff'.

18. Hartmut Stegemann, *Die Entstehung*, p. 26: 'Diese durchweg im Ich-Stil formulierten 'Lehrerlieder' enthalten nun zahlreiche Aussagen über Gegner ihres Autors, die nicht einfach als allgemeine Klagen über die Bösheit seiner Umwelt zu beurteilen sind, sondern auch nach Art der Darstellung konkrete geschichtliche Bezüge haben müssen'.

19. *Ibid.*

20. *Ibid.*

21. *Ibid.*, pp. 12-13.

22. *Ibid.*, p. 13.

23. *Ibid.*, pp. 186-97.

24. R. Smend, 'Über das Ich der Psalmen', *ZATW* 8 (1886), pp. 49-147, esp. 50-53.

25. E. Balla, *Das Ich der Psalmen*, p. 5.

26. H. Birkeland, *Die Feinde des Individuums in der israelitischen Psalmenliteratur*, pp. 3-4, 338.

27. E. Gerstenberger, *Der bittende Mensch. Bittritual und Klagelied des Einzelnen im Alten Testament*, pp. 114, 143-44. Cf. R. Albertz, *Persönliche Frömmigkeit und offizielle Religion*, esp. pp. 165-198.

28. S. Holm-Nielsen, *Hodayot*, pp. 330-31.

29. *Ibid.*, p. 348.

30. Holm-Nielsen, *Hodayot*, pp. 39, 46-47, 50, 64, 89-90, 98, 128, 137; cf. G. Morawe, *Aufbau und Abgrenzung der Loblieder von Qumran. Studien zur gattungsgeschichtlichen Einordnung der Hodayoth*, pp. 108-31.

31. *Ibid.*

32. *Ibid.*, p. 309.

33. *Ibid.*, p. 307.

34. *Ibid.*, p. 308.

35. *Idem*, '"Ich" in den Hodajoth und die Qumran-Gemeinde', in *Qumran-Probleme*, pp. 220-21; 'Ich will nicht leugnen, dass den Gedichten aktuelle Ereignisse und persönliche Gefühle zugrunde liegen können und dass sie möglicherweise noch hier und dort durch den Text hindurch schimmern können. Aber gerade weil diese Gedichte, woraus sie auch entstanden sein mögen, zu Psalmen der Qumrangemeinde geworden sind, also zu Gedichten des Gottesdienstes, sind sie von der konkreten aktuellen Situation gelöst und allgemein geworden, und daher ist das 'Ich' mit jedem in Qumran zu identifizieren, der im gemeinsamen Gottesdienst der Gemeinde Gott für die Erlösung dankt, die ihm zuteil geworden ist, und

dafür, dass er der Gemeinde angehört'. Cf. *idem*, 'Erwägungen zu dem Verhältnis zwischen den Hodayot und den Psalmen Salomos', in *Bibel und Qumran*, p. 117. Concerning the 'I' of the Old Testaments psalms, John H. Hayes (*Understanding the Psalms*, p. 58) says: 'Thus the 'I' that speaks may have been many individuals on different occasions throughout Israel's history. Indeed, many of the very personal psalms could have been employed by the whole congregation or by groups who saw themselves in the 'I' that addresses God'.

36. Stegemann, *Die Entstehung*, p. 188.
37. *Ibid.*
38. *Ibid.*
39. Holm-Nielsen, *Hodayot*, pp. 81 n. 14, 87.
40. Jeremias, *Der Lehrer der Gerechtigkeit*, pp. 211-13.
41. Stegemann, *Die Entstehung*, p. 190.
42. S. Talmon, 'Yom Ha-Kippurim in the Habakkuk Scroll', *Bib* 32 (1951), pp. 542-63: *idem*, 'The Calendar Reckoning of the Sect from the Judean Desert', *Scripta Hierosolymitana* 4, pp. 162-99; William H. Brownlee, *The Midrash Pesher of Habakkuk*, pp. 179-89; Maurya P. Horgan, *Pesharim: Qumran Interpretations of Biblical Books*, pp. 30, 246-47.
43. Bonnie P. Kittel, *The Hymns of Qumran*, p. 96.
44. Stegemann, *Die Entstehung*, pp. 188-89.
45. *Ibid*., p. 189.
46. *Ibid.*

BIBLIOGRAPHY

Abbott, Nabia, *The Rise of the North Arabic Script and its Kur'anic Development, with a Full Description of the Kur'an Manuscripts in the Oriental Institute* (Chicago: Chicago University Press, 1937).

Adam, A. and Burchard, Christoph, *Antike Berichte über die Essener* (2nd edn; Berlin: Walter de Gruyter, 1972).

Albertz, Rainer, *Weltschöpfung und Menschenschöpfung* (CTM, 3; Stuttgart: Calwer, 1978).

—*Persönliche Frömmigkeit und offizielle Religion* (CTM, 9; Stuttgart: Calwer, 1978).

Albright, William F., 'A Biblical Fragment from the Maccabean Age: The Nash Papyrus', *JBL* 56 (1937), pp. 145-76.

—'Comments on Dr. Lacheman's Reply and the Scrolls', *BASOR* 116 (1949), pp. 17-18.

—'On the Date of the Scrolls from 'Ain Feshkha and the Nash Papyrus', *BASOR* 115 (1949), pp. 10-19.

—'New Light on Early Recensions of the Hebrew Bible', *BASOR* 140 (1955), 27-33 = *Qumran and the History of the Biblical Text*, ed. F.M. Cross and S. Talmon, Cambridge: Harvard University Press, 1975, pp. 140-46.

—and Mann, C.S., 'Qumran and the Essenes: Geography, Chronology, and Identity of the Sect', in *The Scrolls and Christianity*, ed. M. Black (London: SPCK, 1969), pp. 11-25.

Allegro, J.M., 'Further Messianic References in Qumran Literature', *JBL* 75 (1956), pp. 174-82.

—'An Unpublished Fragment of Essene Halakhah (4Q Ordinances)', *JSS* 6 (1961), pp. 71-73.

—*Discoveries in the Judaean Desert*, V (Oxford: Clarendon, 1968).

Amoussine, Joseph D., 'A propos de l'interprétation de 4 Q 161 (Fragments 5-6 et 8)', *RQ* 8 (1974), pp. 381-92.

—'The Reflection of Historical Events of the First Century B.C. in Qumran Commentaries (4Q 161; 4Q 169; 4Q 166)', *HUCA* 48 (1977), pp. 123-52.

Amusin, J. = Amoussine, Joseph D., '4 Q Testimonia, 15-17', in *Hommages à André Dupont-Sommer* (Paris: Librairie d'Amérique et d'Orient Adrien-Maisonneuve, 1971), pp. 357-61.

Audet, J.P., 'Qumran et la notice de Pline sur les Esséniens', *RB* 68 (1961), pp. 346-87.

Avenary, H., 'Pseudo-Jerome Writings and Qumran Tradition', *RQ* 4 (1963), pp. 3-9.

Avigad, N., 'The Palaeography of the Dead Sea Scrolls and Related Documents', in *Scripta Hierosolymitana*, IV (Jerusalem: Hebrew University, 1958), pp. 56-87.

Avi-Yonah, M., Avigad, N., *et al.*, *Masada, Survey and Excavations, 1955-1956* (Jerusalem, 1957).

Baer, Y., 'Serek ha Yahad—The Manual of Discipline: A Jewish Christian Document from the Beginning of the Second Century CE' (Heb.), *Zion* 29 (1964), pp. 1-60.

Balla, E., *Das Ich der Psalmen* (Göttingen: Vandenhoeck & Ruprecht, 1912).
Baltzer, K., *Das Bundesformular* (2nd edn; Neukirchen: Neukirchener Verlag, 1964).
Bar-Adon, Pesah, 'The Expedition to the Judean Desert. 1960. Expedition C', *IEJ* 11 (1961), pp. 25-35.
—'Another Settlement of the Judean Desert Sect at 'En el-Ghuweir on the Shores of the Dead Sea', *BASOR* 227 (1977), pp. 1-25 = *EI* 10 (1971), pp. 72-89.
Bardtke, Hans, *Die Handschriftenfunde am Toten Meer*, II (Berlin: Evangelische Haupt-Bibelgesellschaft, 1957).
—'Die Rechtsstellung der Qumran-Gemeinde', *TLZ* 86 (1961), pp. 93-104.
—'Qumran und seine Funde', *TRu* 29 (1963), pp. 261-92.
—'Qumran und seine Funde', *TRu* 30 (1965), pp. 281-315.
—'Literaturbericht über Qumran. IX. Teil. Die Loblieder (Hodajoth) von Qumran', *TRu* 40 (1975), pp. 210-26.
—'Literaturbericht über Qumran. X. Teil. Der Lehrer der Gerechtigkeit und die Geschichte der Qumrangemeinde', *TRu* 41 (1976), pp. 97-140.
Baumgarten, Joseph M., 'The Essene Avoidance of Oil and the Laws of Purity', *RQ* 6 (1967), pp. 183-92 = *idem*, *Studies in Qumran Law* (Leiden: E.J. Brill, 1977), pp. 88-97.
—'The Heavenly Tribunal and the Personification of Sedeq in Jewish Apocalyptic', *ANRW* II.19.1 (1979), pp. 219-39.
—'Hanging and Treason in Qumran and Roman Law', *EI* 16 (1982), pp. 7*-16*.
Beall, Todd S., 'Josephus' Description of the Essenes. Illustrated by the Dead Sea Scrolls' (unpublished Ph.D. dissertation; The Catholic University of America, Washington, 1984).
Becker, J., *Das Heil Gottes. Heils- und Sündenbegriffe in den Qumran-texten und im Neuen Testament* (SUNT, 3; Göttingen: Vandenhoeck & Ruprecht, 1964).
Beegle, D.M., 'Ligatures with Waw and Jodh in the Dead Sea Isaiah Scroll', *BASOR* 129 (1953), pp. 11-14.
Betz, O., 'Die Geburt der Gemeinde durch den Lehrer', *NTS* 3 (1956-57), pp. 314-26.
—'Essenes', *IDBSup*, pp. 277-79.
—*Offenbarung und Schriftforschung in der Qumransekte* (Tübingen: Mohr, 1960).
—'Donnersöhne, Menschenfischer und der Davidische Messias', *RQ* 3 (1961-62), pp. 41-70.
—'Past Events and Last Events in the Qumran Interpretation of History', *Proceedings of the Sixth World Congress of Jewish Studies* (1973; 1977), pp. 27-34.
Bietenhard, H., 'Die Handschriftenfunde vom Toten Meer (Hirbet Qumran) und die Essener-Frage. Die Funde in der Wüste Juda (Eine Orientierung)', *ANRW* II.19.1 (1979), pp. 704-78.
Birkeland, H., *Die Feinde des Individuums in der israelitischen Psalmenliteratur* (Oslo: Grondahl, 1933).
Birnbaum, Solomon, 'The Dates of the Cave Scrolls', *BASOR* 115 (1949), pp. 20-22.
—'The Date of the Habakkuk Cave Scroll', *JBL* 68 (1949), pp. 161-68.
—'The Date of the Hymns as Scroll', *PEQ* 84 (1952), pp. 94-103.
—*The Qumran (Dead Sea) Scrolls and Palaeography* (BASOR Sup. 13-14; New Haven, 1952).
—*The Hebrew Scripts* I-II (London: Palaeographia, 1954-1957-1971).
Black, Matthew, 'The Account of the Essenes in Hippolytus and Josephus', in *The Background of the New Testament and its Eschatology. In Honour of C.H. Dodd*, ed. W.D. Davies and D. Daube (Cambridge: Cambridge University Press, 1956), pp. 172-75.

—'The Patristic Accounts of Jewish Sectarianism', *BJRL* 41 (1959), pp. 285-303.

—*The Scrolls and Christian Origins* (London: Thomas Nelson, 1961), pp. 3-24.

—'The Tradition of Hasidean-Essene Asceticism: Its Origins and Influence', in *Aspects du Judéo-Christianisme* (Colloque de Strasbourg; Paris: Presses Universitaires de France, 1965), pp. 19-33.

Bregman, Marc, 'Another Reference to 'A Teacher of Righteousness' in Midrashic Literature', *RQ* 10 (1979), pp. 97-100.

Brock, Sebastian P., 'Some Syriac Accounts of the Jewish Sects', in *A Tribute to Arthur Vööbus*, ed. Robert H. Fischer (Chicago: Lutheran School of Theology, 1977), pp. 265-76.

Brooke, George J., *Exegesis at Qumran. 4QFlorilegium in its Jewish Context* (JSOTS, 29; Sheffield: JSOT, 1985).

—'Qumran Pesher: Towards the Redefinition of a Genre', *RQ* 10 (1981), pp. 483-503.

Brown, Raymond E., 'The Teacher of Righteousness and the Messiah(s)', in *The Scrolls and Christianity*, ed. M. Black (London: SPCK, 1969), pp. 37-44.

Brownlee, William H., 'The Jerusalem Habakkuk Roll', *BASOR* 112 (1948), pp. 8-18.

—'Biblical Interpretation among the Sectaries of the Dead Sea Scrolls', *BA* 14 (1951), pp. 54-76.

—'The Historical Allusions of the Dead Sea Habakkuk Midrash', *BASOR* 126 (1952), pp. 10-20.

—'The Habakkuk Midrash and the Targum of Jonathan', *JJS* 7 (1956), pp. 169-86.

—'Messianic Motifs of Qumran and the New Testament', *NTS* 3 (1956/57), pp. 12-30.

—*The Midrash Pesher of Habakkuk* (Missoula: Scholars Press, 1979).

—'The Wicked Priest, the Man of Lie, and the Righteous Teacher—The Problem of Identity', *JQR* 73 (1982), pp. 1-37.

Bruce, F.F., *The Teacher of Righteousness in the Qumran Texts* (London: Tyndale, 1956).

—*Die Handschriftenfunde am Toten Meer nach dem heutigen Stand der Forschung* (München: Kaiser, 1957).

Buchanan, George Wesley, 'The Office of Teacher of Righteousness', *RQ* 9 (1977), pp. 241-43.

Bunge, J.G., 'Zur Geschichte und Chronologie des Untergangs der Oniaden und des Aufstiegs der Hasmonäer', *JSJ* 6 (1975), pp. 1-46.

Burchard, Christoph, 'Die Essener bei Hippolyt, Hippolyt, Ref., IX.18, 2-28, 2 und Josephus, Bell. 2,119-161', *JSJ* 8 (1977), pp. 1-41.

Burgmann, H., 'Das Kultmahl der Qumrangemeinde und der politische Gegensatz zum Makkabäer Jonathan', *TZ* 27 (1971), pp. 385-98.

—'Der Josuafluch zur Zeit des Makkabäers Simon (143–134 v. Chr.)', *BZ* NF 1 (1975), pp. 26-40.

—'Gerichtsherr und Generalankläger: Jonathan und Simon', *RQ* 9 (1977), pp. 3-72.

—'Der Gründer der Pharisäergenossenschaft der Makkabäer Simon', *JSJ* 9 (1977), pp. 153-91.

—'Antichrist—Antimessias. Der Makkabäer Simon', *Judaism* 36 (1980), pp. 152-74.

—'Wer war der "Lehrer der Gerechtigkeit"?', *RQ* 10 (1981), pp. 553-78.

Burrows, Millar *et al.* (eds.), *The Dead Sea Scrolls of St. Mark's Monastery*, I (New Haven: ASOR, 1950-51).

—'The Meaning of *'sr 'mr* in *DSH*', *VT* 2 (1952), pp. 255-60.

Butler, H.A., 'The Chronological Sequence of the Scrolls of Qumran Cave One', *RQ* 2 (1960), pp. 533-39.

Cantineau, J., *Le Nabatéen II* (Paris: Leroux, 1930-32).
Carmignac, J., 'Conjecture sur un passage de Flavius Josèphe relatif aux esséniens', *VT* 7 (1957), pp. 318-19.
—'Témoignage de Philon', *RQ* 2 (1960), pp. 530-32.
—'Les éléments historiques des "Hymnes" de Qumran', *RQ* 2 (1960), pp. 205-22.
—'Les citations de l'Ancien Testament, et spécialement des Poèmes du Serviteur, dans les Hymnes de Qumran', *RQ* 7 (1960), pp. 357-93.
—in Cothenet, F. and Lignée, H., *Les Textes de Qumran* II (Paris: Letouzey, 1963).
—'Le genre littéraire du "pesher" dans la Pistis-Sophia', *RQ* 4 (1963-64), pp. 497-522.
—'Le document de Qumran sur Melkisedeq', *RQ* 7 (1969-71), pp. 343-78.
—'Qui était le Docteur de Justice?', *RQ* 10 (1980), pp. 235-46.
—'Précisions', *RQ* 10 (1981), pp. 585-86.
Charles, R.H. (ed.), 'The Zadokite Fragments', in *Apocrypha and Pseudepigrapha of the Old Testament*, II (Oxford, 1913), pp. 785-834.
Charlesworth, James H., 'The Origin and Subsequent History of the Authors of the Dead Sea Scrolls: Four Transitional Phases among the Qumran Essenes', *RQ* 10 (1980), p. 213-33.
Clermont-Ganneau, C., 'Kumran', in *Archaeological Researches in Palestine during the Years 1873-1874*, II (London: Palestine Exploration Fund, 1896).
Cohen, Shaye J.D., *Josephus in Galilee and Rome. His Vita and Development as Historian* (Leiden: Brill, 1979).
Collins, John J., 'Jewish Apocalyptic against its Hellenistic Near Eastern Environment', *BASOR* 220 (1975), pp. 27-36.
—Review of Philip R. Davies, *The Damascus Covenant*, in *JBL* 104 (1985), pp. 332-33.
Colson, F.H., *Philo* (Loeb Classic Series; Cambridge, Mass., 1929-39).
Corpus inscriptionum semiticarum, II (Paris: E. Reipublicae typographa, 1881-1962).
Cowley, A.E. (ed.), *Aramaic Papyri of the Fifth Century B.C.* (Oxford: Clarendon, 1923).
Cross, Frank M. Jr, 'A New Qumran Biblical Fragment Related to the Original Hebrew Underlying the Septuagint', *BASOR* 132 (1953), pp. 15-26.
—'The Oldest Manuscripts from Qumran', *JBL* 74 (1955), pp. 147-72=*Qumran and the History of the Biblical Text*, ed. F.M. Cross and S. Talmon, Cambridge: Harvard University Press, 1975, pp. 147-76.
—*The Ancient Library of Qumran and Modern Biblical Studies* (Garden City: Doubleday, 1958).
—'The Development of the Jewish Scripts', in *The Bible and the Ancient Near East*, ed. G. Ernest Wright (London: Routledge & Kegan Paul, 1961), pp. 133-202.
—*Canaanite Myth and Hebrew Epic* (Cambridge: Cambridge University Press, 1973), pp. 326-42.
—'Alphabets and Pots: Reflections on Typological Method in the Dating of Human Artifacts', *MAARAV* 3 (1982), pp. 121-36.
Crown, Alan D., 'Problems in Epigraphy and Palaeography: The Nature of the Evidence in Samaritan Sources', *BJRL* 62 (1979), pp. 37-60.
Crüsemann, Frank, 'Ein israelitisches Ritualbad aus vorexilischer Zeit', *ZDPV* 94 (1978), pp. 68-75.
Dalman, G., *Neue Petra-Forschungen* (Leipzig: J.C. Hinrichs, 1912).
—'Jahresbericht', *PJ* 10 (1914), pp. 9-12.
—'Jahresbericht', *PJ* 16 (1920), pp. 40-41.
Daumas, François, 'Littérature prophétique et exégétique égyptienne et commentaires

esséniens', in *A la rencontre de Dieu: Mémorial Albert Gelin* (Bibliothèque de la faculté catholique de théologie de Lyon, 8; Le Puy: Xavier Mappus, 1961).

Davies, Philip R., 'Hasidim in the Maccabean Period', *JSS* 28 (1977), pp. 127-40.

—*1QM, the War Scroll from Qumran. Its Structure and History* (BO, 32; Rome: Biblical Institute Press, 1977).

—*The Damascus Covenant. An Interpretation of the 'Damascus Document'* (JSOTS, 25; Sheffield: JSOT, 1982).

—*Qumran* (Cities of the Biblical World: Guildford: Lutterworth Press, 1982).

—'Calendrical Change and Qumran Origins: An Assessment of VankerKam's Theory', *CBQ* 45 (1983), pp. 80-89.

—'Eschatology at Qumran', *JBL* 104 (1985), pp. 39-55.

—'Qumran Beginnings', in *SBL Seminar Papers 1986* (Atlanta: Scholars Press), pp. 361-68.

Delling, G., 'Josephus und die heidnischen Religionen', *Klio* 43-45 (1965), pp. 263-69.

Denis, A.-M., *Les thèmes de connaissance dans le Document de Damas* (Louvain: Louvain University Press, 1967).

Dimant, Deborah, 'Qumran Sectarian Literature', in *Jewish Worship in the Second Temple Period*, ed. Michael E. Stone (Philadelphia: Fortress, 1984), pp. 483-550.

Dombrowski, B.W., 'יחד' in IQS and το κοινόν. An Instance of Early Greek and Jewish Synthesis', *HTR* 59 (1966), pp. 293-307.

Driver, G.R., 'The Number of the Beast', in *Bibel und Qumran* (Berlin: Evangelische Haupt-Bibelgesellschaft, 1958), pp. 75-81.

—*The Judean Scrolls. The Problem and a Solution* (Oxford: Blackwell, 1965).

—'Myths of Qumran', *ALUOS* 6 (1969), pp. 23-48.

Duhaime, J.L., 'Remarques sur les dépôts d'ossement d'animaux à Qumran', *RQ* 9 (1977), pp. 245-51.

Du Mesnil du Buisson, R., *Inventaire des Inscriptions Palmyreniennes de Doura-Europas* (Paris, 1939).

Dupont-Sommer, André, 'Le "Commentaire d'Habacuc" découvert près de la Mer Morte', *RHR* 137 (1950), pp. 129-71.

—'Le Maître de Justice fût-il mis à mort?', *VT* 1 (1951), pp. 200-15.

—'Quelques remarques sur le *Commentaire d'Habacuc* à propos d'un livre recent', *VT* 5 (1955), pp. 113-29.

—'On a Passage of Josephus Relating to the Essenes (*Antiq.* XVIII, 22)', *JSS* 1 (1956), pp. 361-66.

—*Aperçus préliminaires sur les manuscrits de la Mer Morte* (Paris: Maisonneuve, 1959).

—*Observations sur le Commentaire d'Habacuc découvert près de la Mer Morte* (Paris: Maisonneuve, 1959).

—*Les Écrits esséniens découverts près de la Mer Morte* (Paris: Payot, 1959).

—*The Essene Writings from Qumran* (Cleveland: World, 1961).

—'Observations sur le Commentaire de Nahum découvert près de la Mer Morte', *Journal des Savants* (1963), pp. 201-27.

Eisenman, Robert, *Maccabees, Zadokites, Christians and Qumran* (Leiden: Brill, 1983).

—*James the Just in the Habakkuk Pesher* (Leiden: Brill, 1986).

Elliger, K., *Studien zum Habakuk-Kommentar vom Toten Meer* (BHT; Tübingen: J.C.B. Mohr [Paul Siebeck], 1953).

Farmer, W.R., 'Essenes', *IDB*, II (Nashville: Abingdon, 1962), pp. 143-49.

Finkel, Asher, 'The Pesher of Dreams and Scriptures', *RQ* 4 (1963-64), pp. 357-70.
Fitzmyer, Joseph A., '"4Q Testimonia" and the New Testament', *TS* 18 (1957), pp. 513-37=*idem*, *Essays on the Semitic Background of the New Testament* (London: Geoffrey Chapman, 1971), pp. 57-89.
—'The Use of Explicit Old Testament Quotations in Qumran Literature and in the New Testament', in *Essays on the Semitic Background of the New Testament* (London: Geoffrey Chapman, 1971), pp. 3-58.
—*The Dead Sea Scrolls. Major Publications and Tools for Study* (Missoula: Scholars Press, 1975, 1977).
—'Crucifixion in Ancient Palestine, Qumran Literature and the New Testament', *CBQ* 40 (1978), pp. 502-12.
—'The Dead Sea Scrolls and the New Testament after Thirty Years', *Theological Digest* 29 (1981), pp. 357-58.
Flusser, David, 'Pharisees, Sadducees and Essenes in the Pesher Nahum', *In Memory of Gedaliahu Alon. Essays in Jewish History and Philology* (Hakibbutz Hameuchad, 1970), pp. 133-68.
Foerster, W., 'Der heilige Geist im Spätjudentum', *NTS* 8 (1961/62), pp. 117-34.
Ford, J. Massingberde, 'Can we exclude Samaritan Influence from Qumran?', *RQ* 6 (1967), pp. 109-29.
Freedman, David N., 'The "House of Absalom" in the Habakkuk Scroll', *BASOR* 114 (1949), pp. 11-12.
Gabrion, Hervé, 'L'interprétation de l'Écriture dans la littérature de Qumran', *ANRW* II.19.1 (1979), pp. 779-848.
Gaster, Theodore H., *The Dead Sea Scriptures in English Translation* (Garden City: Doubleday, 1956).
—'A Qumran Reading of Deuteronomy XXXIII 10', *VT* 8 (1958), pp. 217-19.
Gerleman, G., 'Der "Einzelne" der Klage- und Dank-psalmen', *VT* 32 (1982), pp. 133-49.
Germann, Heinrich, 'Jesus ben Siras Dankgebet und die Hodajoth', *TZ* 19 (1963), pp. 81-87.
Gerstenberger, E.S., *Der bittende Mensch. Bittritual und Klagelied des Einzelnen im Alten Testament* (Neukirchen: Neukirchener Verlag, 1980).
Ginzberg, L., *Eine unbekannte jüdische Sekte* (New York, 1922) = *An Unknown Jewish Sect* (New York, 1970) (revised and updated).
Golb, Norman, 'The Dietary Laws of the Damascus Covenant in Relation to Those of the Karaites', *JJS* 8 (1957), pp. 51-69.
—'Who Hid the Dead Sea Scrolls?', *BA* 48 (1985), pp. 68-82.
Goldenberg, Robert, 'The Jewish Sabbath in the Roman World up to the Time of Constantine the Great', *ANRW* II.19.1 (1979), pp. 414-47.
Goldstein, Jonathan, 'The Tales of the Tobiads', in *Studies in Judaism in Late Antiquity: Christianity, Judaism and other Greco-Roman Cults*, ed. Jacob Neusner (Leiden: Brill, 1975), pp. 85-123.
—*I Maccabees: A New Translation with Introduction and Commentary* (Garden City: Doubleday, 1976).
Goranson, Stephen, 'On the Hypothesis that Essenes lived on Mt. Carmel', *RQ* 9 (1978), pp. 563-67.
Gordon, Robert P., 'The Targum to the Minor Prophets and the Dead Sea Texts: Textual and Exegetical Notes', *RQ* 8 (1974), pp. 425-29.
Goshen-Gottstein, M.H., 'Anti-Essene Traits in the Dead Sea Scrolls', *VT* 4 (1954), pp. 141-47.
Graf, David, 'The Pagan Witness to the Essenes', *BA* 40 (1977), pp. 125-29.

Grant, F.C., *Hellenistic Religions* (New York: Liberal Arts Press, 1953).

Greig, James C.G., 'The Teacher of Righteousness and the Qumran Community', *NTS* 2 (1955/56), pp. 119-26.

Grözinger, K.E. *et al.* (eds.), *Qumran* (Wege der Forschung, 160; Darmstadt: Wissenschaftliche Buchgesellschaft, 1981).

Groningen, B.A. van, *Short Manual of Greek Palaeography* (2nd edn; Leiden: A.W. Sijthoff, 1955).

Grundmann, Walter, 'The Teacher of Righteousness of Qumran and the question of justification by faith in the theology of Paul', in *Paul and Qumran*, ed. J. Murphy-O'Connor (London: Chapman, 1968), pp. 85-114.

Gunkel, H. and Begrich. J., *Einleitung in die Psalmen* (Göttingen: Vandenhoeck & Ruprecht, 1933).

Haberman, A.M., 'The Dead Sea Scrolls—a Survey and a New Interpretation', *Judaism* 5 (1956), pp. 306-15.

Hadas, Moses, *Hellenistic Culture* (New York: Columbia University Press, 1959).

Halperin, D.J., 'Crucifixion, the Nahum Pesher, and the Rabbinic Penalty of Strangulation', *JJS* 32 (1981), pp. 32-46.

Hanson, R.S., 'Paleo-Hebrew Scripts in the Hasmonean Age', *BASOR* 175 (1964), pp. 26-42.

Harding, G. Lankaster, *et al.*, Archaeological Finds', *Qumran Cave I* (DJD, I), pp. 3-40.

Harris, J.G., 'Early Trends in Biblical Commentaries as Reflected in Some Qumran Texts', *EvQ* 36 (1964), pp. 100-105.

Hatch, N.H.P., *An Album of Dated Syriac Manuscripts* (Boston: The American Academy of Arts and Sciences, 1946).

Hayes, John H., *Understanding the Psalms* (Valley Forge: Judson Press, 1976).

Hengel, Martin, *Judaism and Hellenism* (ET Philadelphia: Fortress Press, 1974).

—'Mors turpissima crucis. Die Kreuzigung in der antiken Welt und die 'Torheit' des Wortes vom Kreuz', *Rechtfertigung Festschrift für Ernst Käsemann* (Tübingen: J.C.B. Mohr [Paul Siebeck], 1976), pp. 125-84.

—'Qumran und der Hellenismus', in *Qumran. Sa piété, sa théologie et son milieu*, ed. M. Delcor (Louvain: Louvain University Press, 1978), pp. 333-72.

Hermann, Siegfried, *Geschichte Israels* (München: Kaiser, 1973).

Hoenig, S.B., 'The Age of Twenty in Rabbinic Tradition and 1QSa', *JQR* 49 (1959), pp. 209-14.

—'The Qumran Liturgic Psalms', *JQR* 57 (1967), pp. 327-32.

—'The Dead Sea Psalm Scroll', *JQR* 58 (1967), pp. 162-63.

—'The Sectarian Scrolls and Rabbinic Research', *JQR* 59 (1968), pp. 24-70.

Holm-Nielsen, S., *Hodayot. Psalms from Qumran* (Aarhus: Universitetsforlaget, 1961).

—'"Ich" in den Hodajoth und die Qumran-Gemeinde', in *Qumran-Probleme* (Berlin: Akademie, 1963), pp. 217-29.

—'Erwägungen zu dem Verhältnis zwischen den Hodayot und den Psalmen Salomos', in *Bibel und Qumran* (Berlin: Evangelische Haupt-Bibelgesellschaft, 1968), pp. 112-31.

—'Religiöse Poesie des Spätjudentums', *ANRW* II.19.1 (1979), pp. 152-86.

Honeyman, A., 'Notes on a Teacher and a Book', *JJS* 4 (1953), pp. 131-32.

Hopkins, D., Dombrowski, 'The Qumran Community and 1 Q Hodayot: A Reassessment', *RQ* 10 (1981), pp. 323-64.

Horgan, Maurya, *Pesharim. Qumran Interpretation of Biblical Books* (CBQMS, 8; Washington: Catholic Biblical Association of America, 1979).

Huppenbauer, H.W., 'Enderwartung und Lehrer der Gerechtigkeit im Habakuk-Kommentar', *TZ* 20 (1964), pp. 81-86.
Isser, Stanley, 'The Conservative Essenes: A New Emendation of Antiquities XVIII.22', *JJS* 7 (1976), pp. 177-80.
Iwry, S., 'Was there a Migration to Damascus? The Problem of שבי ישראל', *EI* 9 (1969), pp. 80-88.
Jaubert, Annie, 'Le Calendrier des Jubilés et de la secte de Qumran: ses origines bibliques', *VT* 3 (1953), pp. 250-64.
—'Le pays de Damas', *RB* (1958), pp. 214-48.
—*La notion de l'alliance dans le Judaïsme* (Paris: Editions du Seuil, 1963).
Jeremias, Gert, *Der Lehrer der Gerechtigkeit* (SUNT, 2; Göttingen: Vandenhoeck & Ruprecht, 1963).
—'Teacher of Righteousness', *IDBSup* (Nashville: Abingdon, 1976), pp. 861-63.
Jongeling, B., *A Classified Bibliography of the Finds in the Desert of Judah 1958-69* (Leiden: Brill, 1971).
Kahle, Paul, *The Cairo Geniza* (London: Oxford University Press, 1952).
—'Zehn Jahre Entdeckungen in der Wüste Juda', *TLZ* 82 (1957), pp. 641-50.
Kallner-Amiran, D.H., 'A Revised Earthquake-Catalogue of Palestine—I', *IEJ* 1 (1950-51), pp. 223-46.
—'A Revised Earthquake-Catalogue of Palestine—II', *IEJ* 2 (1952), pp. 48-57.
Kanael, B., 'Some Observations on the Chronology of Khirbet Qumran', *EI* 5 (1958), p. 93.
Karcz, I. and Kafri, U., 'Evaluation of Supposed Archeoseismic Damage in Israel', *Journal of Archaeological Science* 5 (1978), pp. 237-53.
Keel, Othmar, *Feinde und Gottesleugner. Studien zum Image der Widersacher in den Individualpsalmen* (SBM, 7; Stuttgart: Katholisches Bibelwerk, 1969).
—*Die Welt der altorientalischen Bildsymbolik und das Alte Testament. Am Beispiel der Psalmen* (Neukirchen: Neukirchener Verlag, 1972).
Kennedy, Charles A., 'The Development of the Lamp in Palestine', *Berytus* 14 (1963), pp. 67-115.
Khairy, N.I., 'Inkwells of the Roman Period from Jordan', *Levant* 12 (1980), pp. 155-62.
Kittel, Bonnie, *The Hymns of Qumran. Translation and Commentary* (SBLDS, 50; Chico: Scholars Press, 1981).
Klauck, Hans-Josef, 'Gütergemeinschaft in der klassischen Antike, in Qumran und im Neuen Testament', *RQ* 11 (1982), pp. 47-79.
Knibb, Michael A., 'The Dead Sea Scrolls: Reflections on Some Recent Publications', *ET* 90 (1979), pp. 294-300.
—'Exile in the Damascus Document', *JSOT* 25 (1983), pp. 99-117.
von Koelichen, Johann-Christian, '"Der Lehrer der Gerechtigkeit" und Hos 10, 12 in einer rabbinischen Handschrift des Mittelalters', *ZAW* 74 (1962), pp. 324-27.
Koffmann, E., 'Die staatsrechtliche Stellung der essenischen Vereinigungen in der griechisch-römischen Periode', *Bib* 44 (1963), pp. 46-61.
Kraeling, E.G. (ed.), *The Brooklyn Museum Aramaic Papyri* (New Haven: Yale University, 1953).
Kruse, H., 'Noch einmal zur Josephus-Stelle Antiqu. 18, 1, 5,' *VT* 9 (1959) pp. 31-39.
Kuhn, H.-W., *Enderwartung und gegenwärtiges Heil. Untersuchungen zu den Gemeindeliedern von Qumran mit einem Anhang über Eschatologie und Gegenwart in der Verkündigung Jesu* (SUNT, 4; Göttingen: Vandenhoeck & Ruprecht, 1966).

Kuhn, K.G., *Konkordanz zu den Qumrantexten* (Göttingen: Vandenhoeck & Ruprecht, 1960).
—'Nachträge zur "Konkordanz zu den Qumrantexten", *RQ* 4 (1963), pp. 163-234.
Lacheman, Ernest R., 'Reply to the Editor', *BASOR* 116 (1949), pp. 16-17.
—'A Matter of Method in Hebrew Paleography', *JQR* 40 (1949-50), pp. 15-39.
—'Can Hebrew Paleography be called "Scientific"?', *JQR* 42 (1951-52), pp. 377-85.
—'Hebrew Paleography Again', *JQR* 44 (1953), pp. 116-22.
—'The So-Called Bar Kokhba Letter', *JQR* 44 (1953-54), pp. 285-90.
Lagrange, M.-J., 'La secte juive de la Nouvelle Alliance au pays de Damas', *RB* 9 (1912), pp. 213-40, 321-60.
Laperrousaz, E.-M., '"Infra hos engadda", Notes à propos d'un article récent', *RB* 69 (1962), pp. 369-80.
—*Qumran: L'Établissement essénien des bords de la Mer Morte. Histoire et archéologie* (Paris: Picard, 1976).
—'À propos des dépôts d'ossements d'animaux trouvés à Qumran', *RQ* 9 (1978), pp. 569-73.
—*Les esséniens selon leur témoignage direct* (Paris: Desclée, 1982).
—'Qumran et découvertes au désert de Juda', *DBSup* IX, pp. 745-98.
Lapp, Paul W., *Palestinian Ceramic Chronology* (ASOR Publications of the Jerusalem School, 8; New Haven, 1961).
LaSor, W.S., *Bibliography of the Dead Sea Scrolls. 1948-1957* (Fuller Library Bulletin, 31; Pasadena: Fuller Theological Seminary Library, 1958).
Leaney, A.R.C., *The Rule of Qumran and its Meaning* (London: SCM Press, 1966).
Leszynsky, R., *Die Sadduzäer* (Berlin, 1912).
Levi, I., 'Un écrit sadducéen antérieur à la destruction du Temple', *REJ* 61 (1911), pp. 161-205; 63 (1912), pp. 1-19.
—'Document relatif à la Communauté des Fils de Sadoq', *REJ* 65 (1913), pp. 24-31.
Levine, Baruch, 'The Temple Scroll: Aspects of its Historical Provenance and Literary Character', *BASOR* 232 (1978), pp. 5-23.
Levy, Isodore. *La légende de Pythagore de Grèce en Palestine* (Paris: Honoré Champion, 1927).
Licht, J. 'The Doctrine of the Thanksgiving Scroll', *IEJ* 6 (1956), pp. 1-13, 89-101.
—*The Thanksgiving Scroll* (Jerusalem: Baliak, 1957).
Lidzbarski, M., *Ephemeris für semitische Epigraphik* (Giessen: J. Ricker, 1915).
Lindner, Helgo, *Die Geschichtsauffassung des Flavius Josephus in Bellum Judaicum* (Leiden: Brill, 1972).
Lipscomb, W.H. and Sanders, J.A., 'Wisdom at Qumran', in *Israelite Wisdom. Theological and Literary Essays in Honor of Samuel Terrien*, ed. John G. Gammie, Walter A. Brueggemann, W. Lee Humphreys (Missoula, 1978), pp. 277-85.
Liver, J., 'The Half-Shekel in Biblical and Post-biblical Literature', *HTR* 56 (1963), pp. 191-98.
Loew, E.A. *Studia Palaeographica: A Contribution to the history of early Latin minuscules and to the dating of Visigothic Manuscripts* (München: Verlag der Königlich-Bayrischen Akademie der Wissenschaften, 1910).
Lohse, E., *Die Texte aus Qumran. Hebräisch und Deutsch* (2nd edn; Darmstadt: Wissenschaftliche Buchgesellschaft, 1971).
Longenecker, Richard, *Biblical Exegesis in the Apostolic Period* (Grand Rapids: Eerdmans, 1975).
Lowy, Simeon, 'Some Aspects of Normative and Sectarian Interpretation of the

Scriptures (The Contribution of the Judean Scrolls towards Systematization)', *ALUOS* 6 (1966-68), pp. 98-163.
Luebbe, John, 'A Reinterpretation of 4QTestimonia', *RQ* 12 (1986), pp. 187-98.
Maier, J., *Die Texte vom Toten Meer* (München: Ernst Reinhardt, 1960).
Mansoor, M., *The Thanksgiving Hymns* (Leiden: Brill, 1961).
Marcus, Ralph, 'Pharisees, Essenes, and Gnostics', *JBL* 73 (1954), pp. 157-61.
Margoliouth, G., 'Manuscripts. Materials Used to Receive Writing', *JE* 8 (1904), pp. 304-305.
—'The Calendar, The Sabbath and the Marriage Law in the Geniza-Zadokite Document', *ET* 23 (1911-1913), pp. 553-58; 25 (1913-1914), pp. 560-64.
Marmorstein, A., 'Eine unbekannte jüdische Sekte', *Theologisch Tijdschrift* 52 (1918), pp. 91-122.
Martin, Malachi, *The Scribal Character of the Dead Sea Scrolls* (Louvain: Publications Universitaires, 1958).
Masterman, E.W.G., 'Observations on the Dead Sea Levels', *PEFQS* (1902), p. 161.
—'Notes on some ruins and a rockcut aqueduct in the wady Kumran', *PEFQS* (1903), p. 267.
May, Herbert G., 'Cosmological Reference in the Qumran Doctrines of the Two Spirits', *JBL* 82 (1963), pp. 1-14.
Mazar, B., Dothan, T. and Dunayevsky, I., *En-Gedi, The First and Second Seasons of Excavation: 1961-1962 Atiqot*, V (Jerusalem, 1966).
Mazar, B., 'The Archaeological Excavation near the Temple Mount', in *Jerusalem Revealed. Archaeology in the Holy City. 1968-1974*, ed. Y. Yadin (Jerusalem: Israel Exploration Society, 1975), p. 32.
Mealand, David L., 'Community of Goods at Qumran', *TZ* 31 (1973), pp. 129-39.
—'Philo of Alexandria's Attitude to Riches', *ZNW* 69 (1978), pp. 258-64.
Mendels, Doron, 'Hellenistic Utopia and the Essenes', *HTR* 72 (1979), pp. 207-22.
Meshorer, Y., *The Jewish Coins of the Second Temple Period* (Chicago: Argonaut, 1967).
Metzger, Bruce M., 'The Formulas Introducing Quotations of Scripture in the MT and in the Mishnah', *JBL* 70 (1951), pp. 297-307.
—'The Furniture in the Scriptorium at Qumran', *RQ* 1 (1959), pp. 509-15.
—(ed.), *The Oxford Annotated Apocrypha of the Old Testament* (Oxford: Oxford University Press, 1977).
—*Manuscripts of the Greek Bible. An Introduction to Palaeography* (Oxford: Oxford University Press, 1981).
Meyer, E., 'Die Gemeinde des neuen Bundes im Lande Damaskus: eine jüdische Schrift aus der Seleukidenzeit', *Abhandlung der preussischen Akademie der Wissenschaften*, Phil.-hist. Klasse 9 (Berlin, 1919), pp. 1-65.
Meyshan, J., 'The Symbols on the Coinage of Herod the Great and their Meanings', *PEQ* 91 (1958), pp. 118-22.
—'The Chronology of the Coins of the Herodian Dynasty', *EI* 6 (1960), p. 32.
Milik, J.T. 'Un contrat juif de l'an 134 après J.-C.', *RB* 61 (1954), pp. 182-92.
—*Ten Years of Discovery in the Wilderness of Judaea* (Naperville: Alec R. Allenson, 1959).
—'Deux documents inédits due désert de Judah', *Bib* 38 (1957), pp. 245-68.
—'Milik-sedeq et Milki-reša' dans les anciens écrits juifs et chrétiens', *JJS* 23 (1972), pp. 95-144.
Molin. G., 'Hat die Sekte von Khirbet Qumran Beziehungen zu Ägypten?', *TLZ* 78 (1953), pp. 653-56.
—*Die Söhne des Lichts* (München: Herold, 1954).

Momigliano, A., *Alien Wisdon. The Limits of Hellenism* (Cambridge: Cambridge University Press, 1975.

—'The Second Book of Maccabees', *CP* 70 (1975), pp. 81-91.

Moore, G.F., 'The Covenanters of Damascus: A Hitherto Unknown Jewish Sect', *HTR* 4 (1911), pp. 330-77.

Moorey, R., *Excavation in Palestine* (Cities of the Biblical World; Guildford: Lutterworth, 1981).

Morawe, Günther, *Aufbau und Abgrenzung der Loblieder von Qumran. Studien zur gattungsgeschichtlichen Einordnung der Hodayoth* (Berlin: Evangelische Verlagsanstalt, 1961).

—'Vergleich des Aufbaus der Danklieder und hymnischen Bekenntnislieder (IQH) von Qumran mit dem Aufbau der Psalmen im Alten Testament und im Spätjudentum', *RQ* 4 (1963), pp. 323-56.

Mowinckel, S., 'Some Remarks on Hodayoth 39, 5-20', *JBL* 74 (1956), pp. 265-76.

Muilenburg, James, 'A Qoheleth Scroll from Qumran', *BASOR* 135 (1954), pp. 20-28.

Muraoka, T., '"Essene" in the Septuagint', *RQ* 8 (1973), pp. 267-68.

Murphy-O'Connor, J., 'An Essene Missionary Document? CD II,14–VI,1', *RB* 77 (1970), pp. 201-29.

—'The Translation of Damascus Document VI,11-14', *RQ* 7 (1971), pp. 553-56.

—'The Original Text of CD 7:9–8:2 = 19:5-14', *HTR* 64 (1971), pp. 379-86.

—'A Literary Analysis of Damascus Document VI,2–VIII,3', *RB* 78 (1971), pp. 210-32.

—'A Literary Analysis of Damascus Document XIX,33–XX,34', *RB* 79 (1972), pp. 544-64.

—'The Critique of the Princes of Judah (CD VIII,3-19)', *RB* 79 (1972), pp. 200-16.

—'The Essenes and their History', *RB* 81 (1974), pp. 215-44.

—'Demetrius I and the Teacher of Righteousness', *RB* 83 (1976), pp. 400-20.

—'The Essenes in Palestine', *BA* 40 (1977), pp. 100-24.

—'Judah the Essene and the Teacher of Righteousness', *RQ* 10 (1981), pp. 579-85.

—'The Damascus Document Revisited', in *SBL Seminar Papers 1986* (Atlanta: Scholars Press), pp. 369-83.

Naveh, Joseph, *Early History of the Alphabet* (Jerusalem: Magnes Press, 1982).

Negoitsa, Athanase, 'Did the Essenes Survive the 66-71 War?', *RQ* 6 (1969), pp. 517-30.

Newsom, Carol Ann, *The Songs of Sabbath Sacrifice: Edition, Translation and Commentary* (Atlanta: Scholars Press, 1985).

Nickelsburg, George, 'The Epistle of Enoch and the Qumran Literature', *Essays in honour of Yigael Yadin* (JJS, 39; 1982), pp. 333-48.

—'*1 Enoch* and Qumran Origins: The State of the Question and Some Prospects for Answers', in *SBL Seminar Papers 1986* (Atlanta: Scholars Press), pp. 341-60.

Noll, Stephen F., 'Angelology in the Qumran Texts', Ph.D. Dissertation, Universtity of Manchester, 1979.

Nolland, John, 'A Misleading Statement of the Essene Attitude to the Temple (Josephus, *Antiquities*, XVIII, I, 15, 19)', *RQ* 9 (1978), pp. 555-62.

North, R.J., 'The Qumran "Sadducees"', *CBQ* 17 (1955), pp. 44-68.

—'The Qumran Reservoirs', in *The Bible in Current Catholic Thought*, ed. J.L. McKenzie (New York, 1962), pp. 100-32.

Noth, Martin, *Geschichte Israels* (2nd edn; Göttingen: Vandenhoeck & Ruprecht, 1956).

Osswald, E., 'Zur Hermeneutik des Habakuk-Kommentars', *ZAW* 68 (1956), pp. 243-56.

Osten-Sacken, Peter von der, *Gott und Belial. Traditionsgeschichtliche Untersuchungen zum Dualismus in den Texten aus Qumran* (SUNT, 6; Göttingen: Vandenhoeck & Ruprecht, 1969).

Patte, Daniel, *Early Jewish Hermeneutic in Palestine* (SBLDS, 22; Missoula: Scholars Press, 1975).

Pedersen, J., *Israel: Its Life and Culture*, I-II (London: Oxford University Press, 1926).

Philonenko, M., 'Le Maître de justice et la Sagesse de Salomon', *TZ* 14 (1958), pp. 81-88.

Pixner, Bargil, *An Essene Quarter on Mount Zion?* (Jerusalem: Franciscan Printing Press, 1976).

Ploeg, J. van der, *Funde in der Wüste Juda. Die Schriftrollen vom Toten Meer und die Brüderschaft von Qumran* (Köln: Bachem, 1959).

Polak, A.N., 'The Dead Sea Scrolls: A New Approach', *JQR* 49 (1959), pp. 89-107.

Poole, J.B. and Reed, R., 'The "Tannery" of Ain Feshka', *PEQ* 93 (1961), pp. 114-23.

Qimron, E. and Strugnell J., 'An Unpublished Halakhic Letter from Qumran', in *Biblical Archaeology Today. Proceedings of the International Congress on Biblical Archaeology, Jerusalem, April 1984* (Jerusalem: IEJ, 1985), pp. 400-407.

Rabin, Chaim, 'The "Teacher of Righteousness' in the Testaments of the Twelve Patriarchs?', *JSS* 3 (1952), pp. 127-28.

—'Alexander Jannaeus and the Pharisees', *JJS* 7 (1956), pp. 3-11.

—*The Zadokite Documents* (2nd edn; Oxford: Clarendon, 1958).

Rabinowitz, I., 'A Reconsideration of "Damascus" and "390 Years" in the "Damascus" ("Zadokite") Fragments', *JBL* 73 (1954), pp. 11-35.

—'The Guides of Righteousness', *VT* 8 (1958), pp. 391-404.

—'The First Essenes', *JSS* 4 (1959), pp. 358-61.

—'*Pesher/Pittaron.* Its Biblical Meaning and its Significance in the Qumran Literature', *RQ* 8 (1973), pp. 219-32.

—'The Meaning of the Key ("Demetrius")-Passage of the Qumran Nahum Pesher', *JAOS* 98 (1978), pp. 394-99.

Rajak, Tessa, 'Josephus and the "Archaeology of the Jews"', *JJS* 33 (1982), pp. 465-77.

Rengstorff, K.H., 'Hirbet Qumran und die Bibliothek vom Toten Meer', *Studia Delitzschiana* 5 (1960), pp. 9-81.

Riessler, P., *Altjüdisches Schrifttum ausserhalb der Bibel übersetzt und erläutert* (Heidelberg: F.H. Kerle, 1927).

Robinson, H. Wheeler, 'The Hebrew Conception of Corporate Personality', in *Werden und Wesen des Alten Testaments*, ed. J. Hempel (BZAW, 66; Berlin: Töpelmann, 1936), pp. 49-62.

Rosenbloom, J.R., 'Notes on Historical Identifications in the Dead Sea Scrolls', *RQ* 1 (1958), pp. 265-72.

Rost, Leonard, *Die Damaskusschrift neu bearbeitet* (Berlin: Walter de Gruyter, 1933).

Roth, Cecil, *The Historical Background of the Dead Sea Scrolls* (Oxford: Blackwell, 1958) = *The Dead Sea Scrolls: A New Historical Approach* (New York: W.W. Norton, 1965).

—'Why the Qumran Sect cannot have been Essenes', *RQ* 1 (1959), pp. 417-22.

—'The Zealots in the War of 66-73', *JSS* 4 (1959), pp. 332-55.

—'Were the Qumran Sectaries Essenes? A Re-examination of Some Evidence', *JTS* 10 (1959), pp. 87-93.

—'The Zealots and Qumran: The Basic Issue', *RQ* 2 (1959), pp. 81-84.
—'Did Vespasian Capture Qumran?', *PEQ* 91 (1959), pp. 122-29.
—'The Subject Matter of Qumran Exegesis', *VT* 10 (1960), pp. 51-68.
—'The Historian and the Dead Sea Scrolls', *History Today* 11 (1961), pp. 90-97.
—'The Teacher of Righteousness and the Prophecy of Joel', *VT* 13 (1963), pp. 91-95.
—'Qumran and Masada: A Final Clarification regarding the Dead Sea Sect', *RQ* 5 (1964), pp. 81-88.
Rowley, H.H., *The Internal Dating of the Dead Sea Scrolls* (Louvain: Publications Universitaires, 1952).
—'The Covenanters of Damascus and the Dead Sea Scrolls', *BJRL* 35 (1952), pp. 111-54.
—*The Zadokite Fragments and the Dead Sea Scrolls* (Oxford: Blackwell, 1956).
—'The Kittim and the Dead Sea Scrolls', *PEQ* 88 (1956), pp. 92-109.
—'4QpNahum and the Teacher of Righteousness', *JBL* 75 (1956), pp. 188-93.
—'The 390 Years of the Zadokite Work', in *Mélanges Bibliques rédigés en l'honneur d'André Robert* (Paris: Bloud & Gay, 1957), pp. 341-47.
—*The Relevance of Apocalyptic* (3rd edn; New York: Association Press 1964).
—'The History of the Qumran Sect', *BJRL* 49 (1966), pp. 203-32.
Rubenstein, Arie, 'Urban Halakhah and Camp Rules in the "Cairo Fragments of a Damascus Covenant"', *Sefarad* 12 (1952), pp. 283-96.
—'The Essenes According to the Slavonic Version of Josephus' *Wars*', *VT* 6 (1956), pp. 307-308.
Russell, K.W., 'The Earthquake of May 19, A.D. 363', *BASOR* 238 (1980), pp. 47-64.
Saachi, Paolo, 'Il problema degli anni 390 nel Documento di Damasco I, 5-6', *RQ* 5 (1964), pp. 89-96.
Sachau, E., *Aramäische Papyrus und Ostraka* (Leipzig, 1911).
Sanders, J.A., 'The Dead Sea Scrolls—A Quarter Century of Study', *BA* 36 (1973), pp. 110-48.
—'History and Archaeology of the Qumran Community', *BASOR* 231 (1978), pp. 79-80.
Saulcy, F. de, *Narrative of a Journey Round the Dead Sea and in the Bible Lands; in 1850 and 1851. Including an Account of the Discovery of the Sites of Sodom and Gomorrah*, I (Philadelphia: Parry & M'Millan, 1854).
Sayce, A.H. and Cowley, A.E., *Proceedings of the Society of Biblical Archaeology* 29 (1907), Pl. I-11; 37 (1915), Pl. II.
Schäfer, Peter, 'The Hellenistic and Maccabean Periods', in *Israelite and Judaean History*, ed. John H. Hayes and J. Maxwell Miller (Philadelphia: Westminster, 1977).
Schalit, A., *König Herodes* (Berlin: de Gruyter, 1969).
—(ed.), *The Hellenistic Age. World History of the Jewish People* I (New Brunswick: Rütgers University Press, 1972).
Schechter, Solomon, *Documents of Jewish Sectaries* (New York: Ktav, 1970).
Schiffman, Lawrence, *The Halakhah at Qumran* (Leiden: Brill, 1975).
—'The Temple Scroll in Literary and Philological Perspective', in *Approaches to Ancient Judaism*, ed. W.S. Green (Missoula, 1980), pp. 147-51.
—*Sectarian Law in the Dead Sea Scrolls. Courts, Testimony and the Penal Code* (BJS, 33; Chico: Scholars Press, 1983).
Schneider, Claus, 'Zur Problematik des Hellenistischen in den Qumrantexten', *Qumran-Probleme* (1963), pp. 299-314.

Schubert, K., 'Der Sektenkanon von En Feschka und die Anfänge der jüdischen Gnosis', *TLZ* 78 (1953), pp. 495-506.

—*Die Gemeinde vom Toten Meer, ihre Entstehung und ihre Lehren* (München: Reinhardt, 1958).

Schürer, Emil, *History of the Jewish People in the Age of Jesus Christ*, rev. and ed. G. Vermes and Fergus Millar (Edinburgh; T & T Clark, 1973).

Seeligman, Isaac Leo, 'Voraussetzungen der Midrasch-exegese', *VTSup* 1 (1953), pp. 150-81.

Segal, M.H., 'The Habakkuk "Commentary" and the Damascus Fragments', *JBL* 70 (1951), pp. 131-47.

Sellers, O.R., 'Radiocarbon Dating of the Cloth from the Ain Feshka Caves', *BASOR* 123 (1951), pp. 24-26.

Sharabani, Marcia, 'Monnaies de Qumran au Musée Rockefeller de Jérusalem', *RB* 87 (1980), pp. 274-84.

Siegel, J.P., 'The Employment of Palaeo-Hebrew Characters for the Divine Names at Qumran in the Light of Tannaitic Sources', *HUCA* 42 (1971), pp. 159-72.

—'The Scribes of Qumran. Studies in the Early History of the Jewish Scribal Customs, with Special Reference to the Qumran Scrolls and to the Taanaitic Traditions of *Massekheth Soferim*' (Ph.D. Dissertation, Brandeis University, 1972).

—'Two Further Medieval References to the Teacher of Righteousness', *RQ* 9 (1978), pp. 437-40.

Silberman, Lou H., 'Unriddling the Riddle: A Study in the Structure and Language of the Habakkuk Pesher (1 Q p Hab)', *RQ* 3 (1961-62), pp. 323-64.

Sinclair, Lawrence A., 'A Qumran Biblical Fragment: Hosea 4QXII^{d} (Hosea 1.7–2.5)', *BASOR* 239 (1980), pp. 61-65.

Skehan, P.A., 'The Period of the Biblical Texts from Khirbet Qumran', *CBQ* 19 (1957), pp. 435-40.

—'Two Books on Qumran Studies', *CBQ* 21 (1959), pp. 71-78.

Smend, Rudolph, 'Über das Ich der Psalmen' ZATW 8; (1886), pp. 49-147.

Smith, Morton, 'The Description of the Essenes in Josephus and the Philosophumena', *HUCA* 29 (1958), pp. 273-313.

—'The Dead Sea Sect in Relation to Ancient Judaism', *NTS* 7 (1961), pp. 347-60.

Smith, Robert H., 'The "Herodian" Lamp of Palestine. Types and Dates', *Berytus* 14 (1961), pp. 53-65.

Smyth, K., 'The Teacher of Righteousness', *ET* 69 (1958), pp. 340-42.

Snodgrass, Anthony, 'Archaeology', in *Sources for Ancient History*, ed. Michael Crawford (Cambridge: Cambridge University Press, 1983), pp. 137-84.

Soerenyi, Andreas, 'Das Buch Daniel, ein kanonisierter Pescher?', *VTSup* 15 (1966), pp. 278-94.

Sonne, I., 'A Hymn against Heretics in the Newly Discovered Scrolls', *HUCA* 23 (1950-51), pp. 275-313.

Spijkerman, P.A., 'Chroniques du Musée de la Flagellation', *SBLFA* 12 (1961-62), pp. 323-25.

Starcky, J., 'Inscriptions archaïques de Palmyre', in *Studi Orientalistici in onore di Giorgia Levi della Vida*, II (Rome, 1956).

Steckoll, S.H., 'The Qumran Sect in Relation to the Temple of Leontopolis', *RQ* 6 (1967), pp. 55-69.

—'Preliminary Excavation Report in the Qumran Cemetery', *RQ* 6 (1968), pp. 323-44.

—'Marginal Notes on the Qumran Excavations', *RQ* 7 (1969), pp. 33-40.

Stegemann, Hartmut, 'Rekonstruktion der Hodajot. Ursprüngliche Gestalt und kritisch bearbeiteter Text der Hymnenrolle aus Höhle 1 von Qumran' (Ph.D. Dissertation, Heidelberg, 1963).

—*Die Entstehung der Qumrangemeinde* (Bonn: published privately, 1971).

—'Die Bedeutung der Qumranfunde für die Erforschung der Apokalyptik', in *Apocalypticism in the Mediterranean World and the Near East*, ed. David Hellholm (Tübingen: J.C.B. Mohr [Paul Siebeck] 1983), pp. 495-530.

—'Some Aspects of Eschatology in Texts from the Qumran Community and in the Teachings of Jesus' in *Biblical Archaeology Today. Proceedings of the International Congress on Biblical Archaeology, Jerusalem, April 1984* (Jerusalem: IEJ, 1985), pp. 408-26.

Stendahl, Krister, *The School of St. Matthew and its Use of the Old Testament* (2nd edn; Philadelphia: Fortress, 1968).

Stern, Menahem, *Greek and Latin Authors on Jews and Judaism* (Jerusalem: Israel Academy of Sciences and Humanities, I, 1976; II, 1980).

Strugnell, John, 'Flavius Josephus and the Essenes: Antiquities XVIII.18-22', *JBL* 77 (1958), pp. 106-15.

—'The Angelic Liturgy at Qumran—4QSerek Širot Olat Hassabbat', *VTSup* 7 (1959), pp. 318-45.

—'Notes en marge du Volume V des "Discoveries in the Judaean Desert of Jordan"', *RQ* 7 (1970), pp. 225-29.

Sukenik, E.L., *Megilloth Genizoth* (Jerusalem: Baliak, 1954).

Szysman, S., 'À propos du Karaïsme et des textes de la Mer Morte', *VT* 2 (1952), pp. 343-48.

—'Une source auxiliare importante pour les études qumraniennes: les collections Firkowica', in *Qumran. Sa piété, sa théologie et son milieu*, ed. M. Delcor (Louvain: Louvain University Press, 1978), pp. 61-73.

—*Le Karaïsme. Ses doctrines et son histoire* (Lausanne: l'Age d'Homme, 1980).

Talmon, Shemaryahu, 'Yom Ha-Kipporim in the Habakkuk Scroll', *Bib* 32 (1951), pp. 542-63.

—'A Further Link Between the Judean Covenanters and the Essenes', *HTR* 56 (1963), pp. 313-19.

—'The Calendar Reckoning of the Sect from the Judean Desert', *Scripta Hierosolymitana*, 4, ed. C. Rabin and Y. Yadin (Jerusalem: Magnes Press, 1965).

Teicher, J.L., 'Method in Hebrew Palaeography', *JJS* 2 (1950/51), pp. 200-202.

—'The Habakkuk Scroll', *JJS* 5 (1954), pp. 47-59.

—'Archaeology and the Dead Sea Scrolls', *Antiquity* 37 (1963), pp. 25-30.

Thiering, Barbara, 'The Poetic Forms of the Hodayot', *JSS* 8 (1963), pp. 189-209.

—'The Biblical Source of Qumran Asceticism', *JBL* 93 (1974), pp. 429-44.

—'Once More the Wicked Priest', *JBL* 97 (1978), pp. 191-205.

—*Redating the Teacher of Righteousness* (ANZSTR; Sydney: Theological Explorations, 1981).

—*The Gospels and Qumran* (ANZSTR; Sydney: Theological Explorations, 1981).

—'Qumran Initiation and New Testament Baptism', *NTS* 27 (1981), pp. 615-31.

—*The Qumran Origins of the Christian Church* (ANZSTR; Sydney: Theological Explorations, 1983).

Thomas, D. Winton, 'The Dead Sea Scrolls: What May we Believe?', *ALUOS* 6 (1969), pp. 7-20.

Thorion, Yohanan, 'Der Vergleich in den Hodayot', *RQ* 42 (1983), pp. 193-217.

Thorion-Vardi, Talia, 'The Use of the Tenses in the Zadokite Documents', *RQ* 45 (1985), pp. 65-88.

Toombs, Lawrence E., 'Barcosiba and Qumran', *NTS* 4 (1957/58), pp. 65-71.
—'Earthquake', *IDB* II (Nashville: Abingdon, 1962), p. 4.
Tov, Emanuel, 'The Textual Affiliations of 4QSam[a]', *JSOT* 14 (1979), pp. 37-53.
—*The Text-Critical Use of the Septuagint in Biblical Research* (Jerusalem: Sinor, 1981).
—'A Modern Textual Outlook Based on the Qumran Scrolls', *HUCA* 53 (1982), pp. 29-43.
Trever, John C., 'A Palaeographic Study of the Jerusalem Scrolls', *BASOR* 113 (1949), pp. 6-23.
—'Some Comments on the Palaeography of the Dead Sea Scrolls', *JJS* 2 (1950/51), pp. 195-99.
—'The Spiritual Odyssey of the Qumran Teacher', in *SBL Seminar Papers 1986* (Atlanta: Scholars Press), pp. 384-99.
Treves, M., 'On the Meaning of the Qumran Testimonia', *RQ* 2 (1960), pp. 569-71.
Ulrich, Eugene C., Jr, *The Qumran Text of Samuel in Josephus* (HSM, 19; Missoula: Scholars Press, 1978).
—'4QSam[c]: A Fragmentary Manuscript of 2 Sam 14-15 from the Scribe of the *Serek Hay-yahad* (1QS)', *BASOR* 235 (1979), pp. 1-25.
VanderKam, James C., 'The Origin, Character, and Early History of the 364-Day Calendar: A Reassessment of Jaubert's Hypothesis', *CBQ* 41 (1979), pp. 390-411.
—'2 Maccabees 6,7a and Calendrical Change in Jerusalem', *JSJ* 12 (1981), pp. 52-74.
Vaux, Roland de, 'Post-scriptum. La cachette des manuscrits hébreux', *RB* 56 (1949), p. 234.
—'A propos des manuscrits hébreux', *RB* 54 (1950), pp. 417-29.
—'Fouilles au Khirbet Qumran', *RB* 61 (1954), pp. 206-36.
—'Fouilles de Khirbet Qumran', *RB* 63 (1956), pp. 533-77.
—'Bulletin', *RB* 64 (1957), pp. 623-37.
—'Archaeology and the Dead Sea Scrolls', *Antiquity* 37 (1963), pp. 126-27.
—'Method in the Study of Early Hebrew History', in *The Bible in Modern Scholarship*, ed. J. Philip Hyatt (Nashville and New York: Abingdon, 1965), pp. 15-29.
—'Essenes or Zealots', *NTS* 13 (1966-67), pp. 89-104.
—'On the Right and Wrong Uses of Archaeology', in *Essays in Honor of Nelson Glueck. Near Eastern Archaeology in the Twentieth Century*, ed. James A. Sanders (New York: Doubleday, 1970), pp. 64-80.
—*Archaeology and the Dead Sea Scrolls* (London: Oxford University Press, 1973).
Vellas, Basileios, 'Zur Etymologie des Namens "Εσσαῖοι"', *ZAW* 81 (1969), pp. 99-100.
Vermes, Geza, *Les manuscrits du désert de Juda* (Paris, 1953).
—'The Symbolical Interpretation of *Lebanon* in the Targums: The Origin and Development of an Exegetical Tradition', *JTS* 9 (1958), pp. 1-12.
—'The Etymology of "Essene"', *RQ* 2 (1960), pp. 427-43.
—'Essenes and Therapeutae', *RQ* 3 (1962), pp. 495-504.
—'The Qumran Interpretation of Scripture in its Historical Setting', *ALUOS* 6 (1966-68), pp. 85-97.
—*The Dead Sea Scrolls in English* (2nd edn; Harmondsworth: Penguin Books, 1975).
—'Dead Sea Scrolls', *IDBSup* (Nashville: Abingdon, 1976), pp. 210-19.
—*The Dead Sea Scrolls. Qumran in Perspective* (Cleveland: Collins World, 1978).
—'The Essenes and History', *JJS* 32 (1981), pp. 18-31.

Vogel, Elain K., 'Bibliography of Holy Land Sites', *HUCA* 42 (1971), pp. 54-55.

Vogel, Elaine K. and Holtzclaw, Brooks, 'Bibliography of Holy Land Sites, Part II', *HUCA* 52 (1981), p. 71.

Wacholder, Ben Zion, *The Dawn of Qumran. The Sectarian Torah and the Teacher of Righteousness* (New York: Ktav, 1983).

Wagner, S., *Die Essener in der wissenschaftlichen Diskussion* (BZAW, 79; Berlin: Töpelmann, 1960).

—'ידע' in den Lobliedern von Qumran', in *Bibel und Qumran*, pp. 232-52.

Walker, Norman, 'Concerning the 390 Years and the 20 Years of the Damascus Document', *JBL* 76 (1957), pp. 57-58.

Wallenstein, M. 'A Hymn from the Scrolls', *VT* 5 (1955), pp. 177-83.

Wardy, Bilhah, 'Jewish Religion in Pagan Literature during the Late Republic and the Early Empire', *ANRW* II.19.1, pp. 592-644.

Weill, G. 'Un document araméen de la moyenne Egypte', *REJ* 65 (1913), pp. 16-23.

Weinert, Francis J., '4Q 159: Legislation for an Essene Community Outside of Qumran?', *JSJ* 5 (1974), pp. 179-207.

—'A Note on 4 Q 159 and a New Theory of Essene Origins', *RQ* 9 (1977), pp. 223-30.

Weingreen, J., 'The Title *Moreh Sedek*', *JSS* 6 (1961), pp. 162-74.

Weiss, P.R., 'The Date of the Habakkuk Scroll', *JQR* 41 (1950), pp. 125-54.

Welten, P., *Die Königs-Stempel: Ein Beitrag zur Militärpolitik Judas unter Hiskia und Josia* (Wiesbaden; Harrassowitz, 1969).

Wernberg-Møller, P., *The Manual of Discipline* (Leiden: Brill, 1957).

—'The Contribution of the *Hodayot* to Biblical Textual Criticism', *Textus* 4 (1964), pp. 133-75.

Wieder, Naphtali, 'Notes on the New Documents from the Fourth Cave of Qumran', *JJS* 7 (1956), pp. 75-76.

—'The Qumran Sectaries and the Karaites', *JQR* 47 (1956/57), pp. 97-113, 269-92.

—*The Judean Scrolls and Karaism* (London: East and West Library, 1962).

Wieluch, D., 'Zwei "neue" antike Zeugen über Essener', *VT* 7 (1957), pp. 418-19.

Wiesenberg, E., 'Chronological Data in the Zadokite Framents', *VT* 5 (1955), pp. 284-308.

Winter, Paul, 'The Wicked Priest', *Hibbert Journal* 58 (1959), pp. 53-60.

—'Two Non-Allegorical Expressions in the Dead Sea Scrolls', *PEQ* 91 (1959), pp. 38-46.

Wirgin, W., 'Numismatics and the Dead Sea Scrolls', *RQ* 2 (1959), pp. 69-74.

Woude, A.S. van der, 'Le Maître de Justice et les deux Messies de la Communauté de Qumran', *La Secte de Qumran et les origines du Christianisme* (Recherches Bibliques, 4; 1959), pp. 121-34.

—'Wicked Priest or Wicked Priests? Reflections on the Identification of the Wicked Priest in the Habakkuk Commentary', *JJS* 33 (1982), pp. 349-59.

Wright, G. Ernest, 'A Phenomenal Discovery', *BA* 2 (1948), p. 23.

Yadin, Yigael, *Masada. Herod's Fortress and the Zealots' Last Stand* (New York: Random, 1966).

—'A Note on 4Q159 (Ordinances)', *IEJ* 18 (1968), pp. 250-52.

—'Pesher Nahum (4QpNahum) Reconsidered', *IEJ* 21 (1971), pp. 1-12.

—*Jerusalem Revealed. Archaeology in the Holy City 1968-1974* (Jerusalem: Israel Exploration Society, 1975), pp. 90-91.

—*The Temple Scroll* (Jerusalem: Israel Exploration Society, 1983).

Yamauchi, Edwin M., 'The Teacher of Righteousness from Qumran and Jesus of Nazareth', *ChrTo* 10 (1966), pp. 816-18.

Zeitlin, Solomon, 'Scholarship and the Hoax of the Recent Discoveries', *JQR* 39 (1948-49), pp. 337-63.
—'The Alleged Antiquity of the Scrolls', *JQR* 40 (1949-50), pp. 57-77.
—'The Hebrew Scrolls: Once More and Finally', *JQR* 41 (1950-51), pp. 1-58.
—'The Hebrew Scrolls and the Status of Biblical Scholarship', *JQR* 42 (1951-52), pp. 133-92.
—*The Zadokite Fragments* (Philadelphia: The Dropsie College for Hebrew and Cognate Learning, 1952).
—'The Fiction of the Recent Discoveries Near the Dead Sea', *JQR* 44 (1953-54), pp. 85-115.
—'The Essenes and Messianic Expectations', *JQR* 45 (1954), pp. 83-119.
—'The Propaganda of the Hebrew Scrolls and the Falsification of History', *JQR* 46 (1955/56), pp. 1-39, 116-80, 209-258.
—*The Dead Sea Scrolls and Modern Scholarship* (Philadelphia: The Dropsie College for Hebrew and Cognate Learning, 1956).
—'The Account of the Essenes in Josephus and the Philosophumena', *JQR* 49 (1958-59), pp. 292-99.
—'Josephus and the Zealots: A Rejoinder', *JSS* 5 (1960), p. 388.
Zeuner, F.E., 'Notes on Qumran', *PEQ* 92 (1960), pp. 27-36.

INDEX

INDEX OF BIBLICAL AND QUMRAN REFERENCES

INDEX OF AUTHORS CITED